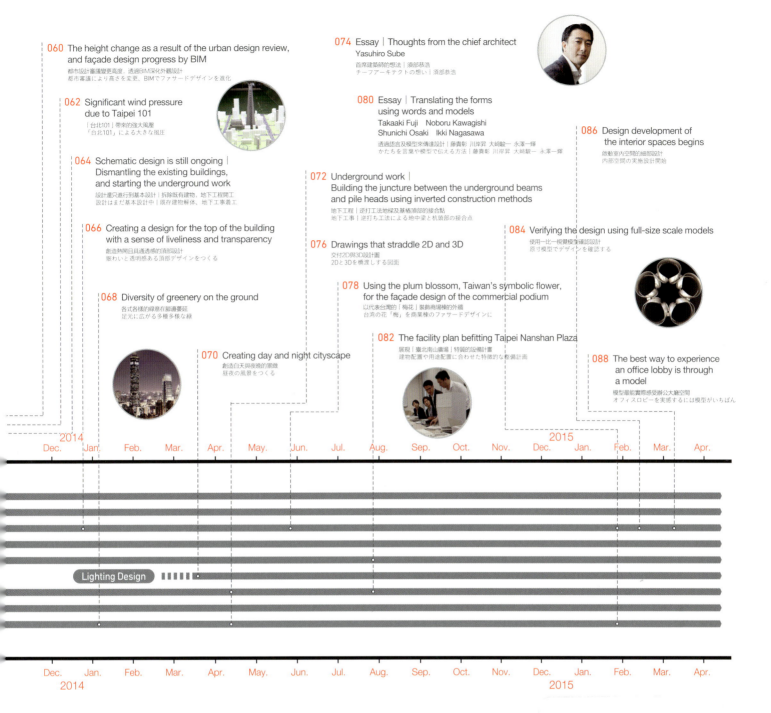

060	The height change as a result of the urban design review, and façade design progress by BIM
062	Significant wind pressure due to Taipei 101
064	Schematic design is still ongoing	Dismantling the existing buildings, and starting the underground work
066	Creating a design for the top of the building with a sense of liveliness and transparency
068	Diversity of greenery on the ground
070	Creating day and night cityscape
072	Underground work	Building the juncture between the underground beams and pile heads using inverted construction methods
074	Essay	Thoughts from the chief architect — Yasuhiro Sube
076	Drawings that straddle 2D and 3D
078	Using the plum blossom, Taiwan's symbolic flower, for the façade design of the commercial podium
080	Essay	Translating the forms using words and models — Takaaki Fuji, Noboru Kawagishi, Shunichi Osaki, Ikki Nagasawa
082	The facility plan befitting Taipei Nanshan Plaza
084	Verifying the design using full-size scale models
086	Design development of the interior spaces begins
088	The best way to experience an office lobby is through a model

Introduction

This book is a diary that traces how Mitsubishi Jisho Sekkei went about designing this project in collaboration with the client, Nan Shan Life Insurance Company, the local Taiwanese architects and the consultants. Our objective here was to record how and when our thought processes unfolded with respect to the creation of a building that began from nothing, from the initial vision and conception up until the final stage where the building was handed over to the client. We take an integrated and holistic approach in conceiving and proposing an interior and exterior, an underlying structure that would make these possible, the necessary lighting fixtures and environmental amenities that would provide the inhabitants with a pleasant environment, and even the surrounding city and landscape. This book demonstrates the design methods that allowed Mitsubishi Jisho Sekkei to communicate repeatedly with the client, and to simultaneously consider a variety of issues ranging from urban scale to the design details with a compact team.

The book is designed so that it can be read starting from either the front or the back, allowing the reader to trace the design process from either the start or the end. The timeline at the bottom of the page shows how a diverse range of issues were considered and taken into account during the same period of time.

This book was edited in three languages, in the hope that it would be useful to children, students, and architectural professionals in Taiwan and elsewhere around the world. Through the example of Taipei Nanshan Plaza, we hope that it would provoke an interest in cities and architecture, and inspire people to visit the actual site.

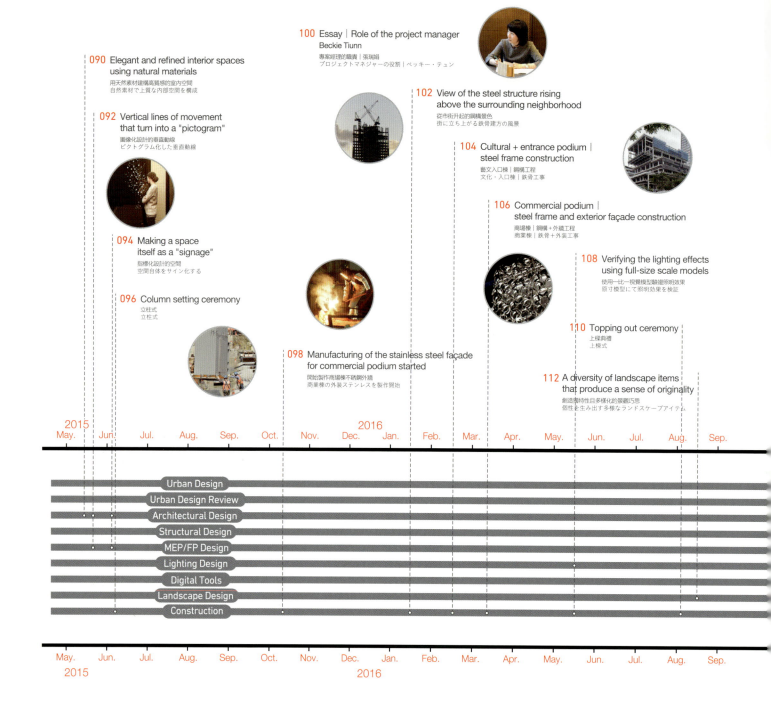

前言

此書是本公司日本三菱地所設計與業主南山人壽及當地建築師、顧問們，對於座落在台灣台北市的「臺北南山廣場」設計過程所做的記錄。書中，我們描寫一座建築物從無到有的構築軌跡：始自「起跑點」的構想階段，直至點交給業主的「終點」為止，於何時、做了何事及如何思考的過程。我們思考了建築物的室內、外牆及其可行的結構系統，還有可讓人們舒適活動的照明及環境設備。此外，並將街道城市及景觀配置納入整體考量後才進行提案。三菱地所設計的建築師們是如何和業主反覆不斷地進行溝通，並組成精簡的專業團隊達成任務；以及從檢討都市規劃的大尺度，到建築本身細部的設計手法等過程，都在書中完整呈現。

本書的編排採用了從前後面皆可閱讀的格式，可自最初的設計過程開始閱讀，亦可從工程結束的頁面逆向閱讀。還可根據頁面下方的時間軸，了解與此同時期進行的多項工作內容。

此書希望從台灣發行擴展到全世界，讓每位對建築有興趣的孩子、學生及建築相關行業的專業從業人員都能人手一本，並期待大家藉由認識「臺北南山廣場」，開始關心都市及建築物的規劃設計，並盼能成為各位造訪本建築的契機，故編輯了中英日三國語言，提供給讀者閱讀。

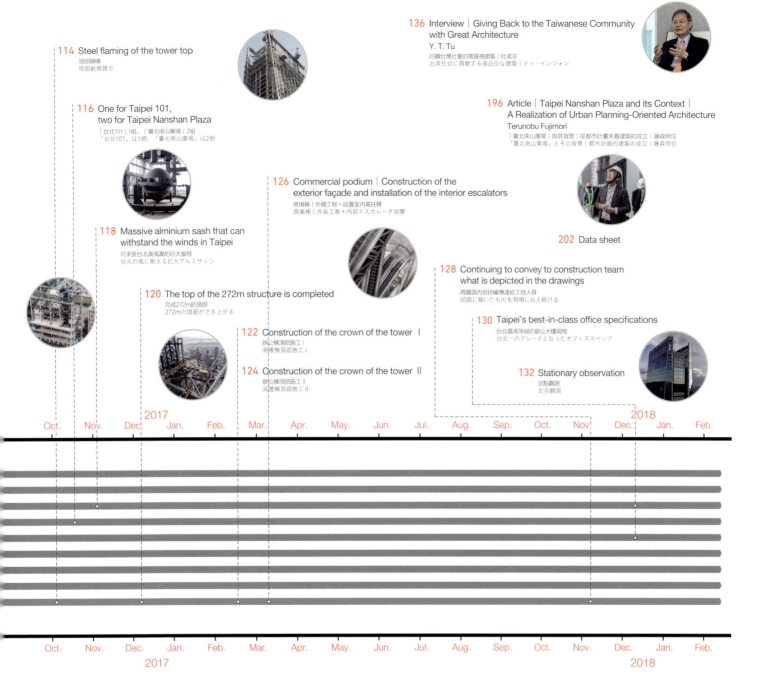

はじめに

この本は、私たち三菱地所設計が、台湾・台北で、クライアントの南山人寿や現地建築家、コンサルタントらとともに、どのように設計活動を行ってきたかを綴った日記である。何もない状態から始まる建築というものづくりを、「始め」の構想段階から、クライアントに建物を引き渡す「終わり」まで、いつ、何を、どのように考えていったかを記したいと考えた。私たちは、建築について、内・外装、これを成り立たせる構造、人びとが快適に過ごすために必要な照明や環境設備、さらには街やランドスケープまで一体に考え、提案する。本書では、三菱地所設計が、どのようにクライアントとのコミュニケーションを繰り返してきたか、いかにコンパクトなチームを組んで、都市スケールからディテールまでを同時に検討してきたか、という設計手法が示されている。

本の前後どちらからでも読める仕様とし、設計プロセスを始めからでも終わりからでも辿れるようにした。誌面の下のタイムラインにより、同時期に多様な検討を行っていたことが分かる。

本書が台湾をはじめ、世界中の子どもたち、学生、そして専門家として建築に携わる方々に手に取っていただけること、「臺北南山廣場」を介して都市や建物をつくることに関心を持ち、当地を訪れるきっかけになることを期待し、3カ国語で編集した。

Correlation Diagram

人物關係圖
人物相関図

Nan Shan Life Insurance Co., Ltd.
Client:
https://www.nanshanlife.com.tw/

Y. T. Tu
Client
Nan Shan Life Insurance

Tsang-Jiunn, Jean
Design Supervisor
Ruentex Development

Chih-Cheng Chen
Client
Nan Shan Life Insurance

Samuel Yin
Chief Technology Officer
Ruentex Group

Tetsuya Okusa
Design Director
Mitsubishi Jisho Sekkei

Yasuhiro Sube
Chief Architect
Mitsubishi Jisho Sekkei

Stan H.H.Lo
Taiwan Architect
Archasia Design Group

Fan Chou Meng
Taiwan Architect
Archasia Design Group

Kuo-Chen Fu
Client
Nan Shan Life Insurance

Chin-Yin Hsu
Client
Nan Shan Life Insurance

Dennis Yeh
Client
Nan Shan Life Insurance

Hao-Ching Wu
Contractor
Fu Tsu Construction

Fu Tsu Construction Co., Ltd.
Constractor:
https://www.futsu.com.tw/

Chin Ti Yang
Contractor
Fu Tsu Construction

Beckie Tiunn
Project Manager
Mitsubishi Jisho Sekkei

Noboru Kawagishi
Architect
Mitsubishi Jisho Sekkei

Takaaki Fuji
Architect
Mitsubishi Jisho Sekkei

Ikki Nagasawa
Project Architect
Mitsubishi Jisho Sekkei

Mitsubishi Jisho Sekkei Inc.
Architect:
https://www.mj-sekkei.com

Shunichi Osaki
Architect
Mitsubishi Jisho Sekkei

Hiroshi Kawamura
Structural Engineer
Mitsubishi Jisho Sekkei

Hiromitsu Mizutori
Electorical Engineer
Mitsubishi Jisho Sekkei

Yukio Moro
Mechanical Engineer
Mitsubishi Jisho Sekkei

Lloyd Lin
Project Manager Cooperator
Mitsubishi Jisho Sekkei

Atsushi Mitsui
Lighting Designer
Sola Associates

Hsi-Ying Kan
Structural Engineer
Evergreen Consulting Engineering

Leif Chen
Taiwan Architect
Archasia Design Group

Zhen-Xing, Liu
Taiwan Architect
Archasia Design Group

Andy Liu
Taiwan Architect
Archasia Design Group

Archasia Design Group
Taiwan Architect:
http://www.archasia.com.tw/

Interview

尹衍樑　潤泰集團 研發長

大草徹也　株式会社三菱地所設計 取締役常務執行役員

Creating a New Skyline in Taipei

創造台北新天際線

台北の新たなスカイラインをつくる

Samuel Yin　　Tetsuya Okusa

——Taipei 101 was completed in 2004, so Taipei Nanshan Plaza is Taipei's first large-scale construction projection in some time. I would like to begin by asking you about what brought the project about and what is the concept behind it.

Samuel Yin: First of all, this project came about because of the property's 50 year land lease. From an investment perspective, our company projected a 2% percent annual loss, but if we had good buildings producing higher rental income, we could increase our return on investment and make up the 2% loss. But by reshaping the Taipei skyline with outstanding architecture, the project will create value that goes beyond return on investment. This was our vision when we first launched the project. Fortunately, we were able to work with Mr. Tetsuya Okusa and his design team at Mitsubishi Jisho Sekkei and construct a building with amazing value-added features. Additionally, right now there is a new plan to build an underground mall that will join together Taipei Nanshan Plaza, Taipei 101, as well as nearby commercial and movie theatres. Underground malls are not common in Taiwan, so once completed it will provide people a new kind of entertainment.

The Chinese word *lita* (利他) means "giving something of value to someone else" or "altruism" in other words. Taipei Nanshan Plaza's underground parking accommodates 31 large-size buses. Before it was built, businesses in the area had no parking and buses had to either drive around and wait for a spot or park on the shoulder and get fined for a traffic violation. The Plaza's underground parking includes clean men's and women's restrooms and a break lounge for drivers. Tourists can get to nearby commercial facilities from the buses that park here. Taipei 101 stands out being self-consciously taller than the buildings around it, but rather than simply striving for height, Taipei Nanshan Plaza comes before the city and the public with a concept that takes into account the site's proportions and relationships to the buildings around it.

——How did Mitsubishi Jisho Sekkei approach this concept?

Tetsuya Okusa: Taipei's Xinyi District is a mixture of offices and commercial facilities as well as a popular nighttime spot for young people. A high-end residential area is also a short walk away and there are mountains close by. The area has enormous potential because it brings together all kinds of elements and functions. Of course, the area has the symbolic Taipei 101 building in the center as well as a certain degree of commercial functions around it, but the area overall lacks cohesiveness. Mr. Yin wanted a building that "provides the missing piece for this prime location," so we focused not just on a building that itself stands out but on one that organically connects to its surroundings and brings cohesiveness to the

——「臺北南山廣場」是「臺北101」（2004年竣工）以來，臺北久違的大規模開發案。首先，想請教「南山廣場」專案開始的契機和理念。

尹衍樑（以下，稱為尹）　這個案子的土地是50年設定地上權。依照本公司在投資上的計算，每年會出現2%的損失，但我們認為設計較佳的建築物能夠得到較高租金收入，投資報酬率（ROI）也會相對提高，就可以用來抵消這2%的損失。事實上，我們對南山廣場除了期待獲得投資衍生的利潤之外，透過優質的建築物能美化臺北市容，帶來了更高的價值。這就是我們在本案最初投標之際的想法。很幸運的，我們能夠遇到三菱地所設計的大草先生及其他夥伴們，為我們設計了具有高度附加價值的建築物。另外，目前「南山廣場」正與「臺北101」、鄰近的商業設施、電影院等共同合作規劃地下街。在臺灣，地下街並不普遍，但是如果這個計畫真的得以實現，會帶給市民新的期待。

在中文有一句話「利他」，也就是說「要提供給別人好的東西」。「南山廣場」在地下停車場提供了31輛大客車停車位。到目前為止，這一帶的商業設施並沒有設置這類的停車位，因此遊覽車經常只能在附近路上巡迴等待或在路邊違規停車而被罰款。這個地下停車場設有乾淨的男女洗手間和司機休息室。遊客可以從車在這裡的遊覽車步行至周邊的商業設施。

「臺北101」標榜的是最高的建築，相對上「南山廣場」則考慮了基地的形狀與周邊建築的協調關係，並不單純地追求高度，而是以市容及市民相呼應作為設計理念。

——對於尹先生的想法，三菱地所設計是如何回應的呢？

大草徹也（以下，稱為大草）　臺北信義區是一個匯聚了許多辦公大樓和商業設施，並且到了晚上是年輕人歡聚的地區。走一小段路就能到達高級住宅區，離山區也很近。是個集中了多樣化要素及功能、並且發展潛力無限大的區域。當初，在這區域中心已經有地標性建築物「臺北101」，周邊商業機能也發展到一定的成熟度，但是整個區域缺乏完整性。於是，對尹先生所說的「想建設一棟適合這個黃金地段中最後一塊拼圖的建築物」，我們考慮的不單單是突顯大樓的設計，而是希望能夠透過這棟建築物有生命力的串連周圍環境，達到整合整個區域的目標。我認為這個想法如能實現，正是回應了尹先生所希望的

——「臺北南山廣場」は、「台北101」（2004年竣工）以降、久々の台北での大規模建設プロジェクトです。まず、「南山廣場」プロジェクトが始まったきっかけ、コンセプトを伺いたいと思います。

尹衍樑（以下、尹）　このプロジェクトでは、土地に50年の借地権設定がなされています。当社の投資上の計算では、年間2%の損失が出るという計算がありましたが、よい建物によって高い賃料収入を得られれば、投資利益率（ROI）も高くなり、この2%の損失を相殺できると考えました。しかし、私たちは「南山廣場」に、投資額から利潤を生む以上に、台北の街の風景を優れた建物によって変えることに対して大きな価値を感じています。それが、私たちがプロジェクトを始めるにあたり考えたことです。幸い、三菱地所設計の大草さんたちに出会うことができ、とても付加価値の高い建物を建てることができました。さらに現在、「南山廣場」と、「台北101」、近隣商業施設、映画館と合同で地下街を設ける新たな計画案があります。台湾では、地下街は一般的ではありませんが、完成したら、人びとに新しい楽しみを提供できることでしょう。

中国語で「利他」、つまり「よいものは他人に差し上げる」という意味の言葉があります。「南山廣場」は、大型バス31台を収容する地下駐車場を提供しています。これまで、この辺りの商業施設にはこうした駐車場がなかったので、バスは路上を周回して待機するか、路肩に駐車して罰金を科されていました。この地下駐車場は、男女別の清潔なトイレや運転手の休憩ラウンジも設けられています。観光客は、ここに駐車したバスから周囲の商業施設へ出かけることができるのです。台北101が、他の建物よりも高いことで主張する建物であるのに対し、「南山廣場」は敷地のプロポーションや周囲の建物との関係を考え、単に高さを求めるのではなく、街や人びとに向き合うというコンセプトでつくられたのです。

——こうした尹さんの考えに、三菱地所設計はどのように応えられましたか？

大草徹也（以下、大草）　台北の信義区は、オフィスと商業施設が混在しながら、夜間には若者が集まる場所です。少し歩けば高級住宅街があり、山も近い。多様な要素や機能が集約する、大きな可能性を持つエリアです。確かに、街の中心として「台北101」という象徴的な建物があり、周囲には商業機能もある程度完成していましたが、エリア全体のまとまりがありませんでした。そこで、尹さんの「この一等

whole district. Mr. Yin wanted to make a positive social contribution, and we started work on the design with the goal of making his wish a reality. Rather than something that stands in opposition the Taipei 101 symbol, our objective was something that would play a supporting role and endow the place with meaning. We could have positioned the tower directly opposite the vibrant commercial axis, but by venturing to slightly skew the angle, we sought to create a line of view toward Taipei 101 and endow the neighborhood with depth and openness. We described to the New York Times the contrast between Taipei Nanshan Plaza and Taipei 101 as that of "queen and king." We can certainly say that this development has succeeded in becoming a new focal point for the area.

Yin: The construction was performed by Fu Tsu Construction, Taiwan's most technologically-advanced general construction contractor. Despite a short 50-month schedule, work was completed without a single accident and within budget. And yet, the quality of the buildings is much higher than expected. It is an amazing accomplishment.

Okusa: We worked closely with Mr. Yin, Mr. Tsang-Jiunn Jean and everyone else throughout the entire project. Such close collaboration is very rare, even in Japan. Specifically, we did comparative studies of every aspect, from interior detail to exterior design, prepared numerous proposals and made every decision based on feedback from Mr. Yin and his team. Even the praying-hands form chosen to symbolize an insurance company dedicated to the well-being of the public was determined by a selection process involving everyone in the project from among five different ideas.

Yin: We debated all kinds of things and made decisions based on majority vote. As a result, a proposal always moved forward with the support of more than 80 percent of project members. The thing that made the greatest impression on me as the project moved forward was the passion of Mr. Okusa and Mr. Yasuhiro Sube, who was also in charge of the design. I was tremendously impressed by how they delved meticulously into every detail.

Taipei Nanshan Plaza uses two of my ideas: the building's "praying hands" form and its "plum blossom" exterior. The initial "plum blossom" proposal was on the level of a very crude sketches, so I am delighted by how they refined into a beautiful form with a three-dimensional surface. I like the idea of enlarging this design and placing it at the entrance as a symbol.

——How did you collaborate on the design and building process?

Okusa: Right now, we are working on installing the "plum blossom" in the lobby as screen art. Coming up with the "plum blossom" motif is a good example of how we repeated a

---

「社會貢獻」，於是著手進行整體的規劃設計。

我們的設計目標並不是要與地標的「臺北101」對抗，而是讓它成為稱職的配角，以形塑真正有意義的中心建物作為目標。當初規劃時，我們原本把塔樓的位置，正對在華納威秀人行步道的熱鬧商業軸線上，但是經過深思檢討，我們把塔樓的位置刻意從軸線上錯開一些，保留望向「臺北101」的視線，創造出街道的立體感及擴展效果。

在《紐約時報》的報導中，也介紹南山廣場和臺北101宛如是"國王和皇后"的對比關係。我希望透過這次的開發可以讓這個區域產生一個新的城市磁場。

尹　這次施工是由在臺灣最好的營造公司互助營造負責施工。即使工期非常的短，大約只有50個月，但完全沒有發生事故，同時也在工程預算之內完工，並且建築物的品質遠遠超越了期待。我們感到非常高興。

大草　這次能夠與尹先生、簡滄圳先生等各位從開始到完工一起討論設計，經歷了在日本也很難得的寶貴經驗。具體來說，我們從細部設計到外觀設計逐一進行比較檢討，準備了多種方案，全部的細節皆是由尹先生和各位的意見做成決定。作為一棟替市民祈福的保險公司大樓，富有象徵性的合掌形狀也是從5個方案之中經過大家的選擇而定案的。

尹　過程中我們討論了很多，且以投票表決決定。因此，一直以來設計方案都獲得5成以上的支持率來進行。

在本案進行中，大草先生和一同負責設計的須部先生的敬業精神，以及對於細節部分也謹慎追求的工作態度，讓我留下了非常深刻的印象。

在「南山廣場」發揮了兩個我的創意。一個是"合掌"的形狀，另一個則是"梅花"的外牆。"梅花"的初期方案簡直是塗鴉程度的東西，但是被設計成立體曲面，做成很漂亮的形狀，我非常滿意。之後也許考慮把這個設計圖案放大，作為象徵物裝飾在大廳。

地にラスト1ピースとなる建物を置きたい」という言葉に対し、単にそれ自体が目立つのではなく、その建物によって周囲が有機的に繋がり、地区全体にまとまりをもたらすことができると考えたのです。その実現こそ「社会に貢献したい」という尹さんの考えに応えることだと思い、設計を始めました。象徴としての「台北101」に対抗するのではなく、脇役としての存在感を持たせ、意味のある中心をつくることを目標としました。高層棟の位置も、賑わいの商業軸に対して、真正面に設置することもできたのですが、これをあえて少しずらすことにより、「台北101」への視点を設け、街の奥行や広がりをつくり出したいと考えたのです。『ニューヨーク・タイムズ』には、「南山廣場」を「台北101」と対比し「キングとクイーン」として紹介しました。今回の開発でこのエリアに新しい磁場を形成するようになってくれるとよいですね。

尹　今回は台湾一の技術力を持つゼネコンである互助営造が施工を行っています。約50ヵ月という短工期にも関わらず、まったくの無事故であり、同時に予算内に収まっていますが、建物の品質は期待をはるかに上回っています。これは素晴らしいことです。

大草　今回、尹さん、簡滄圳さんをはじめ、皆さんと、ものづくりを最初から最後まで一緒に行うことができ、日本でもなかなか得難い経験をしました。具体的に言えば、ディテールから外観デザインに至るまでひとつひとつについて比較検討し、複数の案を準備し、それらをすべて尹さんと皆さんの意見から決定していきました。市民の幸せを祈る保険会社のビルとしての、象徴的な合掌のフォルムも、5案程度の中からみんなで選ぶプロセスを経て決定しました。

尹　多くのことを議論して、多数決で決めましたね。これにより、案は常に5割以上の支持を得た状態で進んでいきました。プロジェクトを進める中で最も印象的だったのは、大草さんと、同じく設計を担当した須部さんの仕事に対する情熱です。細かい部分まで慎重に追求していこうという姿勢はとても記憶に残りました。

「南山廣場」には、ふたつの私のアイデアが生かされています。「合掌」のフォルムと「梅の花」の外壁です。「梅の花」の初期提案は落書き程度のものでしたが、表面を三次曲面とすることで綺麗な形に仕上げていただいてとても嬉しいです。このデザインを拡大し、シンボルとしてエントランスに飾ってみるのもよいかもしれません。

Samuel Yin | Ruentex Group Chief Technology Officer | Born in 1950 in Taipei Taiwan. Chair Professor Department of Civil Engineering, National Taiwan University / International Academy of Engineering / Founder of the Tang Prize / In 2008, Engineering Glory Award by IAE Russian / In 2010, Henry L.Michel Award by ASCE / In2011, Heroes of Philanthropy by Forbes Asia

尹衍樑 | 潤泰集團研發長 | 1950年出生於臺灣臺北 / 台大土木系講座教授，俄羅斯國際工程院第一副院長，唐獎創辦人，台、清、交、北大等多所大學名譽博士 / 2008年獲頒俄羅斯工程之光獎章，2010年獲ASCE頒贈Henry L.Michel Award，2011年富比世亞洲慈善英雄 / 為全球知名的發明家，已獲全球566件專利

サミュエル・イン | ルンテックスグループ チーフ・テクノロジー・オフィサー | 1950年台湾台北生まれ | 台湾大学土木学部首席教授、ロシア国際工学アカデミー第一副院長、唐賞創設者 / 台湾大学、清華大学、国立交通大学、北京大学等の名誉博士 / 2008年ロシアエンジニアグローリー最高栄誉受賞、2010年ASCE Henry L.Michel Award受賞、2011年フォーブスアジア版「慈善事業の英雄」/ 世界的発明家として国際特許566件を持つ

Tetsuya Okusa | Mitsubishi Jisho Sekkei Director, Senior Executive Officer | Born in 1963 in Chiba, Japan / 1988 Master's degree, the University of Tokyo / 1988~2001, Mitsubishi Jisho / 1997, Master of Architecture, the University of Pennsylvania Graduate School of Fine Arts / 2001~, Mitsubishi Jisho Sekkei

大草徹也 | 三菱地所設計 常務董事 | 1963年出生於日本千葉縣 | 1988年東京大學建築研究所碩士 | 1988~2001年任職三菱地所 / 1997年賓州大學藝術研究所碩士 / 2001年~任職三菱地所設計

大草徹也 | 三菱地所設計 取締役常務執行役員 | 1963年千葉県生まれ。1988年東京大学大学院修士課程修了 / 1988~2001年三菱地所 / 1997年ペンシルバニア大学美術学部大学院修士課程修了 / 2001年~三菱地所設計

---

process in which everyone focused on a problem together, exchanged ideas, and then moved ahead with an improved version. It was a very fruitful learning experience. I think we can even say that this process served as the vehicle for creating something excellent.

Yin: It was fascinating. It's probably true that the typical client does not delve into a building to such a detailed extent, but we are deeply interested in architecture and civil engineering, so the mutual growth, the deepening of bonds and the opportunity to form truly good friendships through the design process is intensely satisfying.
Hiring Mitsubishi Jisho Sekkei when we first started was an intuitive decision. We looked into many other design firms as well, but when I looked at the buildings designed by Mitsubishi Jisho Sekkei in Tokyo's Marunouchi district, I realized that that we share the vision of what we seek to create a good building. At the same time, the impression that people make is also very important to a project's success, and when I met Mr. Okusa and Mr. Sube face-to-face, I was convinced that we could rely on them.

Okusa: To be honest, I was every nervous in the beginning (laughs). In Taiwan, Mr. Yin would make sketches in response to the ideas that we had rigorously worked out in Japan and give us advice on how to make them even better. As this process went on, I came to feel that if we followed Mr. Yin's lead, the building would evolve into something beyond what we could achieve on our own. We started with the two building plan that we had prepared according to the design requirements for the project competition sponsored by the Taipei municipal government. But given that the Xinyi District's skyline is getting higher and higher, at some point in the future the skyline would overwhelm two voluminous buildings and they would no longer exert any kind of presence in the city. So, we changed the plan to one tower with a low-rise building and several plazas. That plan was a shot at modifying the original two-tower plan consisting of a company headquarters tower and a second tower for tenants to rent by the floor, and it was at that time that Mr. Yin pushed the single tower idea that gave the building the form that it has today. When he told us to go ahead with that plan, I was really delighted.

Yin: And the results are excellent, including office rental rates that vastly exceeded our expectations and are the highest in Taiwan. Even though the real estate market in Taiwan is said to be in the middle of a downturn, if one builds something truly excellent, it will get a positive response. I think we will reach full occupancy soon. What's more, Breeze Center is scheduled to move into the commercial building as its biggest tenant. There will also be first-class restaurants, including Japanese cuisine. I get excited just thinking about working in a Tower where I can enjoy delicious food from all over the world.

Okusa: I've heard that a high-percentage of tenants are foreign corporations, but the tower's height is not the only reason they like it. Along with the bus terminal that Mr. Yin

---

——設計過程是如何一起進行的呢？

大草 我們當初研究把"梅花"作為藝術金屬簾懸吊在大廳，討論這個問題時候也是一樣，大家一起想辦法，有意見就改善，再反覆提出修改方案，從這過程中我們學習到很多。因為這個改善的機制，讓我們能夠實現更好的設計。

尹 確實是個很有趣的經驗。一般的業主可能對建築不太瞭解，但是我們對建築土木工程非常感興趣，所以透過設計過程的來回討論，互相成長，提升彼此的默契，變成真正的好友，我從心底感到高興。
最初，要把本案委託給三菱地所設計是靠直覺決定的。我們也檢討過其他的設計師事務所，但是在東京丸之內看到了三菱地所設計的建築物後，感受到我們對建築設計有共同的喜好。同時，對人的印象也佔了很大一部分。與大草先生和須部先生初次見面時，我當下覺得交給他們一定沒有問題。

大草 說實話，我一開始非常緊張（笑）。尹先生對我們從日本帶過來並下了很大工夫的設計方案，當場親自繪製手稿反饋意見，並給我們提出了更好的建議。在這樣的交流過程中，我感覺到如果我們跟隨尹先生前進，這棟建築物一定比我們單獨進行還能進化到更完美的境界。當初，在臺北市政府主辦的招標競圖中，根據設計條件而規劃成雙塔的方案雀屏中選。但是，我們考慮到今後的信義區的大樓會有日益高層化的發展，高度較低的雙塔方案容易被未來形成的城市天際線所埋沒，很難在城市裡發揮它的影響力。於是我們提出新的方案，把雙塔方案修正為獨棟方案，並轉化原來的量體，規劃了更多的裙樓和廣場。
這個方案是把原來的總部大廈和出租型辦公大樓的雙塔方案進行優化，當我們當初是硬著頭皮把方案提交出去，但多虧當時尹先生推選了這個獨棟大樓的方案，所以成就了今天的「南山廣場」。猶記得當時尹先生說：「就採用這個方案吧」時，我真的非常高興。

尹 因為有了這個成果，辦公大樓的租金超乎我們的預期變成全臺灣第一。雖然現在的臺灣不動產業界處於不景氣的情況，但由此可知只要做出好的東西，就能得到好評。我估計再過不久，出租率就會達

——ものをつくるプロセスはどのように共有されたのでしょうか？

大草 ロビーに「梅の花」をウインドアートとして吊ることを検討した際もそうでしたが、みなで一緒に悩んで、意見があったら改善し、また改善案を持って行くことをくり返すプロセス自体がとても勉強になりました。よいものをつくり出す仕組みとして機能したのではないかと思います。

尹 とても面白かったですね。おそらく、一般的な施主は建築にそこまで詳しくないでしょうが、私たちは建築や土木にとても興味があるので、設計のやり取りを通じて、互いに成長し、絆も高まり、本当によい友人を得ることができて、心から嬉しいです。
最初、三菱地所設計へのプロジェクトの依頼を決めたのは直感でした。いろいろな設計事務所も検討しましたが、東京の丸の内で三菱地所設計による建物を見て、どういう建物が好ましいか共感できたのがよかったと思います。同時に、人となりの印象も大きいものです。大草さん、須部さんらと顔を合わせて、この人たちに任せたら大丈夫だ、と確信しました。

大草 正直言うと、私は最初、とても緊張しました（笑）。尹さんは、私たちが日本で一所懸命考えてきた提案について、その場でスケッチをして応えて下さったり、その案をさらによくするアドバイスをくれました。こうしたやり取りの中で、尹さんについていけば、この建物は私たちの力以上の進化を遂げるのではないかという気がしました。当初、台北市政府主催の事業コンペでは、設計要件に従って2棟からなる案として、それが採択されていました。しかし、信義区がますます高層化していくであろうということを念頭に置くと、ボリュームを控えた2棟では、今後形成されるスカイラインに埋没、都市の中での影響力を発揮できないと思いました。そこで1棟のタワーにして、その分低層部と広場を多く設ける提案をしたのです。これは、本社テナント棟とフロア貸テナント棟の2棟からなる当初の案を進化させる案として、ダメ元で提案したのですが、この時、尹さんがこの1棟案を推してくださったので今日の姿になりました。「これでいこう」と言っていただけた時は本当に嬉しかったです。

尹 その成果もあり、オフィスの賃料は大幅に想定を超えて、台湾一になりました。台湾が不動産不況と言われるさなかでも、きちんとよいものをつくれば、よい評価をいただくことができるのです。まもなく、入居率も100%に達すると思います。また、商業棟には最大のテナントとして「Breeze Center（微風廣場）」が入居する予定です。日本食をはじめとする高級レストランも出店します。タワーで働きな

mentioned, Taipei Nanshan Plaza has a good deal of public space, including a two-level pedestrian deck and a lobby and other space open to the general public. I think they find this aspect very appealing as well.

──I think Taipei Nanshan Plaza has spurred the development of the Xinyi District. What are your plans for the future?

Yin: Looking ahead, I think development in Taipei will shift to areas with more development potential than the Xinyi District. The Songshan area to the north and the Nangang area to the east, for example. The Nangang District has a Taiwan High Speed Rail station and is a prime location connected to the central Taipei by various forms of public transportation. It is also home to the Academia Sinica, Taiwan's preeminent academic institution. Taipei Nanshan Plaza has indeed brought change to Taipei, but there's no more empty space left in the Xinyi District (laughs).

Okusa: To use Tokyo as an example, the Nangang District that is expected to be the focus of development in the future that Mr. Yin just mentioned is analogous to a place like Shinjuku Fukutoshin or Yokohama Minato Mirai. As is evident from the policy approach applied in Japan, developing outlying areas greatly depends on strengthening the urban core, as has been done in Tokyo's central Daimaruyu (Otemachi, Marunouchi and Yurakucho) area. So, it follows that Taipei's central Xinyi District will need to be transformed into an even more robust hub than it is now.

──If each of you were to sum up the project in a few words, what would they be? Is there a favorite spot in Taipei Nanshan Plaza that you especially like?

Okusa: Building an urban silhouette in a single development that, moreover, has a significant ripple effect on the surrounding area is something that is just not possible in Japan today. It was a pleasure tackling this challenging work together with Mr. Yin. I also think developments that provide outdoor public space on the top floor like Taipei Nanshan Plaza are extremely rare. I look forward to watching Taipei 101's new year's eve fireworks with Mr. Yin from that spot.

Yin: I am very satisfied. In the altruistic spirit of giving "something good to others" that I talked about earlier, I will say that I do not have a particularly favorite spot in Taipei Nanshan Plaza (laughs). I certainly hope to work with Mitsubishi Jisho Sekkei again sometime in the future.

(February 27, 2018 at Ruentex Group, Responsibility for the wording: Shinkenchiku-sha)

到100%。另外，商場最大的租戶"微風廣場"也預定進駐。以日本料理為首的高級餐廳也計畫開店。一邊在辦公大樓上班，一邊可以享受全世界的美食，光是想到就開心。

大草　我聽說外商企業的進駐率很高，但理由應該不僅是塔樓較受歡迎而已。除了剛才尹先生所介紹的「南山廣場」設置有完備的大客車停車場等之外，還有二樓的空橋、對一般民眾開放的大廳等，具有很高的公益性。這些應該也是受到好評的原因。

──「南山廣場」似乎已成為信義區發展的契機。您怎麼看待今後的發展？

尹　我認為，未來臺北的發展會遷移到比信義區還有開發可能性，例如位於北邊的松山區或東邊的南港區。在南港區有高鐵車站，與臺北市中心連接的大眾運輸工具也建置完善。臺灣最高學術研究機構的中央研究院也設置在那裡。「南山廣場」雖然是改變臺北的一個契機，但信義區已經沒有空地了（笑）。

大草　正如尹先生所說的，未來開發上，較受矚目的南港區就像日本東京的新宿副都心或橫濱港灣未來城。如果要實現這類周邊地區發展，最重要的是，必須實施類似日本政府重新加強日本大丸有地區市中心商業特區開發的政策。只要市中心發展成熟，自然而然地周圍也會跟進加強開發。因此，在臺北也應該需要把市中心的信義區建構成為更穩健的據點來進行發展。

──對兩位來說，如果用一句話來形容「南山廣場」，會怎麼表達呢？另外，請兩位和我們分享，在「南山廣場」裡最為特別、最喜歡的地方。

大草　透過一個開發案能創造城市的輪廓，又能帶動周邊環境造成非常大的連鎖反應，在現在的日本是很難實現的。能和尹先生一起進行這個具挑戰性的工作，我感到非常地榮幸。而且，像「南山廣場」一樣，在最頂樓戶外設有公共空間的建案應該很少見。下一次希望能在那裡與尹先生一起欣賞「臺北101」的跨年煙火。

尹　我對這個案子非常滿意。如同我剛才提到的「利他」，也就是我認為「要提供給別人好的東西」，因此我在「南山廣場」"沒有"特別喜歡的地方（笑）。最後，我也希望今後還能與三菱地所設計一起合作。

（2018年2月27日，於潤泰集團總公司／撰文：本誌編輯部）

がら世界中の美味しい食事を楽しめるのは、想像するだけで楽しそうです。

大草　外資系の企業の入居率が高いと聞きましたが、単にタワーの高さだけが好まれているわけではないと思います。「南山廣場」は、先ほど尹さんがおっしゃったバスターミナル整備に加え、2階レベルのペデストリアンデッキ、一般市民へ開放されたロビーなど、高いパブリック性を持っています。こうした側面も評価されているのではないでしょうか。

──「南山廣場」は、信義区の発展のきっかけになっていると思います。今後についてはどのようにお考えですか？

尹　今後の台北の開発は、信義区よりまだ開発の可能性がある、例えば、北側の松山エリアや東側の南港エリアに移っていくのではないかと思います。南港区は、台湾高速鉄道（台湾新幹線）の駅があり、台北と繋がる公共交通機関も整う良所です。台湾の最高学術研究機関である中央研究院も設置されています。「南山廣場」は台北を変えるきっかけになりましたが、信義区にはもう空地がないのですよ（笑）。

大草　尹さんがおっしゃる通り、今後の開発が期待される南港区は、東京で言うと新宿副都心や横浜みなとみらいのような場所にあたります。こうした周辺エリアが発展を遂げるためには、日本の政策にも見られる通り、もういちど大丸有地区のような都心の強化が重要です。ですから、台北でも、都心である信義区をより強固な拠点として進化させる必要があるのではないでしょうか。

──おふたりにとって、このプロジェクトをひと言で言えばどういうものだったのでしょうか。また、「南山廣場」の中で特によいと思われる、お好きな場所を教えてください。

大草　ひとつの開発で都市のシルエットをつくり、さらに周囲への大きな波及効果を持つ開発は、今日の日本ではなかなかできません。こうした挑戦的な仕事を尹さんと一緒にできてとても楽しかったです。そして、「南山廣場」のように、最上階にパブリックなスペースを外部に設けている例は、かなり珍しいと思います。今度はそこで、尹さんと一緒に年末恒例の「台北101」の花火を見たいですね。

尹　とても満足しています。そして、私は先ほども申し上げたように「利他」つまり「よいものは他人に差し上げる」と考えているので、私が南山広場で特別好きな場所は「ない」ということにしておきましょう（笑）。三菱地所設計とは、ぜひ今後とも一緒に仕事をしていきたいですね。

（2018年2月27日、潤泰集團本社にて／文責：本誌編輯部）

08/31/2012

What could be a new icon for the subtropical metropolis of Taipei?

亞熱帶城市・台北新地標
亜熱帯の都市・台北の新たなアイコンとは

Earth   Taiwan

A large basin on a small island

Taiwan is a long and narrow island country measuring 394 km from north to south, and 144 km from east to west, with five mountain ranges in its central region due to an uplift in the terrain. It is highly similar to Japan in terms of its geographical features such as climate, and the prevalence of earthquakes. Taipei, which sits in 243km² basin surrounded by mountains on four sides at a latitude of 25 degrees north and a longitude 121 degrees east, is one of the cities in Taiwan that sees four distinct seasons. Due to the strong sunlight, rainy season and typhoons, and sudden bursts of thunderstorms distinct to the tropical regions, Taiwan has developed a particular genre of covered streetside spaces known as *qilou*. The Xinyi Special District where Taipei Nanshan Plaza stands is required to build pedestrian decks on the second and third storeys by urban planning regulations as the contemporary interpretation of the qilou. . Also important was the provision of shaded green areas. Rooftops planted with greenery and shades under the Banyan trees function as places of rest to find respite from the heat.

Similar to Japan, a high level of safety with respect to earthquakes was demanded. As Taipei also experiences four seasons, our intention was to incorporate something of this warm, humid environment prone to typhoons into the design. Since 2004, Taipei 101 has been a landmark for the city of Taipei. In 2012, when the design for Nanshan Plaza was embarked upon, we wanted to harmonize the design with this symbolic tower standing just next to it, in addition to creating a new icon that would be able to project its own unique identity.

微小島嶼上的巨大盆地

台灣是南北約394公里，東西約144公里的狹長島嶼。中央因地層隆起形成五座山脈，從氣候、地形等地理上的特徵，及地震頻繁的部分看來，跟日本非常相似。

位於北緯25度，東經121度的台北市，為四周有山群環繞面積約243km²的盆地，四季的變化與臺灣其他地區相比尤其顯著。強烈的日照、梅雨和颱風，以及南國特有的突發雷陣雨，造就了店面內縮的走道空間，因此有了特殊的「騎樓」文化。「臺北南山廣場」所在的信義計畫區用現代的概念詮釋「騎樓」，都市計畫法規要求於建築物的二樓及三樓兩個樓層設置空橋。另外，重要的還有創造綠蔭的設計，我們期待在綠化後的屋頂空間及榕樹下，可作為酷暑時節人們休憩的場所。
除此之外，本建築物對於能抵抗地震的高度安全需求也與日本相似，我們思考了能夠對應四季變化、高溫多濕且有颱風來襲的自然環境的最佳設計。

自2004年開始，「台北101」即為台北最著名的地標。我們在2012年著手本案規劃設計時，深切地感受到新的建築物必須能與鄰近的著名地標諧和共存，同時發展出自己的獨特性，於是有了創造新地標的想法。

小さな島の大きな盆地

台湾は、南北約394km、東西144kmと南北に細長く、中央には地層の隆起による5つの山脈を有する島国で、気候や地勢などの地理的特徴や、地震が多い点が日本と大変よく似ている。北緯25度、東経121度にある台北は、四方を山に囲まれた243km²の盆地で、台湾の中では四季の変化が顕著である。強烈な日射、梅雨や台風、南国特有の突発的な豪雨により「騎楼」と呼ばれる屋根付きの側道空間が発達している。
「臺北南山廣場」の建つ信義計画区では、「騎楼」の現代的解釈として、ペデストリアンデッキを2、3階に設置することが都市計画上必須である。また、緑陰の形成も重要で、緑化された屋上やガジュマルの樹の下は、暑さを凌ぐ憩いの場となっている。
日本と同様に地震への高い安全性が求められること、四季があり、高温多湿で台風もある環境をデザインに生かしたいと考えた。
2004年以来、「台北101」は台北のランドマークである。2012年の計画着手時、このシンボルタワーに隣接するものとして、これと調和し、かつ独自性を放つ新たなアイコンをつくりたいと考えた。

09/07/2012 Deciphering the urban planning of Xinyi District

解讀信義區都市計劃
信義区の都市計画を紐解く

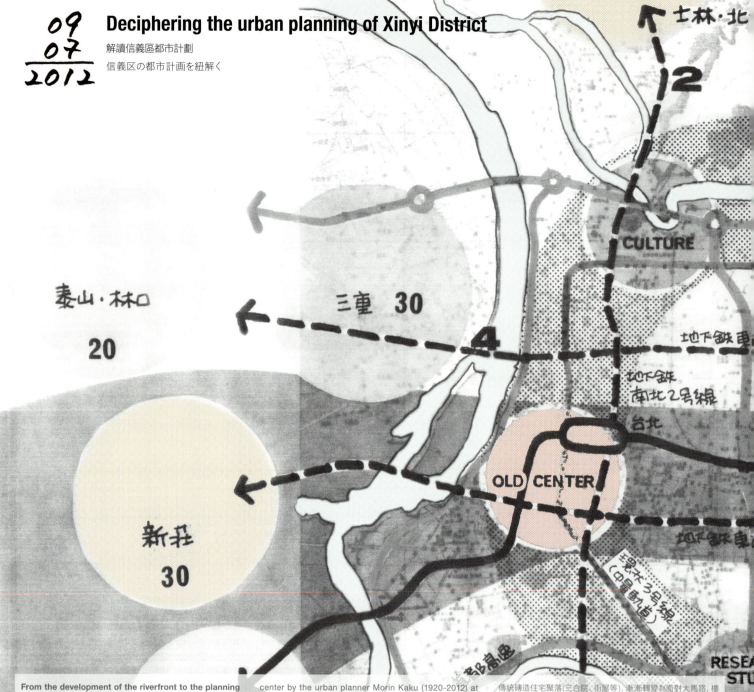

From the development of the riverfront to the planning of a secondary city center

The Taipei basin, where Tamsui River flows out towards the Taiwan Strait, developed economically starting in the early 18th century centering on the northwestern areas (Tamsui, Xinzhuang) due to their water transport links. Starting in the late 1860s, the traditional residential neighborhoods of brick houses (sanheyuan courtyards with structures on three sides, and townhouses) that had expanded to the east and outer edges of the Tamsui riverbank gradually began to transform into two- to three-storey reinforced brick buildings with shops attached known as "shophouses," starting with the sides of major thoroughfares. After the 1970s, these shophouses became mid- and high-rise buildings, thanks to the increasingly common use of reinforced concrete.

Concurrent with the underground construction plan of Taipei City (completed in 1989), which sits along the Taiwan Railway West Coast Line (which began operation in 1908), a redevelopment project that sought to consolidate and streamline the expressways in downtown Taipei and the Taipei Metro (MRT) rail network, as well as utilize land along the railway lines, was undertaken. Xinyi District, which was positioned as Taipei's secondary city center by the urban planner Morin Kaku (1920-2012) at the invitation of the then mayor of Taipei, Mr. Lee Teng-hui (1923-, subsequently President of Taiwan), saw rapid development after 1979, with growth focused on its central area known as Xinyi Special District.

After researching and teaching at the University of Tokyo, Mr. Morin Kaku served as a consultant together with Mitsubishi Jisho (the predecessor of Mitsubishi Jisho Sekkei) on numerous projects, including the skyscraper building Sunshine City (1973) in Tokyo's Ikebukuro, and the underground network in the Zhonghua Road area near Taipei Main Station (1989). Reference was made to the high-rise secondary city center of Tokyo's Shinjuku, in addition to the Marunouchi area, the urban planning and architectural design of which Mitsubishi Jisho Sekkei has been involved with for some 130 years, for the Xinyi Special District, where these ideas and concepts are in full evidence.

沿著河川發展到副都心計畫

台北盆地於18世紀初開始，所有的經濟活動，是以沿著流向台灣海峽的淡水河的西北區域（淡水、新莊）為中心開始發展。1860年代後期，淡水河沿岸的聚落開始往東發展，外緣也開始擴張，傳統磚造住宅聚落（三合院、街屋等），漸漸轉變為面對大馬路，樓高兩、三層的「店屋」。其建築結構是磚造實施補強（加強磚造）且附設店面的住宅。而1970年代後期，隨著鋼筋水泥建築的普及，建築物才進入中高層化的時代。

隨著台灣縱貫鐵路（1908年開通）的台北市內地下化計畫（1989年完成），大台北地區的高速公路、捷運路線也同時整合興建，鐵路沿線的土地也進行了重新開發與再利用。1978年當時擔任台北市長的李登輝先生（1923年～之後成為台灣總統）聘請都市計畫專家郭茂林先生（1920～2012年）將信義區定位成台北市的副都心，並於1979年後，將位處信義區中心區塊的信義計畫區作為副都心的核心，啟動了急速的城市開發。

郭茂林先生於東京大學研究教學後，曾參與東京池袋的超高層大廈「Sunshine City」（1973年），及「台北車站中華路地下街」（1989年）等案，與三菱地所（三菱地所設計的前身）共同參與為數甚多的設計顧問規劃案。郭茂林先生對於信義計畫區的都市規劃，除了參考東京新宿的超高層副都心之外，其規劃理念也蘊含了我們三菱地所設計深耕長達130年，持續進行城市總體營造與建築設計的丸之內特區的精神。

川沿いの発展から副都心計画まで

台湾海峡へ注ぐ淡水河が流れる台北盆地では、18世紀初頭から、

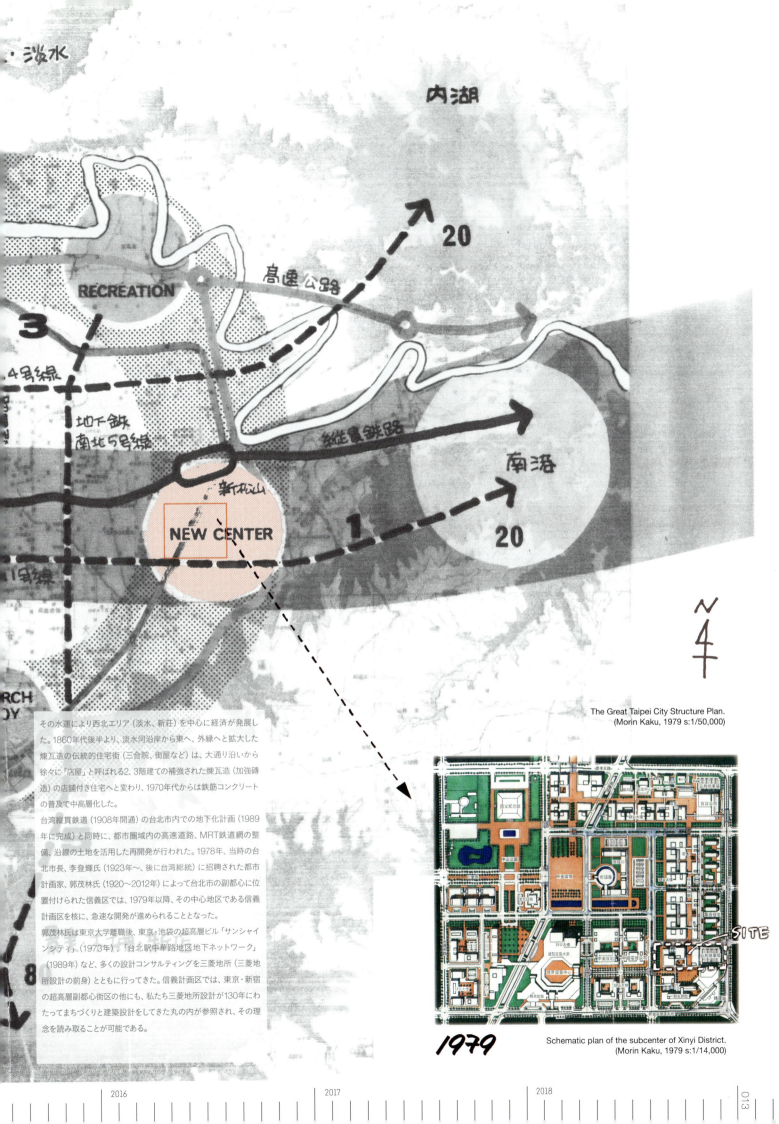

The Great Taipei City Structure Plan.
(Morin Kaku, 1979 s:1/50,000)

Schematic plan of the subcenter of Xinyi District.
(Morin Kaku, 1979 s:1/14,000)

その水運により西北エリア（淡水、新荘）を中心に経済が発展した。1860年代後半より、淡水河沿岸から東へ、外縁へと拡大した煉瓦造の伝統的住宅街（三合院、街屋など）は、大通り沿いから徐々に「店屋」と呼ばれる2、3階建ての補強された煉瓦造（加強磚造）の店舗付き住宅へと変わり、1970年代からは鉄筋コンクリートの普及で中高層化した。

台湾縦貫鉄道（1908年開通）の台北市内での地下化計画（1989年に完成）と同時に、都市圏域内の高速道路、MRT鉄道網の整備、沿線の土地を活用した再開発が行われた。1978年、当時の台北市長、李登輝氏（1923年～、後に台湾総統）に招聘された都市計画家、郭茂林氏（1920～2012年）によって台北市の副都心に位置付けられた信義区では、1979年以降、その中心地区である信義計画区を核に、急速な開発が進められることとなった。
郭茂林氏は東京大学離職後、東京・池袋の超高層ビル「サンシャインシティ」（1973年）、「台北駅中華路地区地下ネットワーク」（1989年）など、多くの設計コンサルティングを三菱地所（三菱地所設計の前身）とともに行ってきた。信義計画区では、東京・新宿の超高層副都心街区の他にも、私たち三菱地所設計が130年にわたってまちづくりと建築設計をしてきた丸の内が参照され、その理念を読み取ることが可能である。

Xinyi District as a secondary city center for Taipei City

With Mr. Morin Kaku's urban planning as a foundation, which made reference to areas such as Tokyo's Marunouchi and Shinjuku, numerous projects were built one after another in Taipei, including the Taipei World Trade Center (1985), TWTC International Trade Building (1988), Taipei International Convention Center (1989), Grand Hyatt Taipei (1990), and the Taipei City Government (1994), which served to create the backbone of the district starting from its western part. Subsequently, commercial and office buildings such as Shin Kong Mitsukoshi were built along the southern edge of the district, and urban transport links including the subway were improved. Although large scale developments came to a halt as a result of economic stagnation after the completion of Taipei 101 (2004), this project for Nanshan Plaza, as the last major development in the area, started to gain momentum in 2011 under the initiative of the Taipei city government.

台北市副都心信義計劃區
郭茂林先生參考東京的丸之内、新宿等地作為信義區都市計劃的基礎，設計了行人可自在步行的街道。「台北世貿中心」(1985

09 / 10 / 2012

The planned site was a node in the urban planning of Xinyi District
基地位置座落於信義計畫區內都市計畫的樞紐
計画地は信義計画区の都市計画における結節点にあった

「國際貿易大樓」(1988年)、「台北國際會議中心」(1989年)、「台北君悅酒店」(1990年)、「台北市政府」(1994年)等陸續完工,由信義計畫區的西側開始形成街道的骨架。之後南側的「新光三越」等商業設施及其他商辦大樓興起,捷運等大眾運輸的建設也趨於完善。「台北101」完工(2004年)後,因為經濟停滯的關係,台北市內大規模的土地開發案皆一度停歇。2011年由台北市政府主導啟動的本案,也被譽為是信義計畫區內最後一處面積廣大且完整的指標開發案。

台北市副都心としての信義計画区
東京の丸の内や新宿などを参考にした郭茂林氏による都市計画を下地に、歩行者に快適な街づくりとして「台北貿易センター」(1985年)、「國際貿易大樓」(1988年)、「台北国際会議センター」(1989年)、「グランドハイアット台北」(1990年)、「台北市政府」(1994年)が次々に建設され、地区の西側から街の骨格が形成されていった。その後、南側に「新光三越」などの商業施設やオフィスビルが建ち、地下鉄などの都市交通が充実した。「台北101」竣工(2004年)後、経済停滞から大規模開発は止まったが、最後の広大なエリア開発として、2011年に今回のプロジェクトが台北市の主導で動き始めた。

Superimposed Mr. Morin Kaku's urban planning scheme onto Xinyi Special District (2015).

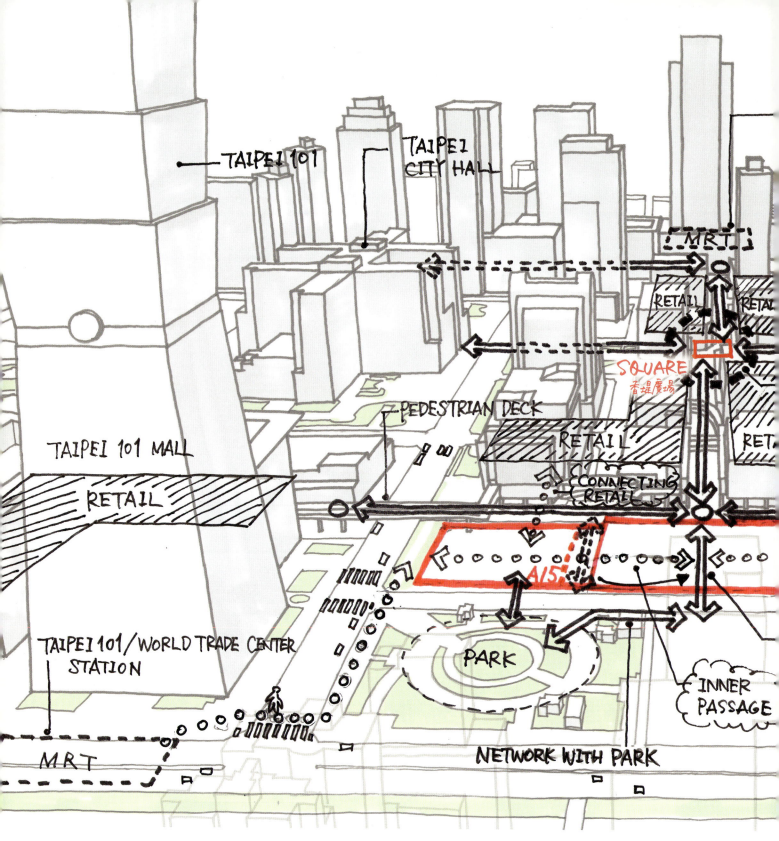

Discovering the axial nature of the city

Previously, Taipei World Trade Center Hall 2 in the A18 area, which occupied part of the site for this project, was built in order to block the "bustling" axis that stretches from the Taipei City Hall MRT station and extends southwards, passing through the plaza. Our attention was drawn to the fact that this plaza occupied the center of Xinyi Special District, and that the axis was slightly staggered at a distance across from the plaza. The plan was to position the newly planned tower (high-rise building) along the axis to the north of the plaza (placing a building at the tip of a road is considered inauspicious for *feng shui*, or geomancy, reasons), so as to ensure a sense of coordination and integration from a distance. Moreover, the axis to the south of the plaza that stretches up until the planned site was positioned as a pedestrian one, connected to the site itself. We considered that by putting the entrances and exits to the bus, bicycle, and car parking spaces in the A20 area, we would be able to segregate foot from vehicular traffic. In addition, by creating multi-layered lines of movement that go through both the site and the interior of the building in an east-west direction, we sought to create a unified sense of bustling liveliness with the lines of pedestrian flow coming from the subway stations on both the eastern and western sides, as well as the commercial activity on the lower levels of Taipei 101.

發現都市的軸向

從圖面上可分析得知本案A18街廓中的舊建物「世貿二館」的位置，過去似乎是阻斷了來自捷運台北市政府站，貫穿香堤廣場往南延伸的「商業活動」的軸線。

我們發現位於信義計畫區中心的香堤廣場，包夾廣場二邊的軸線，呈現些許的偏離。因此，我們將本案的塔樓(辦公棟)，配置於廣場北側那段軸線的延伸位置上(因風水上認為位於道路端點的建築物有路沖問題應予避免)，同時定位廣場南側那段延伸至基地的軸線，作為行人為主的軸線與基地連結。

另外我們也考量到如果將巴士、汽車、機車的停車場出入口設置於A20街廓，就能作到人車分離。再者，如果可以創造出貫穿基地和建築物東西向的複層動線，從捷運站前來的東西向行人動線，就可與「台北101」裙樓的商業活動結合，進而建構成為有整體感的商圈。

Inviting the "bustling" axis in the district, and dividing the site into three

09/14/2012

接納地區商業活動的軸線，將基地分為三區
地区の「賑わい」軸を受け止め、敷地を3つに分割

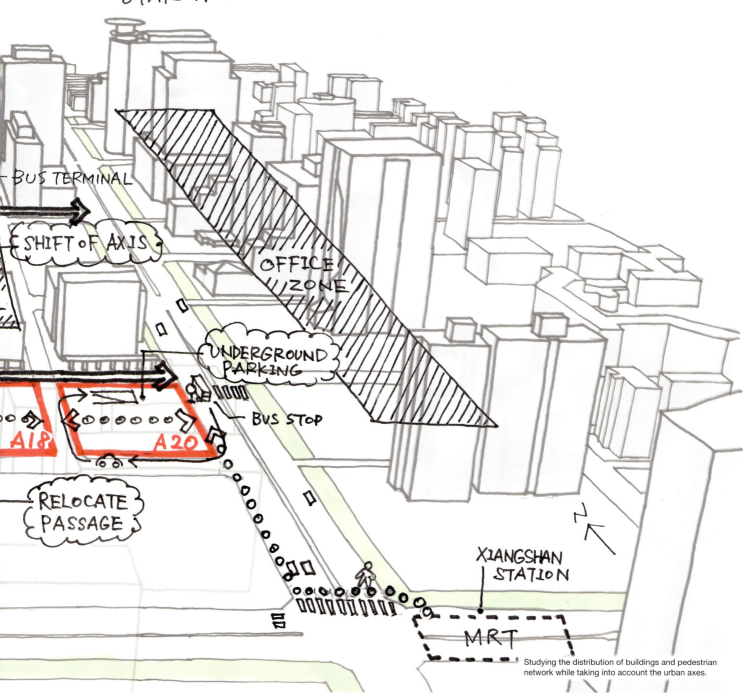

Studying the distribution of buildings and pedestrian network while taking into account the urban axes.

都市の軸性を発見する

かつて、計画敷地の一部であるA18街区にあった「世貿二館」という建物は、MRT台北市政府駅から、香堤広場を経由して南に伸びる「賑わい」の軸をブロックするように建っていた。私たちは、この香堤広場が信義計画区の中心であること、広場を挟んで軸が微妙にずれていることに着目した。そこで、風水上、道の突端に建物を置くことは好まれないため、新たに計画されるタワー（高層棟）を広場より北の軸に合わせて置く。そして、広場より南の、敷地に至る軸を歩行者の軸と位置づけ、敷地に繋いだ。また、バス、自動車、バイクの駐車場出入口をA20街区に設ければ、歩車を分離できると考えた。さらに、敷地・建物内を東西に通り抜けられる多層の動線をつくり、東西双方にある地下鉄駅からの歩行者動線、「台北101」低層部の商業と、一体的な賑わいづくりを目指した。

The site before construction started (2004).

09/21/2012 Seeing the possibilities of two options with tower layout

塔樓配置的兩種可能性浮現
2種類のタワー配置の可能性が見えてきた

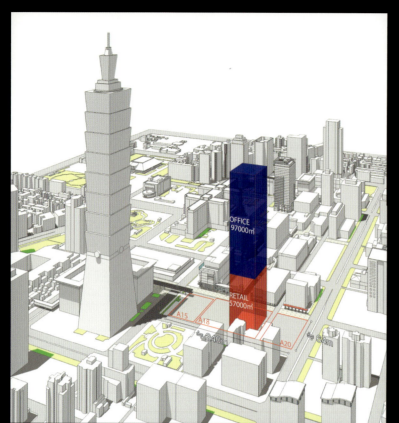
Required program and volume.

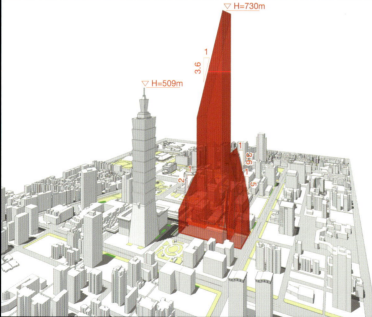
Possible envelope of the building determined by the legal setback limit.

Required volume.

Proposal to add a cultural facility to the city.

Proposal to make up the skyline with three office blocks.

Proposing a cultural facility that would create added value for the client into the future

Based on a set of given conditions, we made repeated studies using physical models and 3D modeling. The initial client's brief mainly required for offices and commercial spaces, but as the discussion progressed, the idea to build a cultural facility that would attract a larger crowd and bring added value to the offices and commercial activities came about. After analyzing the surrounding area, we settled on a fundamental plan that involved positioning the commercial spaces on the western side of the site, with the offices and cultural facility on the eastern side.

As we continued to study the appropriate building volumes, we investigated the optimum distribution and configuration that would enhance their value to the highest potential. The conditions stipulated by the client for the competition of Taipei Nanshan Plaza was to propose two office towers, the head office tower of approximately 150m, and 120m office tower for the lease. We began to think that it was better to aggregate both functions into one tower.

業主提案設立未來能產生附加價值的藝文設施

依據各種設計條件，我們反覆利用模型及電腦進行模擬。
一開始業主的需求是以辦公及商業機能為主，但在雙方研究的過程中，激盪出可以設立能吸引更多人群聚集的藝文設施，並賦予

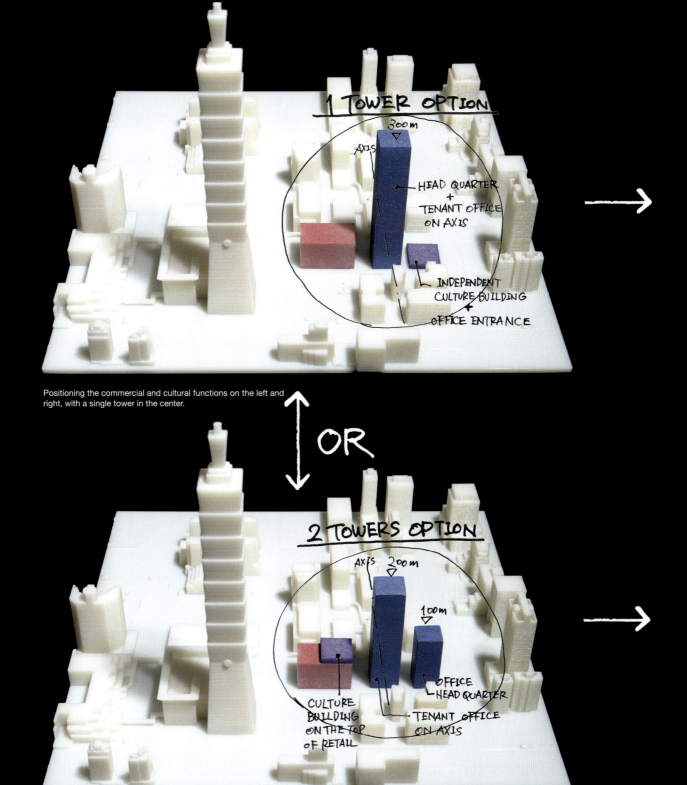

Positioning the commercial and cultural functions on the left and right, with a single tower in the center.

Dividing the tower into two blocks. Positioning the commercial and cultural functions and an additional tower on the left and right, with the main tower in the center.

辦公及商業高度附加價值的創意想法。同時解讀區域周邊的特性,決定了基地的西側作為商業,東側則為辦公及藝文設施之基本配置的方向性。
研究量體的過程中,我們思考了最能提昇建築物價值的配棟方案。最初業主所提出的「臺北南山廣場」備標條件是設計高度約150公尺的總部大樓,以及高度約120公尺的租賃型大樓的雙塔規劃,但我們提出了將兩棟機能整合為一棟較為有利的想法。

クライアントへ未来にわたり付加価値を生み出す文化施設も提案した

条件を基に、模型とコンピュータ上でのスタディを繰り返した。当初、クライアントの要望はオフィスと商業がメインだったが、検討を進めるうち、多くの人を集める文化施設を設け、オフィスや商業に高い付加価値を与えるアイデアが生まれた。エリア周辺を読み込み、敷地の西側に商業、東側にオフィスと文化施設を配する基本的な方向性が定まった。

ボリューム検討を進めつつ、最も建物の価値を高める配棟・高さ、新しい用途である文化施設を提案した。当初、クライアントからの「臺北南山廣場」のコンペ与件は、高さ約150mの本社ビルと、高さ約120mの賃貸ビルの2棟構成だったが、私たちは両方の機能を1棟のタワーに集約した方がよいと考えるようになった。

1 TOWER OPTION

2015

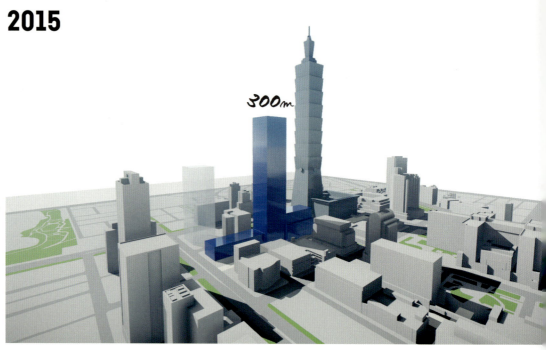

300m

2 TOWERS OPTION

2015

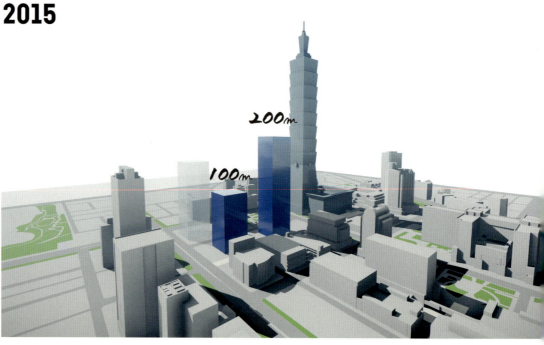

200m
100m

10 05 2012

Proposal for 1 Tower Option allows the project to coexist with Taipei 101, and create a fitting Taipei skyline

正因是單棟方案才能與「台北101」共存，創造出台北的風景
1棟案こそが「台北101」と共存し、台北の風景をつくり出す

Imagining changes of the urban landscape 20 years from now

By simulating the future Taipei urban images, we predicted that buildings in the area would gradually become high-rise buildings by 2030. Nanshan Plaza would be buried in the flock of skyscrapers if we were to proceed with the 2 Towers Option . Therefore, we deliberately chose to submit a proposal for a 1 Tower Option, in contradiction to the conditions stipulated by the client. We placed a particular emphasis on the creation of a new skyline based on a cluster of sculptural forms together with the symbol of Taipei, Taipei 101, in order to enhance its visual distinctiveness and recognizability from a distance. There may be a possibilities that the silhouette of all but the top crown of Nanshan Plaza to disappear from sight as a result of the future transformation of the entire area into skyscrapers. Accordingly, we concluded that the solution would be to emphasize the crown design of the tower, while ensuring a certain balance with the entire proportion.

The act of designing architecture might be said to be equivalent to far-sighted urban design. What is important is to analyze how urban development occurs around the world in order to predict the future, and to enhance the long term value of a given area as a whole in addition to the building being designed.

In October 2012, we obtained approval from the client for our design proposal for 1 Tower Option.

想像20年後城市的變化

我們透過模擬台北未來的模樣，預測2030年左右周圍建築物將會持續高層化，假設現在採用原先業主設定的雙塔方案並執行

▶▶ **2025**　　　　　　　　　　　　　　▶▶▶ **2035**

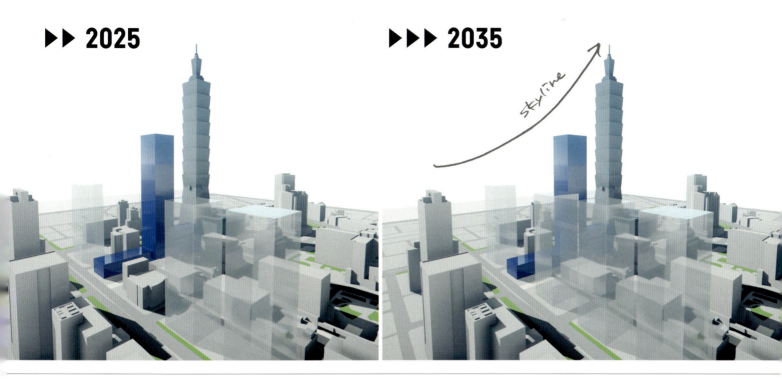

▶▶ **2025**　　　　　　　　　　　　　　▶▶▶ **2035**

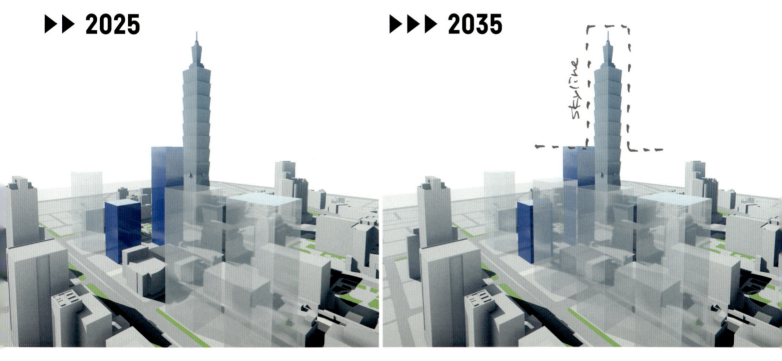

它，預料將來「臺北南山廣場」將埋沒於眾多高層建築之中。因此，我們也嘗試向業主提出單棟的設計方案。
我們重視提高從遠景眺望建築物的辨識度，並期待與台北的象徵「台北101」形成群狀的新天際線。同時，我們預測了此地區整體高層化的結果，可能最後只能看見「臺北南山廣場」頂部的輪廓，因此認為應該特別強調頂部的造型設計並與整體設計取得平衡。建築設計也可說是展望未來的都市設計。我們分析了世界各地的都市開發並從中預測未來，用長期的觀點貫注於建築物本身，並認為提升區域整體的價值甚是重要。在2012年10月，終於說服業主同意單棟的超高層大廈的設計方案。

20年後の都市の変化を想像する

私たちは、台北の将来像のシミュレーションを通して、2030年頃にはこの周囲の建物が続々と高層化すること、仮にここでクライアントの要求である2棟案を採用すると「臺北南山廣場」はその中に埋没することを予測し、1棟案も提案することにした。
台北のシンボルである「台北101」と、群造形的に新たなスカイラインを形成し、遠景からの視認性を高めることを重視した。将来的なエリア全体の高層化で、「臺北南山廣場」は頂部のシルエットしか見えなくなることも予想できる。そこで、頂部のデザインを強調し、全体とのバランスをデザインすべきという結論に至った。

建築の設計は、未来を見据えた都市デザインだと言える。世界中の都市開発を分析し、そこから未来を予測すること、長期的視野で建築そのものに加え、地域全体の価値を向上させることが重要だ。2012年10月、クライアントから、超高層1棟とする設計提案の了承を得た。

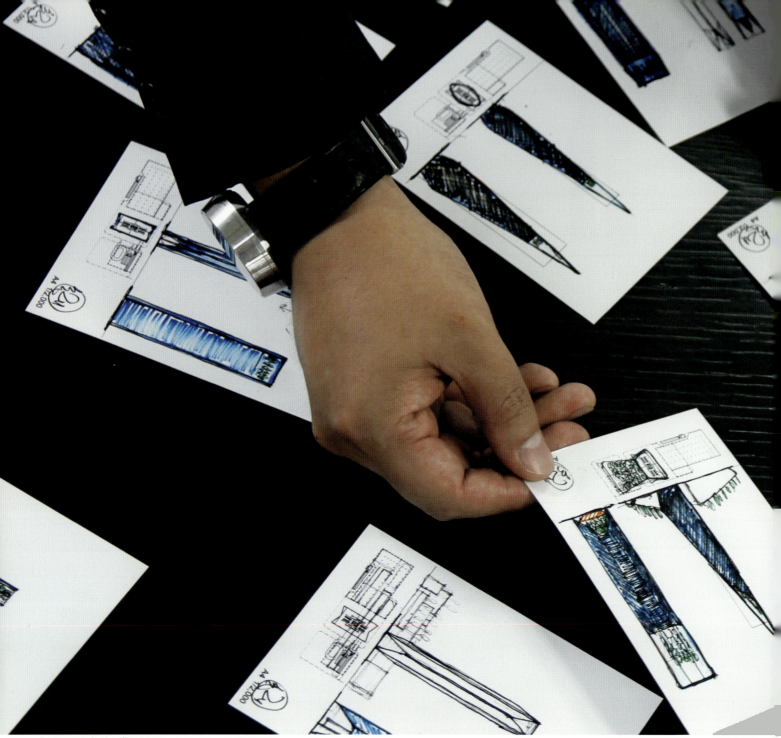

Design study for the office tower.

Repeated studies in Taiwan using models and 3D.
Mr.Kaino and our collarborators rushed to Taiwan.

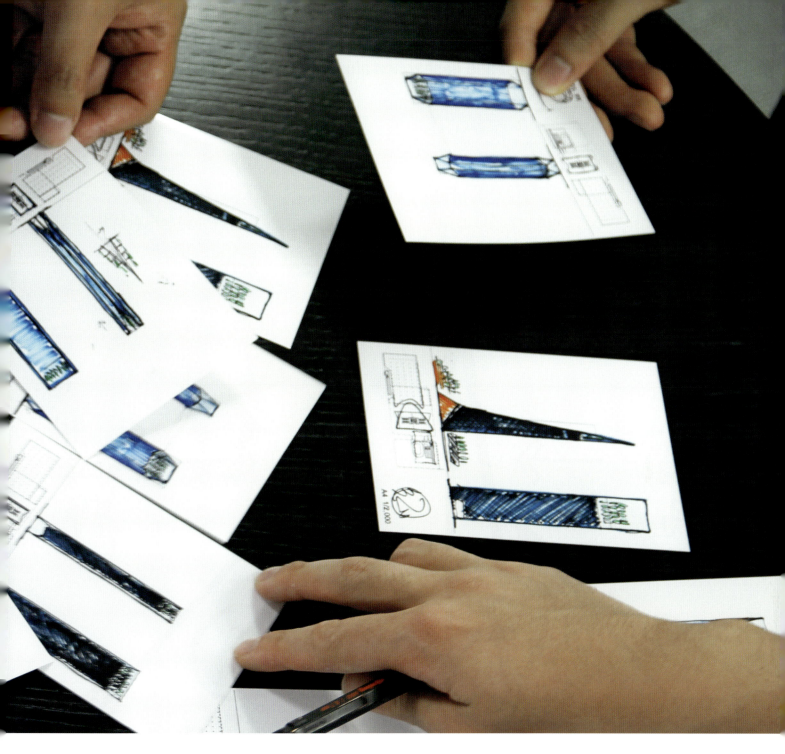

10/12/2012 What would be the concept and the tower design with a long lasting impression?

烙印心中的概念及塔樓設計

心に残るコンセプトとタワーデザインとは

High speed two-weeks design team
The proposal for a 1 Tower Option was accepted. The client proceeded to review the construction plans, review by the city council, and other aspects of the overall schedule, and instructed us w to "compress the design stage into two weeks" - an extremely short timeframe. We concentrated our efforts on exploring what a design that could further enhance the value of this building while activating the entirety of the surrounding area would be. Thanks to the support of a group of trusted collaborators who rushed over from Japan, we immediately formed a team in a small rented office in Taiwan that worked on the design. What would a concept and design for a tower that creates a lasting impression with the client look like?

What followed was a repeated process of trial and error that involved making sketches and models.

為期兩週的高速設計專業團隊
單棟塔樓的方案定案後，業主調整了施工計畫及都市設計審議等的整體時間表，並對我們下達了「兩週內完成設計」的指示。這是極度被壓縮的時間，我們集中摸索如何能更進一步提升建築物的價值，並思考如何才能更加活化週邊整體地區的設計。
我們在台灣狹小的租賃辦公室中，與從日本趕來支援的同事，即時組成了設計小組，思考能夠深刻烙印在業主心中的概念和塔樓的設計，到底該怎麼做？我們反覆地透過繪圖及製作模型等進行檢討，也嘗試了不少錯誤。

2週間の高速でデザインを行うチーム
1棟のタワーを提案することが決まった。クライアントが施工計画、都市審議などの全体スケジュールを見直し、私たちのもとに「2週間でデザインを詰めるように」と指示が入った。きわめて短い時間である。私たちは、この建物の価値をさらに向上させ、周辺地区全体をさらに活性化できるデザインとは何か、集中して模索した。
台湾の小さな貸しオフィスで、日本から駆けつけた仲間たちのサポートにより、デザインを進めるチームを即時に結成した。クライアントの心に残るコンセプト、タワーのデザインとはどのようなものだろう。スケッチや模型づくりなど、試行錯誤を繰り返した。

Integrating the west and east zones along an urban axis

融合都市軸上的東西區塊
都市軸上で東西のゾーンを融合する

10/24/2012

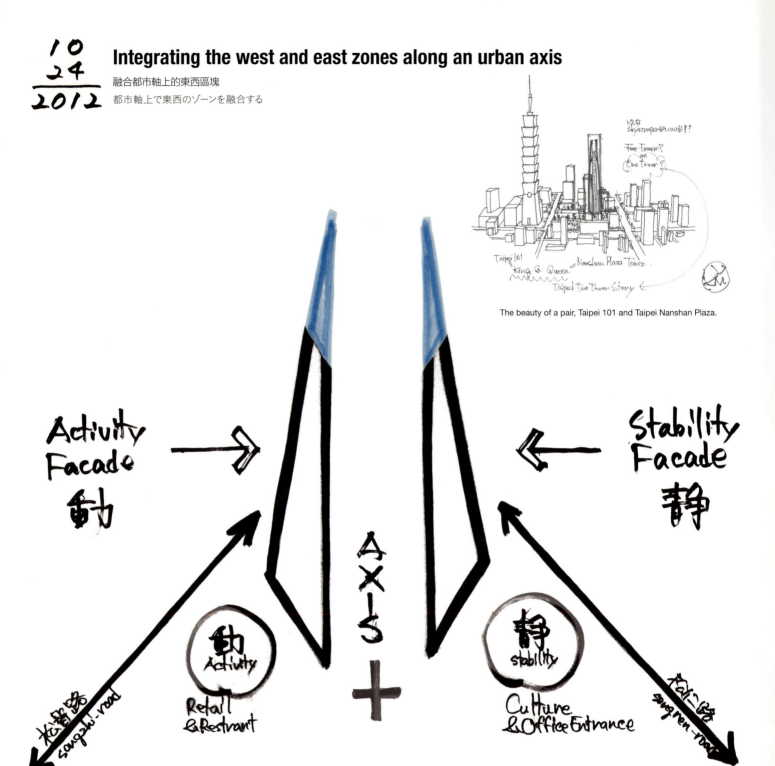

The beauty of a pair, Taipei 101 and Taipei Nanshan Plaza.

The design concept of the office tower is based on the idea of combining two places together.

A "mountain" design where two become one

One week left until the final presentation. The design needs to be refined and given more depth. What would a design that creates a lasting impression with the client and the Taiwanese be? The originality of design was still lacking.

After agonizing over this for several days, we went to the head office of our client, Nan Shan Life Insurance, to meet with the person in charge of the project. As soon as we stepped into the lobby, a piece of calligraphy depicting the Chinese characters for "Nan Shan (南山)" hanging on the wall leapt into view. The tip of the character for "Shan (山)" resembled two triangles fused together, and it was also looked as if two hands joined in unison.

After agonizing over this for several days, we went to the head office of our client, Nan Shan Life Insurance, to meet with the person in charge of the project. As soon as we stepped into the lobby, a piece of calligraphy depicting the Chinese characters for "Nan Shan" hanging on the wall leapt into view. The tip of the character for "Shan" resembled two triangles fused together, and it was also looked as if two hands joined in unison.

The site for Taipei Nanshan Plaza, which stretches some 270m from east to west, connects the bustling western zone where Taipei 101 stands with the quieter western zone populated by many office buildings and high-end residences. As a node on the urban axis conceived by Mr. Morin kaku, we wanted to design this project so that these two zones would become one.

二者合一的「山」型設計

離最後簡報的時間只剩下一週，必須要讓設計進一步深化，到底甚麼才是可以留存在業主跟台灣民眾心中的設計？設計上還是缺乏獨創性…。

煩惱了數日後，為了與專案窗口開會，我們前往南山人壽的總公司。踏入大廳的瞬間，掛在牆上的書法墨寶「南山」兩字映入眼簾，「山」字是由兩個三角形結合而成，傳達了雙手合十般的意境。

「台北101」與「臺北南山廣場」、「業主」和「建築師」、「本地設計

團隊」和「三菱地所設計」……「成雙」的關係成了後續我們設計的主軸。業主的保險公司因有加入保險的保戶支持得以成立，所以「成雙」的形狀也可視為南山人壽與台灣民眾的關係。宛如雙手合十的「山」字，又可以解讀成表達感謝之意。東西向長度約270公尺的「臺北南山廣場」的基地，同時連接了西側「台北101」的商業鬧區，及東側聚集眾多辦公大樓、高級住宅的寧靜區域。我們參考郭茂林先生所思考的都市軸線的節點，希望展現兩個區塊結合為一的設計。

ふたつがひとつになる「山」のデザイン
最終プレゼンテーションまで残り1週間。さらにデザインを深めなくてはならない。クライアントや台湾の人びとの心に残るデザインとはどのようなものか？　まだまだオリジナリティが足りない。悩むこと数日、担当者との打合せのためにクライアントである南山人寿の本社に向かった。ロビーに足を踏み入れた瞬間、壁に掲げられた「南山」の書が目に飛び込んできた。その「山」の字の先端は、ふたつの三角形が合わさったかたちをしており、両手を合わせているようでもあった。
「台北101」と「臺北南山廣場」、クライアントと建築家、現地設計チームと三菱地所設計……。「ふたつ」の関係は常にテーマとなっていた。クライアントは、生命保険会社として加入する人びとにより会社を成り立たせる。ふたつのかたちを南山人寿と台湾の人びととして見ることもできるだろう。合掌するような「山」の字は、感謝を表しているようにも見えた。「台北101」が建つ西側の賑わいのゾーンと、オフィスビルや高級レジデンスが多い東側の静かなゾーンを、東西約270mにわたる「臺北南山廣場」の敷地が繋ぐ。郭茂林氏が考えた都市軸の結節点として、このふたつのゾーンがひとつになるデザインとしたいと考えた。

The way that two mountains overlap with each other was superimposed onto studies of their peaks.

Tower design that fuses two mountains is accepted

決定兩個合而為一的山型設計

ふたつの山が合わさったデザインで決定

The direction of the proposal that was decided on.

Our design on the form of two overlapping objects is based on the Nan Shan calligraphy piece in the lobby of Nan Shan Life Insurance. We presented a total of 5 design options. Three of these designs featured uniform standard floors with only the tip of the building given a conspicuous shape. One featured standard floors that gradually became smaller toward the top, so that it resembled a mountain, and the final one was based on the shape of two mountains combined to form one.

在南山人壽總公司的大廳與「南山」墨寶相遇後，我們將兩個重疊成為一個的概念作為後續的設計基礎。我們向業主說明了五款不同的設計方案，包括三組以相同的標準層平面，但僅有頂部較為顯眼的設計方案，和標準層平面往頂層漸縮漸小宛如山峰般造型的方案，以及另一組則是兩座山合而為一的設計。

南山人寿本社のロビーで出会った「南山」の書から、ふたつのものが重なることをデザインのベースとした。
基準階が同一で頂部だけが目立つものを3つ、基準階を少しずつ頂部に向けて小さくして、山のようにしたものがひとつ、ふたつの山が合わさりひとつの山となるデザインの合計5つの案を説明した。

10/24/2012 Presentation that would decide the architectural design
決定外觀設計的簡報
建築デザインを決めるプレゼンテーション

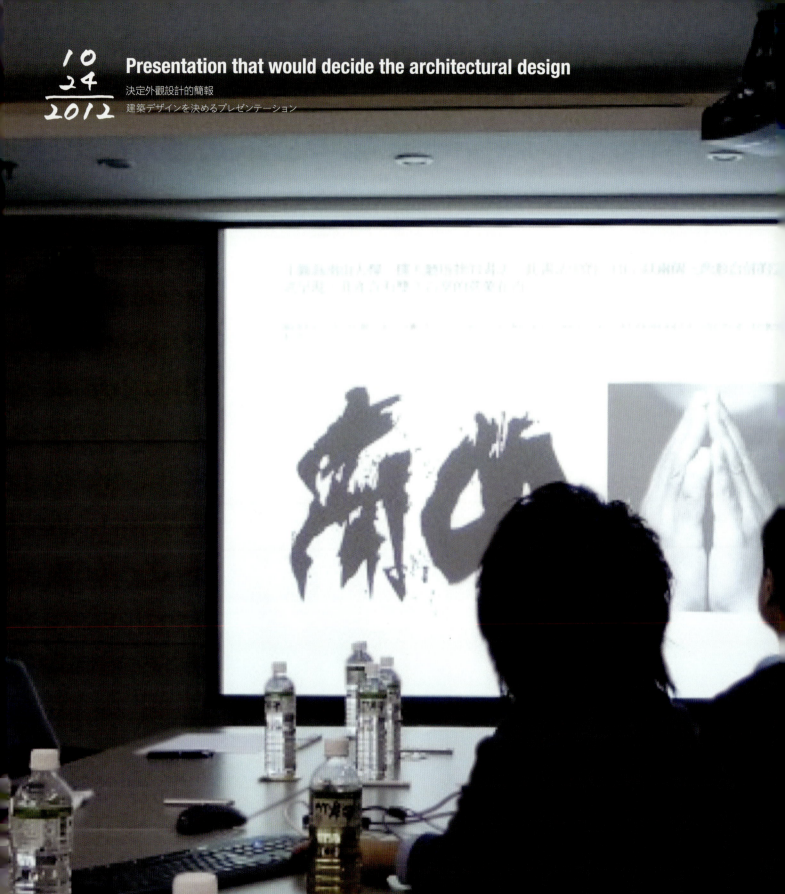

October 24, 2012 was the date of the fateful presentation. Our encounter with the calligraphy piece at the head office of Nan Shan Life Insurance, the question of how to create the "Shan" character in "Nan Shan"... conveying the form of a building is a difficult task.
Using perspective renderings and physical models, we explained our proposal in great detail, together with the several other options.
The final decision on the design was made through a vote by all those present, after the top leadership on the client side shared their thoughts on the project. As a result, the proposal that we had anxiously hoped would succeed was chosen. Our two weeks of trial and error had paid off, while our dream of realizing this building also started to harbor the promise of reality.

2012年10月24日，親臨這場攸關設計命運的簡報。在南山人壽總公司與「山」字墨寶的相遇，以及南山的「山」到底要怎麼呈現？要傳達造型這件事情著實困難。我們使用了透視圖及模型進行複數個設計方案的詳細說明。
最終設計方案的決定方式，是業主方決策長官與在場的所有人，分享業主對於本專案所寄託的期待，最後讓出席者進行舉手投票。結果，我們熱望的方案獲得業主採用，為期兩週的反覆摸索分析，終於結成果實，我們的夢想就此開始奔馳。

2012年10月24日、運命のプレゼンテーションである。南山人寿の本社での書との出会い、南山という山をどのようにつくるのか……。かたちを伝えることは難しい。パースと模型を用いて、複数の検討案とともに、じっくりと説明した。
最終的なデザインの決定は、クライアントのトップが本プロジェクトに託す想いを一同に共有した後、出席者による挙手により決まった。結果、私たちが切望した案が採択された。2週間の試行錯誤が実を結んだのと同時に、さらに夢が膨らみ始めた。

10/24/2012 — Conceiving of the commercial podium that would boost footfall, and the cultural podium that serves as an entrance to the development

吸引人潮的商場棟及成為入口的藝文棟

人を引き上げる商業棟、入口となる文化棟を考える

Study of commercial podium.
Reviewing forms that would ensure a large roof surface together with greenery.

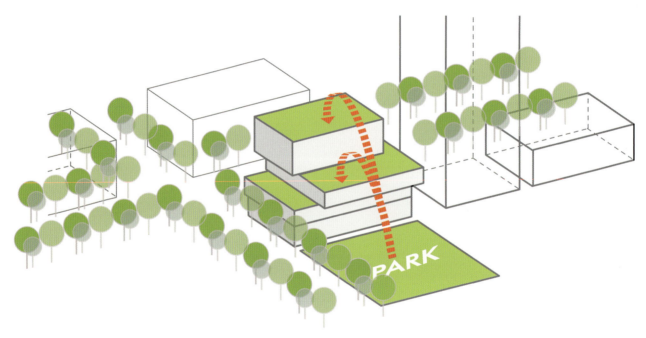

The three-dimensional plants and greenery that connect to the park on the south side are enticing to both people and birds.

Design super high rise in one week
One of the requirements stipulated by the planning and zoning commission was the necessity for a "place of rest where birds and insects and come and gather" ——a condition quite unique to Taipei, surrounded as it is by mountains.
By stacking the retail and restaurant boxes and staggering them, we were able to increase the floor area of the rooftop, and create a variety of different floor levels. Installing a terrace on the roof surface and positioning trees and greenery throughout, we sought to entice people at ground level towards the upper levels. The concept behind this was to form an urban green belt integrated with the existing park on the south side.

與人共生生物多樣性
在台北市的都市發展願景綱要計畫中，有提到因為臺北盆地四面環山，建議開發案應提供「鳥類及昆蟲飛來時可以棲息休憩的場所」。利用商場棟的疊箱設計，將箱體錯開的部分擴大作為屋頂平台，形成各種不同高程的樓層。我們將屋頂規劃為露臺，透過種植樹木植栽，吸引地面層人流至此。這是呼應南側既有的公園，並形成整體城市綠帶的概念。

人の活動と共生する生物多様性
「鳥や虫が飛来でき、憩う場も必要である」という周辺が山々に囲われた台北ならではの都市発展政策の項目がある。
商業の箱を積層し、箱をずらすことで屋根面積を大きく、多様なレベルの床ができる。屋根面にテラスを設け、木々を配置することで地上の人を上層階に誘導できると考えた。南側にある既存の公園と一体となった都市の緑地帯も形成するコンセプトとした。

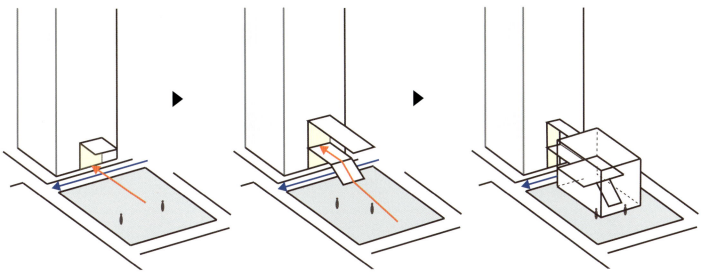

Study of cultural + entrance podium.
The bridge straddling the road, the approach to the office tower, and the cultural functions were combined to make up the cultural + entrance podium.

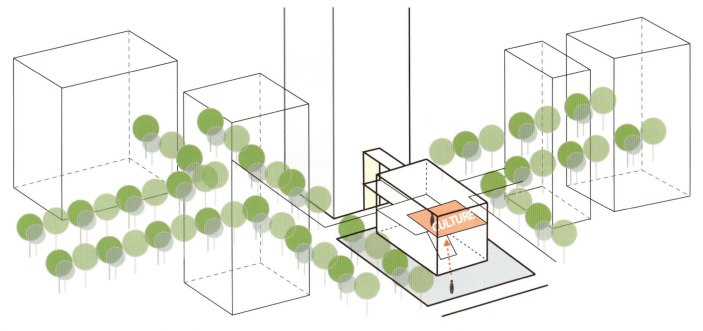

The low-rise cultural + entrance podium pulls people towards the cityscape where high-rise buildings stand.

A voluminous presence that is immediately recognizable as the entrance to the tower
Typically, the office entrance is accessed by visitors through the street out in front, from which they can quickly get on the elevator. Since a road runs through the site for this project, we situated the office lobby on the second floor, and designed a bridge that would lead up to it. Taking in the consideration of the climate of Taiwan, we decided to make the bridge as the interior space. This space is the cultural facility (Nanshan Hall), which serves not only as the approach to the offices, but also a place to welcome people and visitors.

超高樓層入口外型的量體
一般來說，來訪者會從辦公大樓的正面入口進出，並馬上能搭乘電梯是最常見的規劃方式。但本案的規劃是在基地內設計可穿越的通道，故辦公大樓的大廳設置於二樓並與空橋銜接。因考慮到台灣的氣候，將空橋的設計室內化，同時建築物內設置藝文中心（Nanshan Hall），因此，並非只是單純前往辦公大樓的通道，同時擁有歡迎款待來訪者的功能。

タワーのエントランスと分かる佇まいのボリューム
オフィスのエントランスといえば、来館者は正面の通りからアクセスし、すぐにエレベータに乗るのが一般的だ。しかし今回の計画では敷地内に道路が走っていることから、オフィスロビーを2階に設け、ブリッジで渡す計画とした。その際、台湾の気候を考慮し、ブリッジを内部化することとした。ここには文化施設（Nanshan Hall）を併設し、単なるオフィスのアプローチではなく、人をもてなす場としても機能することとした。

10/24/2012 · The design of the tower, as well as the commercial podium and the cultural + entrance podium, is decided

商場棟、藝文入口棟的設計也和辦公棟同時定案
タワーと共に商業棟と文化・入口棟のデザインが決定

Design study of commercial podium.

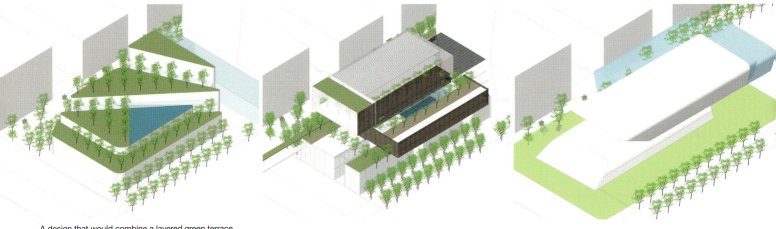

A design that would combine a layered green terrace with the interior plan was sought.

Making people gather | Commercial podium with stacked greenery
When designing the commercial podium, we decided to create a simple stack of three boxes, taking into account the lines of movement in the interior and the location of stairwells and escalator voids. The concept was to create a commercial podium that would entice people, with a green terrace where birds and insects could come as well.

聚集人潮的設計 | 綠意堆疊的商場棟
商場棟的設計需要思考內部動線及挑高的問題,我們決定用簡單的三個箱子堆疊的方式,其概念是建造出可吸引人群,並擁有可讓鳥類及昆蟲停留棲息的綠色露臺的商場棟。

人が集まるデザイン | 緑を積層した商業棟
商業棟をどのようにデザインするか、内部の動線や吹き抜けなども配慮しシンプルな3つのボックスを積層したもので決まった。コンセプトは人を誘い、鳥や虫も飛来できる緑のテラスがある商業棟である。

Design study of cultural + entrance podium.

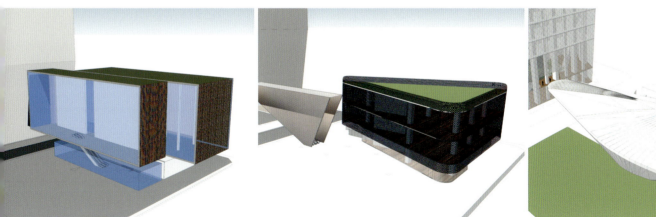

Exploring designs that would prove enticing to people, while also holding its own as a standalone cultural facility.

Designing a polyhedron similar to how the tower was designed

In addition to the proposal of a cultural facility that would give the office entrance added value, the client also requested that the facade of the cultural facility to be symbolic. We proposed three designs: staggered-box scheme similar to the commercial podium, the detached scheme that the office entrance and cultural facility were separated, and a scheme based on the polyhedron form of the tower, with a large overhang that serves as a rain canopy.

與辦公棟相同的多面體設計

除了在辦公大樓入口棟設置藝文設施以創造附加價值的提案外，業主提出希望創造具有象徵性外觀的需求。我們向業主提出了與商場棟相同語彙的箱體錯列的設計，及辦公大樓入口與藝文設施分棟的設計，還有與辦公棟同樣為多面體，像是雨庇般由建築量體向外突出的三種設計方案。

高層棟のデザイン同様の多面体デザイン

オフィスのエントランスに付加価値を与える文化施設を設ける提案に加えて、クライアントからは象徴的なファサードがほしいという要望があった。商業棟と同じく箱をずらしたデザインや、オフィスエントランスと文化施設が分棟しているデザイン、そしてタワーと同じ多面体で、雨除けのキャノピーとなるように建物をせり出したデザインの3つを提案した。

10/31/2012

Using physical paper models to convey what could not be completely expressed using perspective images

使用紙製模型來傳達透視圖無法表現的空間感

パースで表現しきれない空間を紙製の模型で伝える

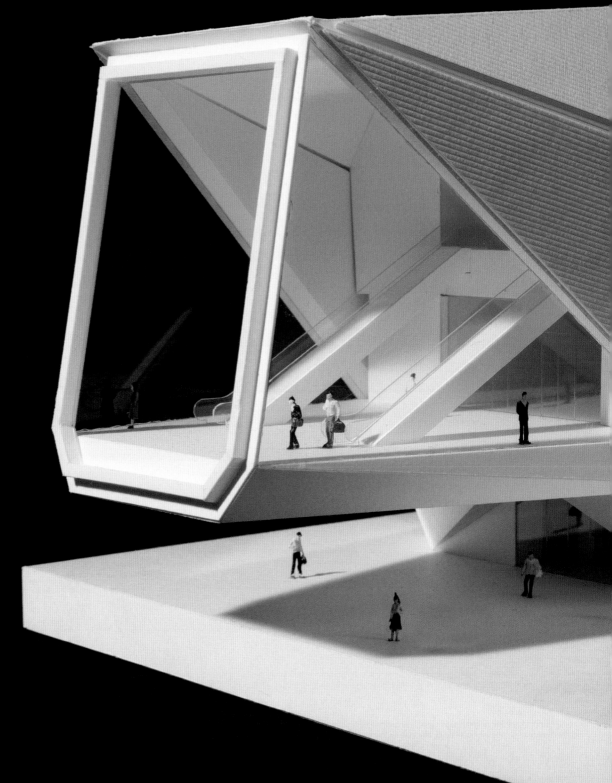

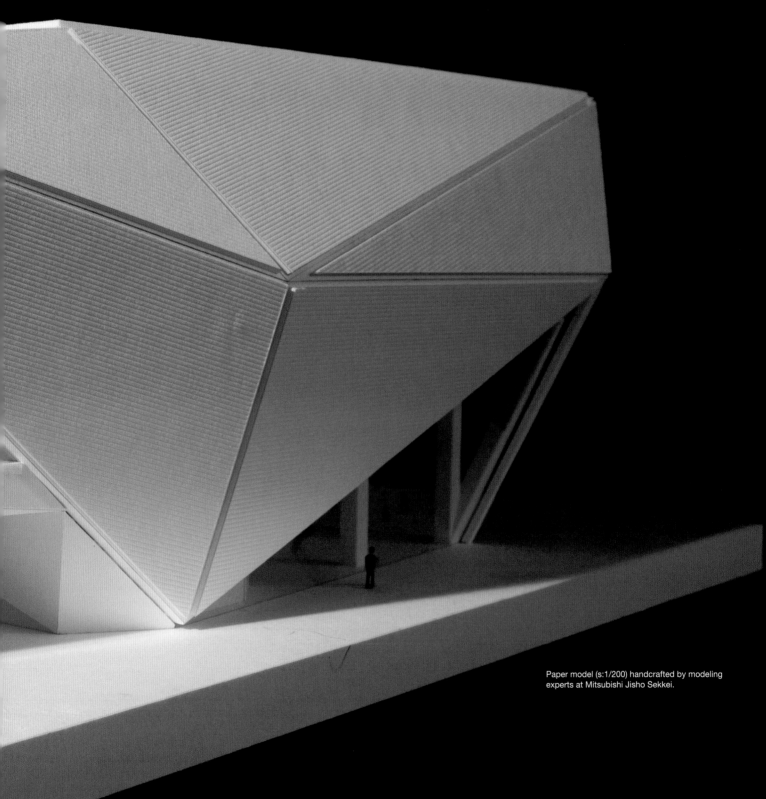

Paper model (s:1/200) handcrafted by modeling experts at Mitsubishi Jisho Sekkei.

Making a strong impression with high-precision physical paper models
We used precise physical models to present the beautiful polyhedral form and its details, to which much design effort was devoted. The accuracy of the physical paper models and delicate shading casted on the models, which are typical presentation methods in Japan, lent our presentation a great deal of persuasiveness. It was, no doubt, one of the major factors that led our presentation to a successful outcome.

高精準度的紙製模型令人印象深刻
為了傳達在「臺北南山廣場」專案中，我們尤下功夫的多面體之美及其個別構件之間的收頭處理，我們盡量以精緻的模型來做簡報。在日本普遍可見的紙製模型的精準度及立體感，眼見為憑可說是最具說服力，這應該也是我們簡報得以成功的很大的因素之一。

高精度の紙製模型が感銘を与える
「臺北南山廣場」で特に力を入れた多面体の美しさやそれぞれの部材の取り合いを、緻密な模型でプレゼンテーションすることを心がけた。日本では一般的に見られる、紙でつくる模型の精度や陰影感が、見るものに与える説得力は、私たちのプレゼンテーションを成功へと導いた大きな要因のひとつである。

10/31/2012 Three-building design is decided

決定三棟的設計
3棟のデザインが決定

Design By Hands

In Asia, clasped hands express gratitude, harmony, and peace. Modeling the form of the building after this motif, we expressed the client's sentiments of gratitude and peace towards the world. The "Nan Shan" in the company name of the client, moreover, comes from the name of a sort of utopia that is eulogized in Chinese poetry. By making the tower resemble both a palm and a mountain at the same time, the symbolic nature of "Nan Shan" was evoked.

In today's 21st century environment, buildings may seem to be mass produced by computers and machinery. In fact, it is the individual workers and engineers who put their hands for the finishing touches in each process. This skyscraper represents an aggregation of the "handiwork" of numerous architects, manufacturers, and builders. The architects make sketches and use models and design drawings to decide on the appropriate shapes and forms. The manufacturers procure the precise components used in everything from the structure to the finish, while the builders assemble the parts to produce a building like a piece of craft. This tower is perhaps the ultimate expression of the wonder of handmade, artisanal construction, accomplished by all these "hands."

Design By Hands

在東方，雙手合掌代表感謝、融和、和平之意。取此文字之形，用建築物決達彰業主對全世界達感謝、及祈求和平的信念。另外，業主的公司名稱「南山」的由來，則為漢詩中被歌詠的烏托邦。塔樓的造型與合掌概念，同時取於山的形體，作為表現「南山」的標誌。21世紀當下，猶如電腦及機器大量生產的建築物卯應林立。但，事實上每一座建築物都是透過個別的工程，及每一位專業技術者的雙手完成。這座超高層大廈是凝聚了建築師、建材製造商、施工者的「雙手」結晶。建築師透過繪圖、模型及設計圖決定義造型。建材製造商則準備從結構體到裝修面材等建造用的精密材料，施工者將其組裝後呈現如工藝品般的建築物。這座超高層大廈，可說是透過眾多的「手」，所展現出來最極致的作品。

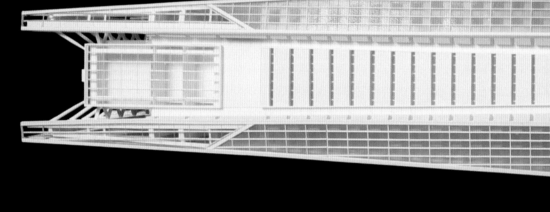

Design By Hands

東洋において「手」を合わせる合掌は、感謝・調和・平和の意を表す。これをかたどり、クライアントの世界に向けた感謝や平和への祈念を表現した。また、クライアントの社名にある「南山」は漢詩に詠まれる理想郷「南山」が由来とされる。タワーを漢と同時に山に見立て、シンボルとしての「南山」を表現した。

21世紀の現在、あたかもコンピュータや機械による大量生産で建物がつくられているかのようだが、実はそれぞれの工程で、一人ひとりの技術者の手を通して完成する。この超高層ビルは、建築家やメーカー、施工者たちの「手」の集の凝集である。建築家がスケッチを描き、模型や設計図でかたちを定める。メーカーは構造体から仕上げまでの精密な部材を用意し、施工者はこれを組み上げ、工芸品のような建物が出来上がる。このタワーは、数々の「手」によるものづくりの素晴らしさを最大限に表現するものになるだろう。

Models produced in Japan. These models helped to facilitate communication among those involved through various presentations.

Mitsubishi Jisho Sekkei's design philosophy |
Creating the vitality pioneered in Tokyo's Marunouchi

孕育自於東京・丸之內創造熱鬧的三菱地所設計的設計哲學

東京・丸の内で培った、賑わいをつくり出す三菱地所設計のデザインフィロソフィー

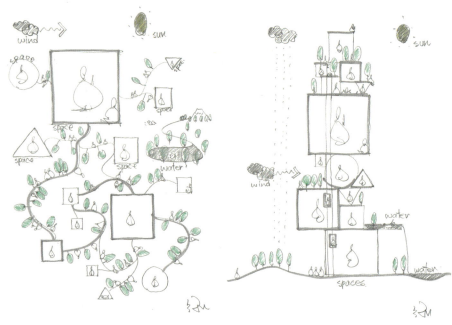

Creating a sense of bustling activity by building ground-level links between multiple uses, just like the Marunouchi area of Tokyo.

Layering multiple uses over each other in order to create a fully three-dimensional sense of liveliness.

Designing cities and skyscrapers

It is the diverse sense of bustling vitality stemming from a mix of multi-cultural and multi-functional uses that gives Tokyo's international financial center, the Marunouchi district, its particular appeal. It is not only the necessary functions such as offices, hotels, residences, and train stations — whether in terms of an entire city or the planning of a single skyscraper — but also the act of combining these with spaces for pause and leisurely strolling, that attracts a large volume of people. For instance, by stacking various functions to create a multi-use environment, even on a single, small plot, it is possible to create a vertical interior city where many cultures are overlaid on each other, and a sense of bustling vitality. We create enjoyable, engaging urban spaces on a plots of land that permit a certain density of use — a philosophy that also underlines Taipei Nanshan Plaza.

Marunouchi Kenchikusho, the predecessor to Mitsubishi Jisho Sekkei, was launched around 130 years ago in a bid to shape and create Tokyo's Marunouchi district. Subsequently, this company went on to create urban neighborhoods, mixed-use buildings in front of train stations, and skyscrapers in Japan as the in-house design organization of a real estate developer. In order to bring

The Marunouchi area of Tokyo, where the design philosophy of Mitsubishi Jisho Sekkei is in evidence (2017).

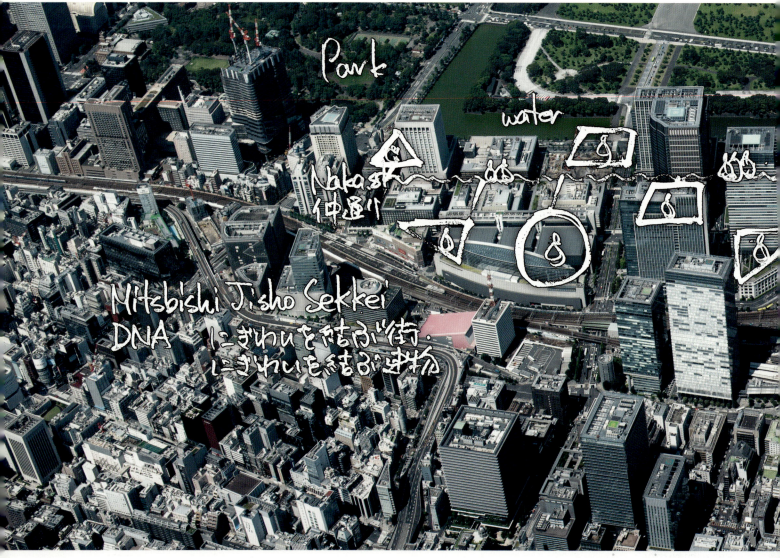

"multi-cultural and multi-use vertical cities" to life, a composite team with a wide range of professional expertise and knowledge is indispensable, in addition to the architects, structural engineers who can tease out rational structures that can realize their designs, and environmental engineers who can propose solutions for reducing environmental impact in addition to controlling the thermal environment.

何謂都市設計與超高層大樓設計

位於國際金融中心的東京・丸之內，因為多種文化、複數機能的混合存在，才造就出多樣化熱鬧商圈的魅力。不僅是於都市，進行超高層大樓的規劃時，除了設計辦公、飯店、住宅、車站等必要空間機能外，需整合成為人們可以散步或駐足的場所，才能匯聚更多的人潮。即使是一塊很小的土地，透過層疊的空間安排使其多功能化，在室內空間堆砌許多文化機能，創造立體都市，自然就能營造熱鬧氛圍。我們擔長在都會區高度密集使用的土地上，創造出人們可以享受生活的空間，這也是「臺北南山廣場」的構思基礎。

大約130年前，為了打造東京・丸之內特區，創立了「丸之內建築所」，也正是三菱地所設計的前身。爾後，整納作為不動產開發商內部的設計部門，完成了街道及站前之複合建築，並建造了幾座日本的超高層建築。為實踐「多種文化・複數用途立體城市」的想法，除了建築師之外，研究出合理結構系統，得以實現建築設計的結構工程師，以及可掌控環境舒適度，且提出減少環境負擔的設備工程師等…擁有豐富專業知識及專業見解的複合團隊是不可或缺的。

都市の設計と超高層ビルの設計は同じである

国際的な金融センターとしてつくられた東京・丸の内に都市的な魅力を与えるためには、多文化・多機能が混在する多様な賑わいを生むことが必須である。都市の設計、超高層ビルの設計の双方で、人が散策し、たたずむことのできる「文化」的な場所とオフィスやホテル、住宅、駅などの必要用途を複合することが、人を集め、賑わいをつくるためには大変重要である。

ひとつの小さな土地であっても、これを積層化して、内部に文化が積層する多用途からなる立体都市をつくれば、賑わいを生むことができる。われわれは、都市部の高度利用可能な土地に、人びとが楽しむことのできる空間を生み出している。「臺北南山廣場」もこのような思想がベースとなった。

三菱地所設計のルーツである130年前の「丸ノ内建築所」は、東京・丸の内をつくるために発足し、その後、デベロッパーのインハウス設計組織として、街や駅前の複合建築、そして日本の超高層建築をつくり上げてきた。こうした「多文化・多用途立体都市」を実現するためには、建築家だけでなく、デザインを実現する合理的なストラクチャーを導き出すことのできる構造エンジニアや温熱環境をコントロールできるだけでなく環境負荷低減の提案を行える環境エンジニアなど、幅広い専門性に富んだ知見を持つ複合チームが不可欠である。

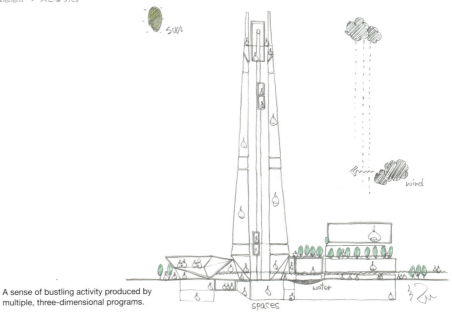

A sense of bustling activity produced by multiple, three-dimensional programs.

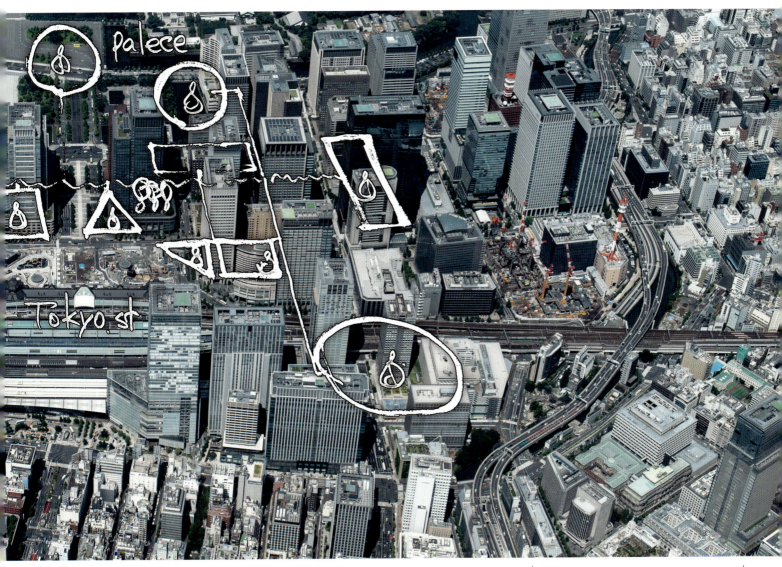

05 / 2012 Design methodology to create a new cityscape for Taipei
創造台北新風景的設計手法
台北の新しい風景をつくり出す手法

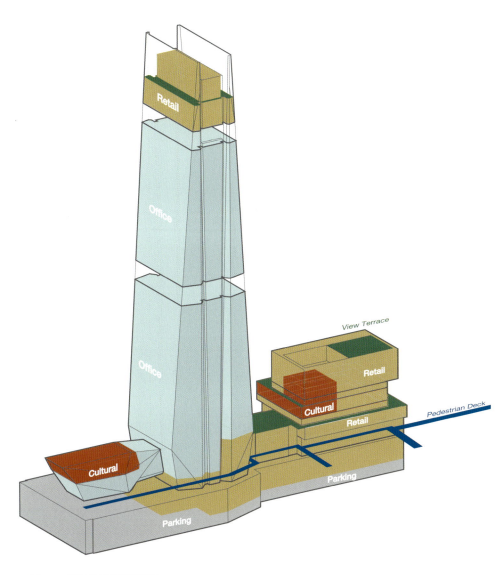

Diagram of the required programs.
The overlaying of multiple uses in order to entice people towards the upper floors constitutes a kind of program that literally gives a form to the building.

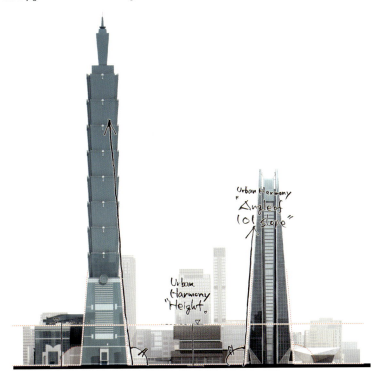

A design that respects the surrounding context.

Although it was the predecessors of Mitsubishi Jisho Sekkei that laid the foundations for Tokyo's Marunouchi, which has been in existence for some 130 years, we have also renewed these fundamentals. While colors and designs vary with the times, the overall framework and adjoining buildings that serve as a height benchmark are respected. It is our belief that cities evolve and progress through this symbiosis between the old and the new. This is the design philosophy that we have cherished in the context of the Marunouchi district.

Tower architecture has served as a symbolic landmark for cities since ancient times. What is important is not the height of these towers, but their silhouette and form, which we consider to have the potential to symbolize and encapsulate a particular city. As a new tower that adjoins Taipei 101, which stood alone as a symbol of Taipei for some 14 years, Taipei Nanshan Plaza harmonizes with Taipei 101 while also seeking to become a new emblem for the city.

On this front, we incorporated the conflict between two entirely different spatialities — the bustling activity on the western side (Songzhi Road) where Taipei 101 and administrative and commercial functions are located, and the quieter eastern side (Songren Road) where corporate head offices are concentrated — into the "mountain" design of the tower, while taking the angle of the elevation of Taipei 101 as a key benchmark. This silhouette was arrived at through numerous simulations that analyzed the design of the surrounding area and the landscape views.

塔樓建築自古以來即為城市發展的象徵。重要的不僅只是高度，「這座建物的輪廓剪影＝造型是否足以成為城市的象徵」，也是重要的思考觀點。我們考量「臺北南山廣場」，該如何與緊鄰已歷時十四年，台北的唯一地標「台北101」保持調和，並成為台北的城市新象徵。

三菱地所設計的先進們在發展長達130年的東京・丸之內特區建置了基礎。而我們將其持續煥新，營造新舊建築共存的商圈，雖然建物的顏色及設計有所不同，但我們仍以主要架構及相同尺度的簷高線設計，向週邊相鄰的建物表示致敬尊重之意。我們深信這種新舊共存的方式，會讓城市更加地進化，這就是丸之內特區一直以來我們很重視的設計思想。

我們將此設計思想也應用在台北。除了延續「台北101」立面的斜角，對於「台北101」，及基地西側(松智路)較為熱鬧的行政及商業設施，與聚集較多企業總部大樓，環境相對幽靜的東側(松仁路)，面對這兩個場所之間的差異性，我們藉由塔樓外觀的「山」型設計來回應。所以塔樓的外觀輪廓(造型)，是透過分析周邊建物設計及從立足周邊景觀的角度等，經過無數的模擬所做出的設計。

古の時代から、タワーの建築はそれが建つ都市においてシンボリックな存在である。ここで、都市のランドマークとして重要なのは高さではなく、それが「都市のシルエットとして印象が残るものであるか」だと考える。14年もの間、たったひとつの台北のシンボルであった「台北101」の隣に建つタワーとして、「臺北南山廣場」は存在感を示しつつ調和するものにしたいと考えた。

130年続く東京・丸の内は、三菱地所設計の前身の先達がその根幹をつくり、われわれがこれを更新した新旧混合の街である。色やデザインは違っていても、軒の高さや大きな骨格は隣接する建物を尊重する。こうして共存させることで、街は進化し続けると信じている。それが、丸の内でわれわれが大切にしている設計思想である。この思想を台北でも生かそうと考えた。「台北101」や行政施設がある西側の松智路と、企業の本社が集まる閑静な東側の松仁路の異なる場所性や、「台北101」の立面の角度などを継承し、「臺北南山廣場」のタワーにおける山のデザインとして取り入れた。このシルエット＝形態は、周辺のデザイン分析や、周囲からの視点の分析など、さまざまなシミュレーションにより導き出して行った。

Creating a three-dimensional pedestrian network that produces bustling activity

創造熱鬧的立體行人步道網絡
賑わいを生む立体的な歩行者ネットワークをつくる

11/2012

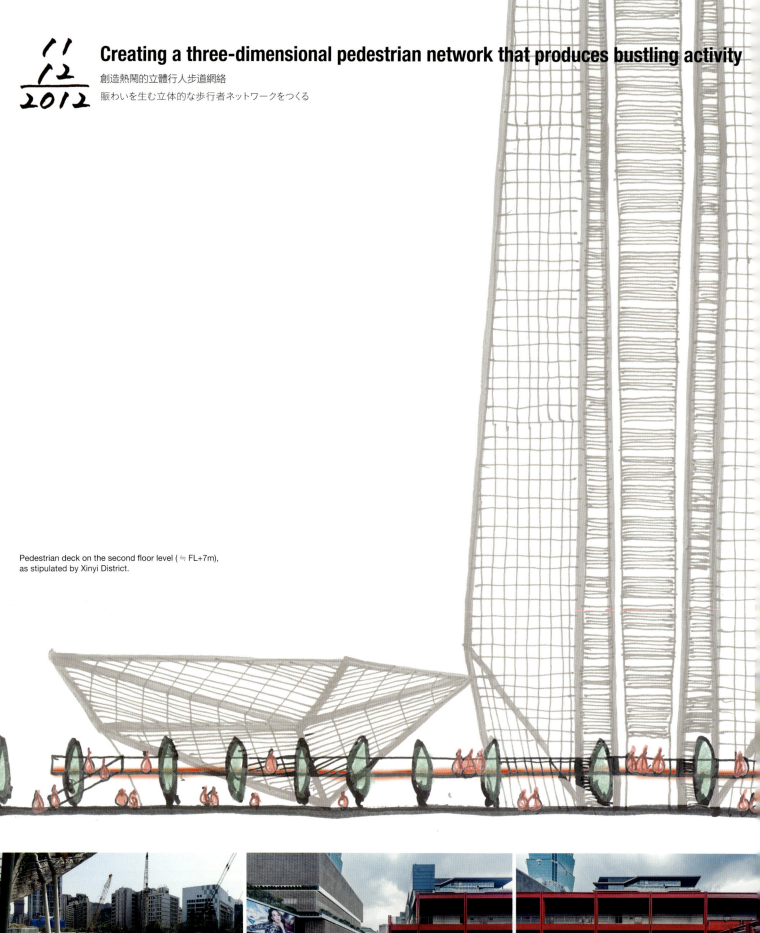

Pedestrian deck on the second floor level (≒ FL+7m),
as stipulated by Xinyi District.

● View A (Under construction)

● View B

● View C

2012　　2013　　2014　　2015

As an urban contribution to the area, we were asked to create a pedestrian network spanning two storeys, from the ground up until the second floor. "Multicultural, multi-purpose three-dimensional cities" require mechanisms that lure people to the upper floors. We felt that a flat, two-layered network would not be able to produce a sufficient level of activity, so we put in place mechanisms on the inside and outside of the building that would allow the unbridled movement of people across multiple levels, such as the commercial terraces with stacked greenery, and interior passageways in the culturai + entrance podium that remain open 24 hours a day.

依照信義區的都市畫規定，必須設置設計地面層與二樓兩個樓層的行人步道系統。基於「多樣文化及複合用途立體城市」的理念，我們認為將人群引導至上層的機制是必要的。如僅在二樓規劃平面連通網，創造出的熱鬧氣氛仍顯不足，因此我們透過層層綠意的商場露台，及藝文入口棟24小時全天候開放通行可貫穿室內的通道等⋯透過多個樓層的動線安排，在建築物的室內和室外建構了大眾可以縱橫交錯穿梭往來的空間機制。

信義区の都市計画として、地上と2階で2層分の歩行者ネットワークをつくることが求められた。「多文化・多用途立体都市」には人を上層階へと誘う仕組みが必須である。2層のみの平面的なネットワークでは賑わいを生むには十分ではないと感じ、緑を積層した商業棟テラス、文化・入口棟の24時間開放する内部貫通通路など、多層にわたって、縦横無尽に人が行き交うことのできる仕組みを建物の内外に構築した。

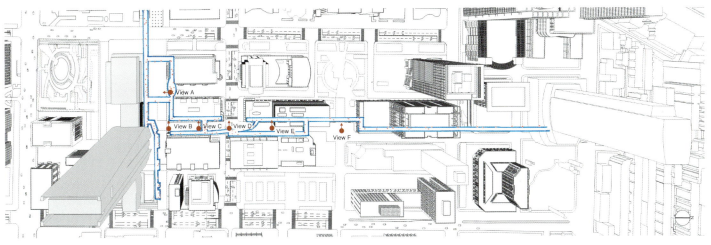

Network of pedestrian decks (s:1/400).

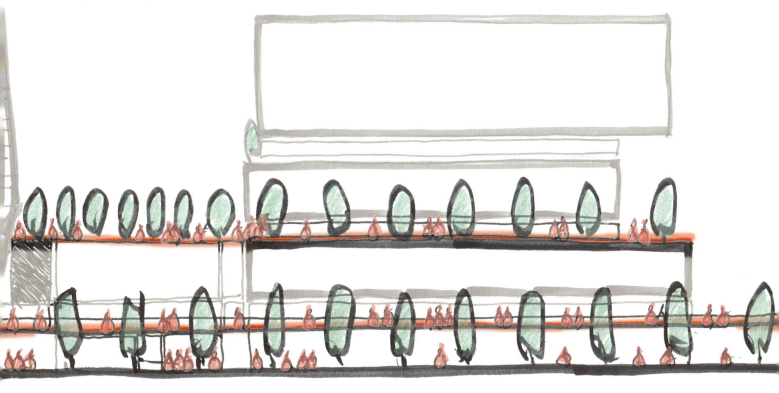

● View D

● View E

● View F

Interview

簡滄圳 潤泰創新國際股份有限公司 董事長

Achieving the Ideal Architecture with Japanese Craftsmanship

日式精工精神，實現理想的建築
日本のものづくりによる、理想的な建築の実現

——The client, designer and builder collaborated throughout the Taipei Nanshan Plaza project. Please tell us your impressions of the project as its client and as one of its collaborators.

Taipei Nanshan Plaza is the biggest construction project in Taiwan since Taipei 101. While this was not the first time that we worked with a foreign designer on a building project, we were impressed by how Mitsubishi Jisho Sekkei consistently presented forward-looking plans for the development concept, site plan, interior and exterior designs, landscaping, and everything else, even before the ideas had occurred to us. They have extensive experience with extremely large-scale projects, and had we worked with a team with little experience, we can be sure that the project would have been quite chaotic.

The world is full of designers, but designers who can present exceptional proposals with the client in mind are very rare indeed. My sense is that there are a lot of talented designers but most of them lack good communication skills and the right attitude for collaborating with other people. Our collaboration involved different cultures and at the beginning there are some things that I regret, but over time we talked to one another and worked as a team so that by the end we were able to overcome every problem that came along.

——What do you think of Mitsubishi Jisho Sekkei from your view of what makes the ideal architect?

For an architect, I focus on "attitude." In other words, an architect has not only design talent but the ability to coordinate and motivate the design and construction teams while also taking into account the client's intentions. Extensive experience and an international perspective are also extremely important, because one cannot make creative decisions without experience and, moreover, because making such decisions requires knowing how far to look ahead. In this regard, Mr. Okusa and Mr. Sube of Mitsubishi Jisho Sekkei are both exceptionally talented designers and excellent team leaders.

At the same time, the client isn't good at making simple "yes" or "no" decisions and can become overwhelmed by all the alternatives. I took part in every design meeting as well as every on-site meeting, and on these occasions they would put together all kinds of tools and provide easy-to-understand presentations so that we could make sound decisions. This is the first time that we have contracted with Mitsubishi Jisho Sekkei, but when I listened to their presentation at the initial project competition, I was convinced that if we put them in charge things would be fine.

It is my impression that since the 1980s Japanese organizational design firms have stood out for their steadily increasing ability to execute international, large-scale projects. What is really impressive, moreover, is that each of these firms is a single company that can comprehensively meet the client's needs, from urban design and development to M&E design, structural engineering, and detail design. They can execute projects on both the micro- and macro-level. When creating a material thing, detail design is very important. The detail work

——在「臺北南山廣場」專案進行過程中，業主、設計團隊和施工單位之間密集地溝通和共享設計施工的內容。身為業主，同時也是合作者，您有什麼樣的印象？

「臺北南山廣場」對臺灣來說是自臺北101完工以來的指標大案。對我們來說，雖不是第一次與外國設計團隊一起合作，但是三菱地所設計的設計團隊，在開發理念、配置、室內、外觀以及景觀設計等各方面，在我們想到之前，就提出了更有前瞻性的計劃，讓我們留下很深刻的印象。他們在設計大規模建案上具有豐富的經驗，若這次是由缺乏經驗的團隊來操刀的話，這案子是肯定是混亂到無法想像的地步。世界上有許多設計師，但是能夠「站在業主的立場」，為業主想出優質方案的設計師則極少。我認為大多數設計師即便能力很好，但是缺乏溝通技巧或是真誠地對待別人的態度。我們因為有文化的差異，合作初期時多少有一點遺憾的部分，但經過長時間的對話和協調，到最後，大家能同心協力一起來克服種種的問題。

——對於簡先生心目中理想的建築師形象來說，您覺得三菱地所設計如何？

我非常重視建築師的「處事態度」。也就是說不僅是設計能力，還需具備統合相關的設計、施工團隊以及理解業主的需求等，能夠整合人心並提升團隊的能力。此外，豐富的經驗與具有國際觀的先見之明也是很重要的。若缺少經驗的話，就無法做出有創意的判斷，而且業主也會期待到設計師能提出具有多少前瞻性的方案。就這一點而言，三菱地所設計的大草先生、須部先生們不僅設計能力非常優秀，人品也很好。

很多時候，業主無法決定Yes或No，常在A或B或C中猶豫不決。每次的設計會議及工地會議我都會參加，他們為了讓我能夠做出正確的判斷，巧妙地搭配各式各樣的表達工具，讓簡報淺顯易懂。雖然這是第一次委託三菱地所設計，但從當時競標階段聆聽他們的簡報開始，我就已經對他們非常有信心了。

1980年代以後，日本的組織型設計事務所給我的印象，是擅長於處理國際化且大規模的案子。而且由單一大型建築師事務所可以從事城市規劃、開發到設備、結構、細部設計等，多元且完整的回應客戶需求，這一點是非常理想的，這樣可以同時滿足宏觀和微觀雙方面。對於從事設計工作者來說，細部設計是非常重要的。三菱地所設計團隊對於細部設計的處理，比我想像的還要細緻許多。為了設計一個東西，做了模型

——「臺北南山廣場」プロジェクトでは、施主と設計者と施工者が常にプロセスを共有していました。施主として、協働者として、どのような印象を持たれましたか？

「臺北南山廣場」は、台湾にとって台北101以来の一大プロジェクトです。私たちにとって、海外の設計者との協業による建設プロジェクトははじめてのことではありませんが、三菱地所設計の設計者は、開発のコンセプト、配置、内外観、ランドスケープなどの様々な部分で、より将来性のある計画を、常に私たちが思いつく前に先行して提案してくれたことが印象でした。彼らは圧倒的に大規模プロジェクトの経験が豊富です、もし、これが経験の少ないチームだったら、このプロジェクトは混迷を極めたのではないでしょうか。

世の中には数多くのデザイナーがいますが、「施主にとっての」優れた提案を出せるデザイナーはとても少ない。高い能力を持っていても、そこにコミュニケーションのスキルや、人に向き合う姿勢がついていかない人が多い気がします。私たちの連携は、文化の違いもあり、初期は多少悔いの残る部分もありましたが、時間をかけた対話と協業により、最終的には、皆でひとつひとつ問題を乗り越えていけるようになりました。

——簡さんの理想とする建築家像から見て、三菱地所設計はいかがでしたか？

私は建築家の「姿勢」を重視します。つまり設計能力だけではなく、プロジェクトに関わる設計・施工チーム、施主の意向といった人の心をまとめる上げる力のことです。また、豊富な経験や国際的な見通しも大切です。経験なくして創造的な判断はできませんし、彼らがどれだけ先を見ているかが求められますから。その点、三菱地所設計の大草さん、須部さんたちは技術も人柄も大変優れていました。

とはいえ、施主はYesかNoを決断できるものではなく、AかBかCかを迷ってしまうものです。私は設計会議と現場の立ち会いに毎回参加しましたが、彼らは私たちがきちんと判断できるよう、さまざまなツールを組み合わせ、分かりやすくプレゼンテーションをしてくれました。三菱地所設計へ設計を依頼するのは初めてでしたが、最初の事業コンペでプレゼンテーションを受けた時から、彼らなら任せても大丈夫だという確信を得ていました。

1980年代以降、日本の組織設計事務所は、より国際的かつ大規模なプロジェクトに長けるようになった印象があります。また、1社で都市計画・開発から設備、構造、ディテールに至るまで、顧客ニーズに包括的に応えられるのが素晴らしい。マクロとミクロ双方を満たすことができるのです。ものづくりにとって、ディテールはとても大切です。三菱地所設計のそれは、私の想像以上に緻密なものでした。ひとつ

Tsang-Jiunn, Jean | Chairman, Ruentex Development | Born in 1963 in Yi-lan Taiwan / In 2001, President, Ruentex Interior Design / In 2001, President, "C-STORE" Combienience Store, China / In 2007, President, Ruentex Development / 2012~, Chairman

簡滄圳｜潤泰創新國際股份有限公司董事長｜1963年出生於臺灣宜蘭｜1991年，創立潤德設計並擔任負責人／2001年，創立中國喜士多便利商店並擔任總經理／2007年，擔任潤泰創新國際股份有限公司總經理／2012年起出任董事長

カン・ソウジュン｜ルンテックス・デベロップメント董事長｜1963年台湾宜蘭生まれ｜1963年潤德設計を創設、総経理に就任／2001年中国にてコンビニエンスストア「C-STORE」を開設、総経理に就任／2007年ルンテックス・デベロップメント総経理／2012年より現職

of Mitsubishi Jisho Sekkei has a precision that completely surpassed my expectations. I was impressed by how much time they took to go over the same mock ups, prototypes and the like again and again.

They could be interesting to work with, too. There was a design meeting where we decided on the shape of the tower. 7 or 8 proposals had been prepared by the local architect, and over the phone Mr. Okusa said, "we're really busy right now with other project proposals and we haven't prepared anything, so do you mind if we don't bring anything this time?" I said, "If you do not design exterior, what do you design as an architect? I want to you to make every effort to bring something, even it's just one idea." At the meeting, that was the idea that we settled on, and since then they have done an excellent job developing it and it is what the final design is based on. If not for that phone call, Taipei Nanshan Plaza would not have taken the form that it is today. There were aspects of the project that we as the client had determined to be of value, and even though bringing these aspects to fruition meant going somewhat over our budget estimate, we decided to bear the cost and have the designers work hard on them.

——A lot of the building products for this project were made by Japanese manufacturers.

I once studied architectural design in Japan and have a high opinion of the quality control and product performance of Japanese companies. Although the building's architectural design had many challenging aspects, this was not a cause of concern because we could use the products of Japanese manufacturers and so we had the designers move ahead. The designers, manufacturers and builders all pushed their limits and achieved a remarkable final product. For example, the exterior curtain wall was made by YKK AP, with whom we have a relationship going back 30 years. I think places where members are jointed at a slant were especially hard to execute, but with them in charge I felt confident that things would go smoothly even for those very complicated design drawings.

The construction professionals faced many challenges, and I often said to them, "A person will probably live no longer than 100 years, but a well-constructed building stands for centuries. What do you wish to leave behind for future generations?" We were always aware that the project had a very important spiritual dimension. People do leave their DNA behind in their grandchildren, but what do they leave behind spiritually? I wanted this project to be an answer to that question.

——As a final question, what kind of future do you see for Taipei Nanshan Plaza?

The project employed the most advanced technologies and includes ample public space. It therefore has an appeal that should attract a great number of people both from here in Taiwan and from abroad. I want it to become Taipei's leading business center. I think Taipei Nanshan Plaza will become Taipei's most prized location and the most recognized landmark in all of Taiwan.

(February 27, 2018 at Ruentex Development, Responsibility for the wording: Shinkenchiku-sha)

的檢討、實品試做等，反反覆覆地花了很長的時間，讓我留下了深刻的印象。有一次，我們與三菱地所設計的設計團隊曾有很有趣的交流。在一個需要決定大樓外觀造型的設計會議上，台灣當地的建築師事務所準備了七、八種方案，同時也接到大草先生的電話，他說：「我正在忙著提交其他的設計方案，實在忙得不可開交，這次三菱地所設計可以不提出設計方案嗎？」我說：「作為建築師，放棄了外觀其他還有什麼能設計的，即使只有1個方案也可以，希望你能夠傾全力提交。」後來，在會議上就通過這個唯一的方案，這個在關鍵性出現的好方案也持續發展至今。如果當時沒有這通電話，「臺北南山廣場」就不是今天看到的這個外觀型態了。作為業主，當我們判斷這設計是有價值的時候，就算是稍微超出預算也不惜成本來支持設計師的創意。

——「臺北南山廣場」，採用了許多日系廠商的產品。

我曾經在日本學過設計，非常信任日本企業的品質管理及產品功能。雖然本案的建築外觀造型極具挑戰性，但因為使用日系廠商的建材，讓大家可以安心地進行施工。設計師、廠商以及施工單位各自挑戰極限，成就了非常完美的工程。例如，外牆的玻璃帷幕採用了YKK AP的產品，我們與他們的合作關係從30年前持續到現在。特別是這次設計中，傾斜部分的框料收頭處理其實難度很高，但是我非常相信他們對於高難度的設計也不會有任何問題。

我經常對辛苦的施工負責人說：「人生一輩子最長也不過100年左右，但是好的建築物可以留存幾百年後。你有想過要留下什麼給後代嗎？」我經常注重這種精神層面上的重要意義。人類留下DNA給子孫。那麼，在精神層面上我們會留下什麼呢？我想透過這開發案，傳達一些思維給後代。

——最後，您看今後的「臺北南山廣場」會有怎樣的未來發展呢？

這個案子採用最先進的技術，且在基地裡規劃了一個很大的公共空間。透過這樣的魅力，將會吸引許多人從國內外到訪。我希望「臺北南山廣場」可以成為臺北的一大商務據點。今後發展成為一個引領臺北黃金地段、並且成為臺灣最頂級的地標性建築。

（2018年2月27日、於潤泰集團總部／撰文：本誌編輯部）

のものをつくるために、模型での検討や試作など、時間をかけ繰り返しているのが印象的でした。

彼らとの面白いやり取りがありました。ある設計会議でタワーのかたちを決めることになりました。地元の建築事務所が7、8種類くらいの案を用意している中、大草さんが電話をかけてきて「他の提案作業で手一杯で時間がないから、今回は私たちは案を持っていかなくてもよいだろうか？」と言うのです。私は「建築家として、外観デザインを諦めて他に何を設計するのですか、1案だけでも、全力で出してほしい」と言いました。会議ではその1案に決まり、そこから今に繋がるよい提案に発展しました。この電話がなかったら、「臺北南山廣場」は今日のかたちになっていません。私たちも施主として価値があると判断した場面では、想定予算を多少超えても、コストをかける決断をして設計者の仕事に応えました。

——今回のプロジェクトでは、日本のメーカーの製品が数多く使用されていますね。

私は、かつて日本で設計を学び、日本企業の品質管理や製品性能に関して高い信頼を持っています。建築のかたちとしては非常に挑戦的な今回のプロジェクトですが、日系メーカーの製品を使用できたので安心して進めてもらうことができました。設計者、メーカー、施工者それぞれが限界に挑み、素晴らしい仕上がりになっています。例えば、外壁のカーテンウォールではYKK APの製品を使用しましたが、私たちと彼らの関係は30年前から続いています。特に、斜めに部材がぶつかるところは大変苦労したと思いますが、彼らなら難しい図面でも大丈夫だという確信がありました。

私は、苦労を重ねる施工担当者に対して「人の一生はせいぜい100年程度だが、いい建物は何百年と残るものだ。あなたたちは後世に何を残したいのか？」とよく話しました。こうした精神的な重要性は常に意識しましたね。人間は子孫にDNAを残す。では、精神としては何を残すのか、このプロジェクトを通して伝えたいと思いました。

——最後に、「臺北南山廣場」はこれからのようになっていくと思われますか？

このプロジェクトは最先端の技術を用い、また共用空間に大きな余裕を設けています。こうした魅力により、国内外から多くの利用者が訪れるでしょう。ここが台北における一大ビジネス拠点になってほしいです。「臺北南山廣場」は、今後台北の一等地の先頭にたつ、そして台湾でも最高のランドマークとなる建築になると思います。

（2018年2月27日、潤泰創新國際にて／文責：本誌編輯部）

A skyscraper design that coexists with the wind
與風共存的超高層大廈設計
風と共存できる超高層ビルのデザインとは

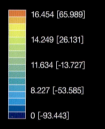

Wind simulation that can activate the city
For the design of a skyscraper, it is crucial to control the wind. Would it be possible to overturn the common logic regarding the wind damage caused by locally strong winds in the vicinity of a large building, and create a pleasant environment?
In anticipation of the wind environment in Xinyi District, based on the buildings standing in the area, we were able to produce a design that activates the city from an environmental standpoint. Deftly allowing the wind to escape overhead was also advantageous in terms of the design of the structure and facade.

讓都市Activate的風場模擬
超高層大廈的設計中如何駕馭風場是很重要的環節。我們可否顛覆傳統「建造大型建物就會產生大樓風風切效應」的常識，並創造出大眾覺得舒適的環境呢？
透過調查週邊的建物及預測信義區的風場環境，我們認為環境面的都市活化＝活性化設計有可能實現。規劃設計上巧妙地讓風排向上空，這對結構及立面外觀的設計也十分有利。

都市をActivateできる風のシミュレーション
超高層ビルのデザインは、風を制御することが重要である。これまでの「大きな建物を建てれば、ビル風による風害が生じる」という常識を覆し、過ごしやすい環境ができないだろうか。
周辺に建つビルをも踏まえた信義区の風環境を予測により、環境面でも都市をActivate＝活性化できるデザインが可能となった。風をうまく上空へと逃がすことにより、構造やファサードの設計にも有利となる。

Reviewing designs that will not cause strong winds to occur at the bottom of buildings, where people gather.

Meeting at the office onsite between Mr. Hiroshi Kawamura (Mitsubishi Jisho Sekkei), Evergreen Consulting Engineering, and the builders.

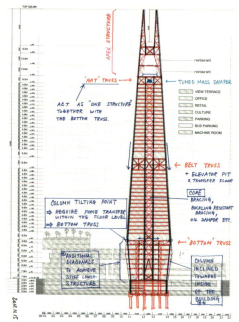

Structure of the office tower. An early concept for the framework.

Structural design collaboration between Taiwan and Japan

台灣與日本的結構設計合作

台湾と日本の構造設計のコラボレーション

Structural engineers that make the design a reality

We envisioned a collaboration with the structural engineers from Taiwan's Evergreen Consulting Engineering starting from the concept design stage, with the preliminary structural schemes verified by Mitsubishi Jisho Sekkei.

Based on the structural concepts prepared in Japan, we repeatedly exchanged opinions with the Taiwan team. The respective experiences of the two quake-prone countries of Japan and Taiwan were combined, and a high level dialogue was held.

Office tower | Double Tube + Outrigger with TMD

In addition to the double tube structure, peripheral belt truss system and internal outriggers were installed on intermediate machine room floors, where pillars are bent at the top, middle, and bottom of the building, ensuring the horizontal and torsional rigidity of the tower. In addition, two tuned mass dampers (TMDs) were installed on the upper floors with trusses in order to suppress the vibration caused by strong winds and earthquakes. At the tip of the building, which is a distinctive feature of the design, back mullions more than 30m high are supported by horizontal trusses and oblique pillars, allowing us to achieve the transparency.

實現設計的結構工程師

從概念設計的階段開始，三菱地所設計先驗證大型結構系統的可行性，並與台灣永峻工程顧問的結構工程師們攜手合作。

我們以在日本準備的結構概念為基礎，與台灣的團隊反覆不斷地進行意見交換，融合同為地震國的台灣與日本的各自經驗，進行了高層次專業水準的溝通。

辦公棟 | Double Tube + Outrigger with TMD

包括雙管結構，建築物的上、中及下層的柱子發生轉折作為中繼機房的樓層，在其外圍設置了帶狀桁架及內部懸臂支架，以確保整體的水平剛性及內部扭轉剛性。另外，上方的桁架層，裝設兩座調諧質量阻尼器TMD（Tuned Mass Damper），可以抑制強風和地震時的搖晃。設計重點之一建築物頂部，則透過在最頂端附近的水平桁架與斜柱來支撐高度超過30公尺的帷幕鋼背擋展現透明感。

デザインを実現する構造エンジニア

コンセプトデザインの段階から、三菱地所設計では大きな構造ス

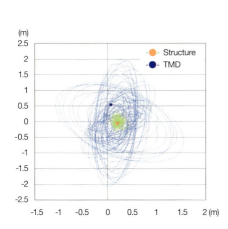

Displacement of the Structure and TMD
(Tuned Mass Damper)

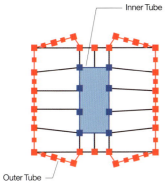

Double tube structure: Diagram (plan)

Comparison of criteria in Japan and Taiwan's Building Law

	Japan: Building Standards Act	Taiwan: ASCE
Story Drift	100 years: ≦1/200 500 years: ≦1/100	475 years: ≦1/200 2,500 years: ≦1/50
Seismic Load	100 years: 0.25G 500 years: 0.5G	475 years: 0.3G 2,500 years: 0.4G

*ASCE: Seismic Load is calculated individually for each building.

キームを検証し、台湾永峻工程顧問の構造エンジニアらとのコラボレーションを図った。
私たちが日本で用意した構造コンセプトをベースに、台湾のチームと意見交換を重ねた。ともに地震国である台湾と日本のそれぞれの経験が融合し、ハイレベルなコミュニケーションが行なわれた。

高層棟｜Double Tube + Outrigger with TMD

ダブル・チューブ構造に加えて、建物の上・中・下部の柱が折れ曲がる階に配置される中間機械室階には、外周ベルトトラスと内部アウトリガーを設けてタワー全体の水平剛性とねじれ剛性を確保する。また、上部のトラス設置階にTMD (Tuned Mass Damper) を2基設置し、強風・地震時の揺れを抑える。デザインのポイントとなる建物頂部は、高さ30mを超えるバックマリオンを最上部付近の水平トラスと斜め柱で支持し、透明感を実現した。

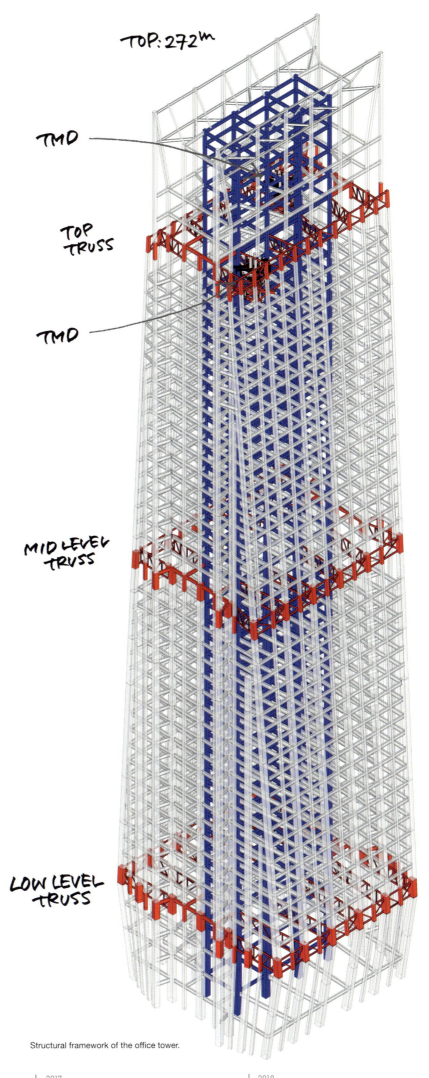

Structural framework of the office tower.

01/31/2013 Structural design of the stacked commercial podium and the diamond-shaped cultural + entrance podium

決定層疊的商場棟及鑽石造型的藝文入口棟的結構

積層する商業棟とダイヤモンド型の文化・入口棟の構造が決定

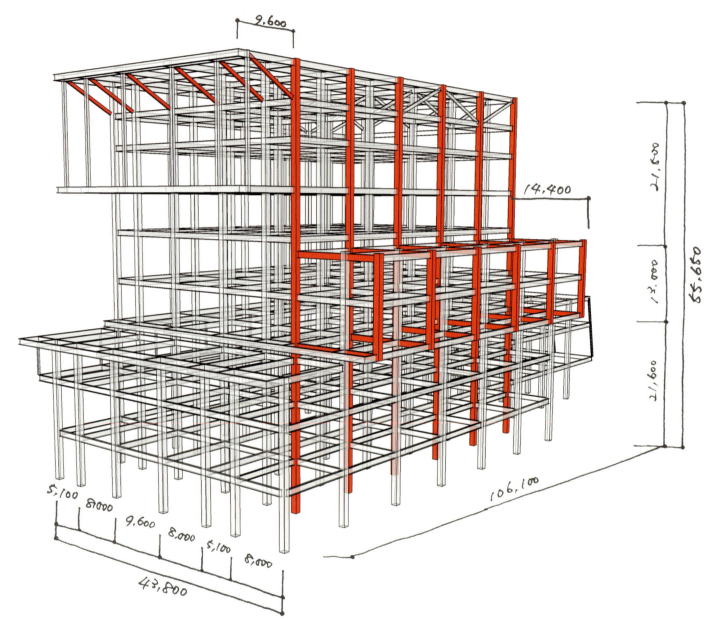

Structural framework of the commercial podium.

Commercial podium | Portal Frame with cantilever
Three layers of floor plates, each around 66×50m, are stacked. A pure rigid frame consisting of modules measuring 8.8×11m was adopted. Each unit was staggered at each floor, producing an overhang of a maximum of 10m. Various types of frames system, such as suspension frames by triangle-shaped trusses, Vierendeel trusses, and cantilevered beams, were used effectively in accordance with the length of the overhang.

商場棟 | Portal Frame with cantilever
66×50公尺左右大小的三塊樓板交錯疊砌；使用8.8×11公尺模矩的純樑柱框架結構；交錯移位的各個樓板單元，創造出最大10公尺左右的出挑。我們將三角桁架的垂吊構架、范倫第構架、懸臂樑等種種的結構型式有效地運用在不同長度的出挑設計上。

商業棟 | Portal Frame with cantilever
66×50m程のフロアプレート3層を積層。8.8×11mモジュールの純ラーメン構造を採用。フロアユニットを各層でずらし、最大10m程度の跳ね出しを生む。三角トラスによる吊り架構、フィーレンディールトラス、片持梁など種々の架構を、跳ね出し長さに応じて効果的に用いた。

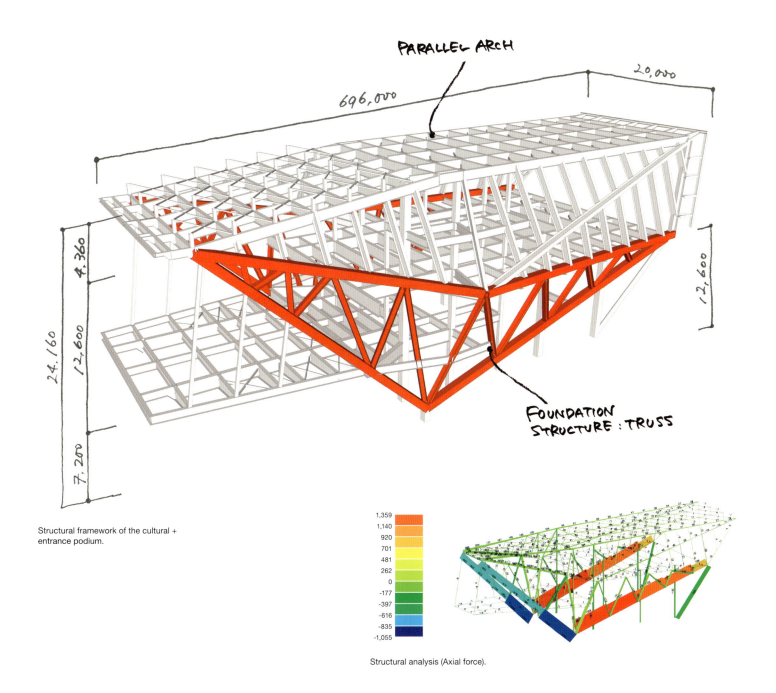

Structural framework of the cultural + entrance podium.

Structural analysis (Axial force).

Cultural + entrance podium | Outer Shell with triangle-shaped truss

As we wanted to integrate the distinctively shaped facade with the structural system, we adopted an outer shell structure which eliminates interior pillars as much as possible. Because a driveway and parking for large buses were located directly beneath the building, the location of pillars at the upper level were restricted. The large triangle-shaped trusses was formed as the foundation of the outer shell, with arches arranged Parallely on top. The framing system was very complicated, handing over the data of the 3D analysis models to the Taiwanese structural engineers allowed information to be transmitted smoothly.

藝文入口棟 | Outer Shell with triangle-shaped truss

我們考量將形狀具有特徵的外觀與結構系統一體化，因此盡量避免內部落柱，並採用了殼體結構。因建築物正下方已規劃有大型巴士停車場及車道，故上方的柱位受到限制，所以我們使用殼體結構作為基礎，建構了大型的三角桁架，並於其基礎上平行配置拱型桁架。因其架構複雜，需透過3D分析模型的數據才能將資訊清楚地傳達給台灣的結構工程師。

文化・入口棟 | Outer Shell with triangle-shaped truss

特徴的な形状のファサードと構造システムを一体化したいと考え、内部の柱を極力排除した、外殻シェル構造を採用。建物直下に大型バス駐車場と車路が計画されるため、上部の柱の位置は制約された。そこで、外殻シェルは土台となる大きな三角トラスで構成し、その土台の上にアーチを平行に配置した。複雑な架構であったため、3Dの解析モデルのデータを台湾の構造エンジニアに渡すことでスムーズな情報伝達を行なうことができた。

Office tower typical floor plan (1/400).

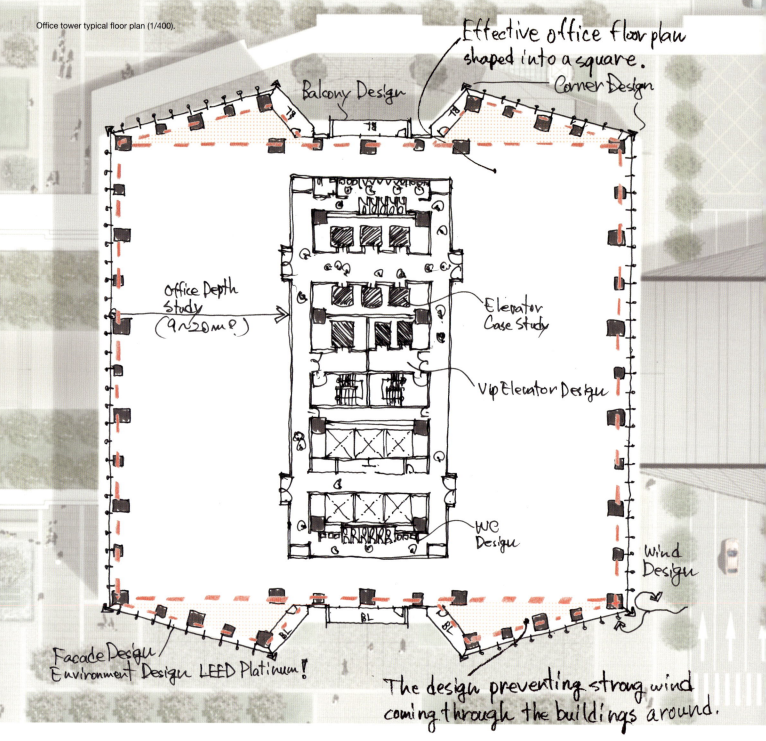

Direction for competitive floor plans and sections

02/05/2013

決定未來有競爭力的平面・剖面圖的方向性

将来的に競争力ある平面・断面の方針を決める

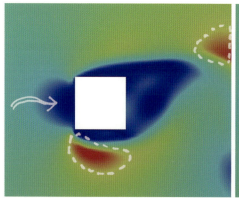

Square plan. Strong winds occur in the vicinity.

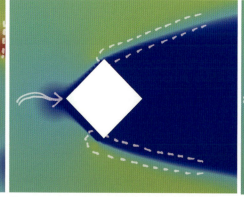

Rhomboid plan. Less the strong winds but the pressure exerted on buildings is large.

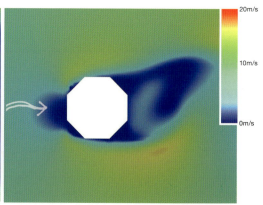

Octagonal plan. Low speed turbulence occur. The load on the periphery is small.

Plans (s: 1/5,000)

Exploring the shape of floor plans to reduce the impact of downdraguth effect with unique Taiwanese approach

Typically, a square shape floor plan is required for a building that will be leased out. Here, however, although square shape floor plans were followed, expanding the corners to form an octagonal shape and allowed us to reduce the impact of wind effect, in addition to giving the silhouette of the building a unique touch.
According to building regulations in Taiwan, balconies allow the floor area ratio to be mitigated by up to 5%, balconies are often requested. In addition, designs that take feng shui (geomancy) considerations into account are preferred. In order to suppress the wind effect and take feng shui into account, a policy regarding floor and section plans was determined that would allow us to realize a building that could remain competitive into the future.

思考台灣的獨特性及摸索減少大樓風的平面規劃

一般來說，租賃用的商辦大樓通常會被業主要求是四角方整的平面形狀。但是，這次我們追求方型平面的同時，轉角的部分稍微膨脹接近八角形的設計，除能減低大樓風的影響，還同時創造出建築物獨特的輪廓特色。
依照台灣的建築法規，陽台面積5%可免予計入容積，所以本案也規劃了陽台。另外，台灣也注重風水的設計，我們一方面抑制風切的影響，一方面顧慮風水的設計，終於決定了具有未來競爭力的超高層大樓平面與剖面設計的方向性。

台湾特有の考えとともにビル風を低減する平面を模索

一般的に、賃借用オフィスビルには四角い平面形状が求められる。しかし、ここでは方形の平面形状を踏襲しつつも、コーナー部分を少し膨らませて八角形に近づけることでビル風の低減に寄与するとともに、ビルのシルエットにも独自性を与えた。
台湾の建築法規では、バルコニーが容積率の5％まで除外となるため、バルコニーの設置が求められる。また風水に配慮したデザインが好まれる。風の影響を抑えつつ、風水に配慮すること。未来にわたり競争力を保持できるビルを実現する平面・断面の方針が定まった。

The importance of efficient vertical circulation planning and preventive measures to avoid drafts in elevators

有效率的垂直動線及電梯井的煙囪效應對策甚是重要

効率的な垂直動線とエレベータのドラフト対策が重要

An interior environment to prevent drafts
One of the problems for a skyscraper is drafts. Elevator shafts and stairwells become wind tunnels due to differences in air pressure between the upper and lower levels. The draft causes difficulties with operating doors, causes vibrations in elevators, and creates wind noises. Mitsubishi Jisho Sekkei has a long track record of designing skyscrapers. The interior wind environment is one of the important issues in determining the competitiveness of a building; Mitsubishi Jisho Sekkei has accumulated know-hows to ensure preventing the wind to enter into the building and get into elevator shafts. We examined to reduce the draft adequately without installing a vestibule by by taking in consideration of factors such as the distance from the entrance to the elevator shafts, the number of objects that obstruct or intercept the wind.

避免產生煙囪效應的室內環境規劃
超高層大廈最容易產生的問題是煙囪效應。所謂的煙囪效應就是電梯井及樓梯間產生風洞，高樓層及低樓層之間因為氣壓壓差的關係，致使門的開關變得困難，而電梯的震動等也會產生風切的聲音。三菱地所設計在超高大廈的領域，有為數豐頓的設計經驗。因為大樓室內風場環境的好壞，對於具有高度競爭力的商辦大樓來說是很重要的環節，我們希望將能抑止風流向電梯井的設計訣竅也應用在本大樓。
我們考量了入口到電梯井的距離，可作為擋風的物體數量等因素，驗證了即便不設置風除室，亦能有效減少煙囪效應的方式。此外，藉由頂部高度約30公尺，覆蓋屋頂露台的玻璃牆面設計也可以減少其效應。

ドラフトを起こさない内部環境
超高層建築で問題となる現象にドラフトがある。ドラフトは、エレベータシャフトや階段室が風洞となり、高層部と低層部で生じる気圧差が原因で、これにより扉の開閉が困難になったり、エレベータの振動や、風切音を生じさせる。三菱地所設計には数多くの超高層の設計実績がある。内部の風環境も高い競争力を持つビルの重要なポイントなので、エレベータシャフトにビル内に入る風を流さないノウハウを応用したいと考えた。
エントランスからエレベータシャフトの距離、風遮蔽物数などを考慮し、風除室を設置せずにドラフトを十分に軽減する検証を行った。また、頂部のルーフトップテラスを覆う高さ30mのガラス壁面もその軽減に一役買っている。

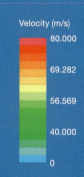

Velocity (m/s)

80.000
69.282
56.569
40.000
0

Simulation of drafts that occur in the interior of the building.

Comparison of three elevator systems and the shape of the core (s:1/2,500).
Double deck system (option C) is able to achieve a high level of efficiency with an average of 17% (as opposed to the typical 11%) and an average operation interval of about 25 seconds (as opposed to under 45 seconds in a typical situation) when looking at transport capability over a period of five minutes.

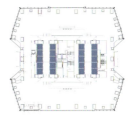

A, Conventional Zoning System
Bank: 5 Elevators * 4 Banks
Total: 20 Elevators
Elevator Lobby: 2nd Floor
Effective Rate (Typical Floor): 65% (Invalid)
Accesibility: ○ (Valid)

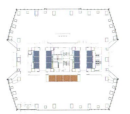

B, Sky Lobby System
Bank: 6 Elevetors * 2 Banks + 4 Shuttle Elevators
Total: 16 Elevators
Elevator Lobby: 2nd Floor, 24th Floor
Effective Rate (Typical Floor): 73% (Valid)
Accesibility: △ (Invalid)

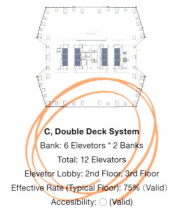

C, Double Deck System
Bank: 6 Elevetors * 2 Banks
Total: 12 Elevators
Elevator Lobby: 2nd Floor, 3rd Floor
Effective Rate (Typical Floor): 75% (Valid)
Accesibility: ○ (Valid)

Elevators | efficient vertical circulation for skyscrapers

The proper planning of elevators is key to enabling people to reach their destination floor with minimal stress. Working on the assumption of a lobby use suit to Taiwanese customs, we considered three options of conveyance. As a result, an internationally cutting edge method that combines a destination announcement system and double deck was adopted. This method involved installing two carriages at the top and bottom and reducing the number of elevators on the floor plan in order to boost the efficiency of each standard floor, while also ensuring efficient operations by using a computer controlled system to reduce the number of empty carriages.

電梯 | 有效率的超高層大廈動線

電梯設計的關鍵在於能讓使用者輕鬆順暢的前往目的地樓層。以符合台灣當地的電梯使用習慣為前提，我們研究了三種運送模式，並搭配使用世界最先進的智慧分配乘車控制系統及雙層車廂電梯。如此一來，上下二層皆有車廂的方式可以減少平面上的電梯數量，並提升標準層的坪效。透過電腦控制可減少無人車廂運作的機率，讓電梯有效率地的運行。

エレベータ | 超高層ビルの効率的な動線

利用者がストレスなく目的階に移動するために超高層ビルの鍵となるのはエレベータの計画だ。台湾の慣習にあったロビーの使い勝手を前提に、コンベンショナルゾーニング方式、スカイロビー方式、ダブルデッキ方式の3つを検討し、行先予報システムとダブルデッキを複合した世界最先端の方式を採用した。この方式は、上下にふたつのかごが設けられているため平均的なエレベータの台数を減らすことで基準階有効率を高めると共に、人が乗っていないエレベータのかごを減らし効率的に運行するコンピュータ制御を行うものである。

06 / 24 / 2013 Designing a curtain wall considering environment and maintenance

同時考慮清掃方式及適合環境的帷幕牆設計

清掃性と環境に配慮したカーテンウォールをデザインする

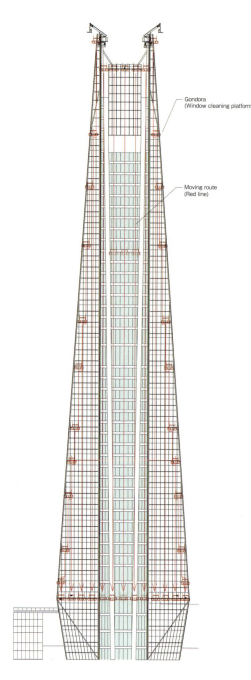

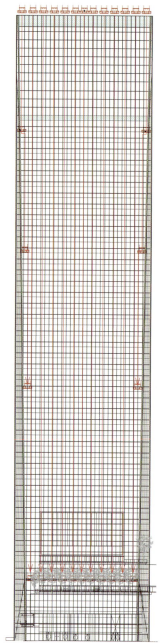

South and east elevation (s:1/400). All the routes taken by the gondola along the exterior walls of the office tower are designed along with the design of the building.

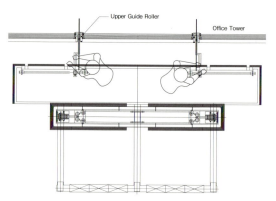

Gondola that travels between the 43rd floor and the roof of the building (s:1/20). The upper guide rollers are inserted into the guide, which holds the gondola in place as it moves.

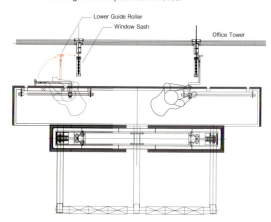

Gondola that travels between the lower levels and the 42nd floor. When traveling downwards from the 43rd floor, the lower guide rollers are set into the guides installed in the window sashes, while the upper guide rollers are stored inside the cage.

Gondola with shock absorbing material installed on the exterior as a safety measure against collisions, an idea that came from Samuel Yin of Ruentex Group.

Design of a gondola and exterior to reduce maintenance costs

In addition to the strength of the components, another important consideration is the reduction of long term maintenance costs. Together with a Taiwanese curtain wall consultant, we analyzed the initial costs incurred by the exterior and its maintainability.

From the moment that the design for the tower was finalized, detailed requirements at the level of the construction drawings came one after another from the local architects and building consultants. We simultaneously studied both "macro" and "micro" perspectives, the form of the tower from urban design points of views and details of the window sash.

The exterior aluminium window sash with sunshade louvers were designed by taking into account the strength in withstanding typhoons, ability to reduce wind noise, and the cost of cleaning. The detail of the sashu was studied with Japanese manufacturers using full-size scale models. These models were extremely effective as a tool of communication that deepened understanding between all those involved.

減低維修成本的洗窗機及外牆系統規劃

增加構件強度減少長期的維修成本也是重要的討論事項。於是我們與台灣的帷幕牆系統顧問共同分析了外牆的初期成本及維

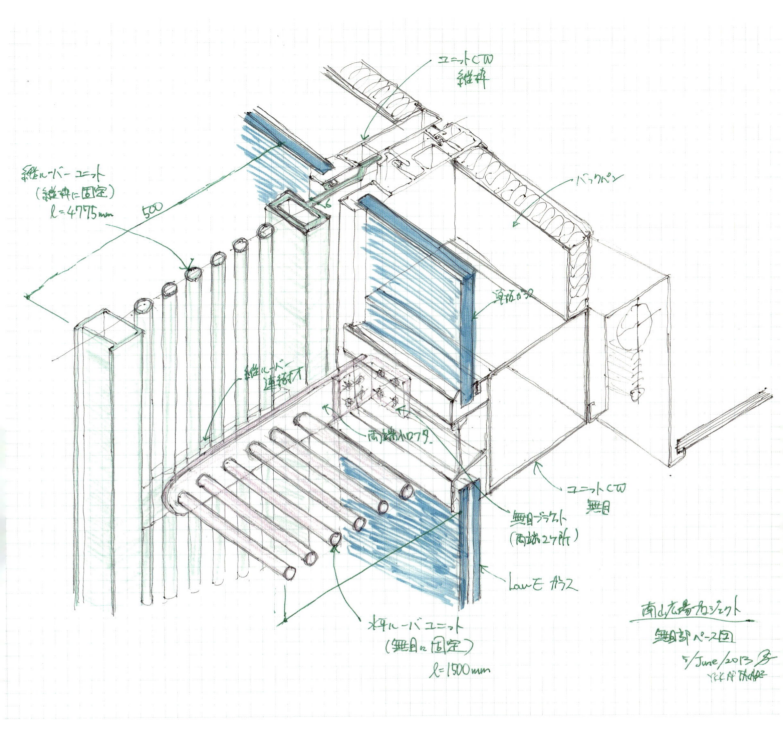

Sketch of the aluminium sash windows on the exterior wall.

修性。
從決定塔樓設計的那一刻開始，本地建築師及工程顧問陸續地提出細部設計規格的詳細需求。從「巨觀」的都市設計觀點決定辦公棟的外觀輪廓，到以「微觀」的角度確認門窗的細部收頭等…我們同時進行了多種驗證。
考量到可以承受颱風的強度，風切聲對策和清潔成本，我們使用將遮陽板加裝在外牆鋁窗框上的設計方式，並與製造鋁框的日本帷幕廠商使用一比一視覺模型進行模擬，透過這種實體模型，可以加深相關參與人員對於帷幕牆的理解，是非常有效的溝通工具。

メンテナンスコストを低減するゴンドラと外装の計画
部材強度に加え、長期的なメンテナンスコストの低減も重要な検討事項である。台湾のカーテンウォールのコンサルタントと外装のイニシャルコストやメンテナンス性を分析した。
高層棟のデザイン決定の瞬間から、現地建築家、施工コンサルタントから実施設計レベルの詳細な要求が次々に出てきた。タワーのシルエットを決める「マクロな」都市デザインの視点と、「ミクロな」サッシのディテールを検証する視点で、多くの同時検証を行った。
日射ルーバーを付加した外壁のアルミサッシは、台風に耐える強度、風切音対策、清掃コストを意識して設計。サッシを製造する日本のメーカーと、原寸模型で詰めていった。こうした模型は、関係者らと理解を深めるコミュニケーションツールとして非常に有効である。

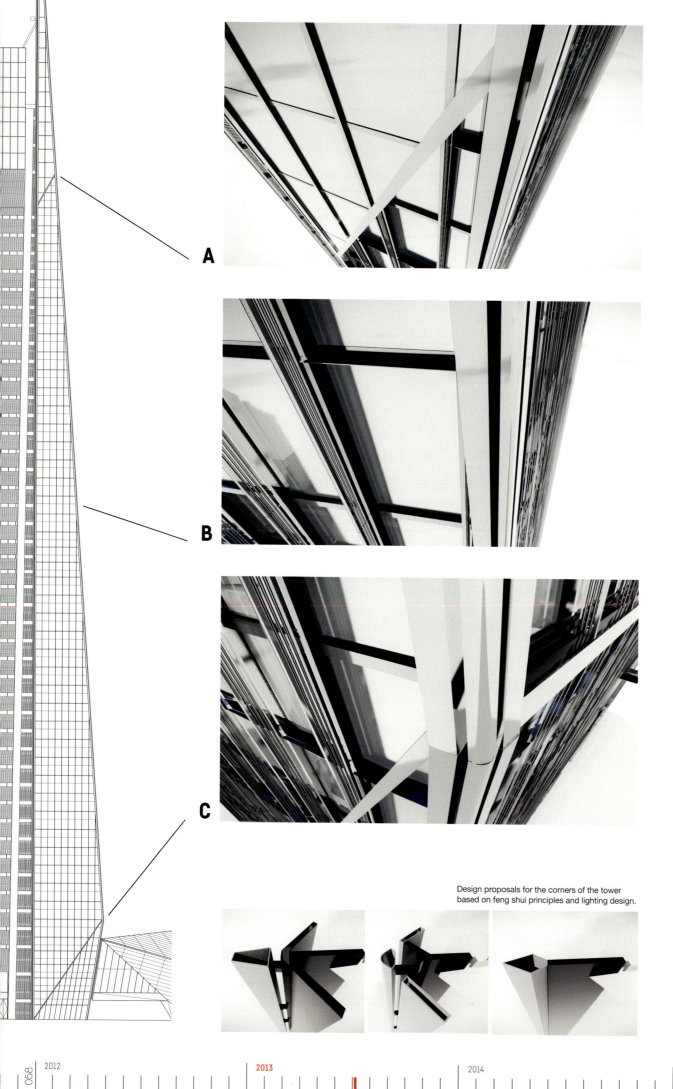

Design proposals for the corners of the tower based on feng shui principles and lighting design.

Thinking to design outline that minimize the wind effect

The facade of a high rise building made up of polygonal shapes takes on an even more complex appearance due to the curtain wall louvers. We studied a corner details that would make it easy to resolve the joints of different surfaces. We also considered sizes and forms to minimize the impact of wind effect, and install lighting boxes at the slits.

For *feng shui* considerations, the corners were designed to be rather soft. Through a process of trial and error, we arrived at a design that allowed for a certain degree of nuanced shade. The design of the corners that create a series of contours is an important factor in determining the silhouette of the city as a whole.

減少風切的外觀設計

呈現多角形的辦公棟外觀形狀加上外牆帷幕的遮陽板，形成了複雜的細部構造。因此，我們討論如何將不同面向的遮陽板細部收頭接合，並讓轉角更容易處理。同時，還思考了可降低大樓風的大小與形狀，並於縫隙間設置了照明燈箱。

另外，因為風水的考量，我們用柔和的設計來表現轉角造型，並進行可出現陰影的重覆測試。建築物外觀輪廓的轉角設計，可說是決定整座城市的剪影重要因素。

風を低減する輪郭デザインを考える

多角形で形成された高層棟のファサードは、カーテンウォールのルーバーにより、さらに複雑な納まりとなる。そこで、異なる立面のルーバーとの取り合いを処理しやすいコーナー部を検討。ビル風を低減する大きさと形状も考え、スリットには照明ボックスを設置した。

また、風水上の理由でコーナーは柔らかいデザインとしつつ、陰影ができるデザインを試行錯誤した。輪郭ができるコーナー部のデザインは、その都市全体のシルエットを決める重要な要素である。

07 05 2013 Outline design to determine the silhouette of the city

決定城市剪影的外觀設計
都市のシルエットを決める輪郭のデザイン

Reviewing the details for the corner elements of the tower. Checks conducted when Mitsubishi Jisho Sekkei supervised the drawings.

08 30 2013 The height change as a result of the urban design review, and façade design progress by BIM

都市設計審議變更高度，透過BIM深化外觀設計
都市審議により高さを変更、BIMでファサードデザインを進化

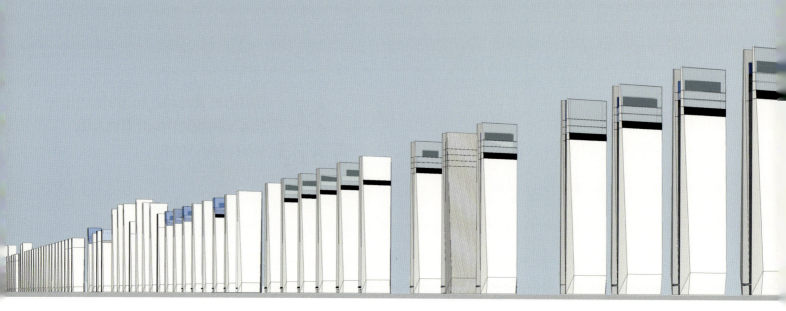

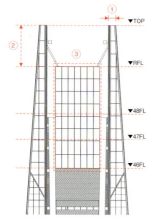

Rules for the design of the top of the building.
① Keeping the width of the crown narrow.
② Providiing height difference.
③ Insterting the glass box.

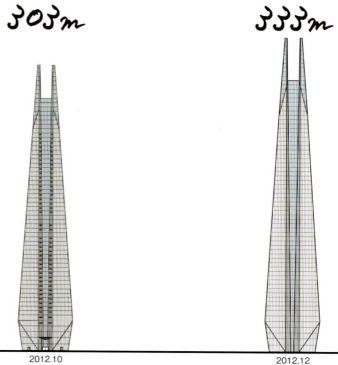

303m — 2012.10

333m — 2012.12

Due to the floor area ratio amendments as a result of the city council review, changes must be made repeatedly that led to changes in the height of the building and angle of inclination of the walls. Because of the polyhedron shape, each floor plate is different. BIM was utilized to progress the design, which allowed us to make design decisions and calculate floor area efficiently.

After the final deliberations, an agreement was reached with the client on the following three points; ①The height of the building to be 272m, an auspicious number for feng shui, ②Offices depth on the top floor to be 9.5m for lease conditions. ③The height difference between the glass crown of the roof and the penthouse to be 10m, for cost reduction.

After making more than 100 studies, building height was greatly lowered, the transparent glass crown that represented the "nails" of the clasped hands was also greatly reduced, and which led to a dramatic reduction of the floating sensation. In order to enhance the overall proportions, we decided on the design by ①keeping the width of the crown narrow, ②providing height difference between the center and two edges, and ③inserting the glass box into the top of the gable side in order to attract lines of sight.

因為都市設計審議決定了容積總量，突然之間，我們面臨建築物的高度及斜牆的角度也必須連帶做出變更的情況。因為外觀為多面體的關係，各樓層標準層的平面大小都不相同，我們使用了讓設計及面積計算更有效率的BIM來深化設計。

Multiple proportions were reviewed in 3D. Rules for the design were formulated as things progressed.

285m　　　　272m

2013.8

2013.11

因應都審最終的結果,我們與業主達成以下的共識:
①建築物高度為風水上的吉祥數字272m
②考量將來利於出租,最頂層的辦公室進深,至少保有9.5m
③顧慮到成本,屋頂的玻璃工作物與屋突高差為10m。
研究超過100種的方式後,我們降低了高度,將雙手合十造型的頂端,象徵「指甲」部份的透明玻璃範圍縮小,漂浮的感覺也大大減弱。
因此,為了提高整體建築的比例,透過①頂部的寬度盡量作細。②凸顯中間與兩端的高度差異。③設計玻璃箱插入頂部的形態讓視線聚焦等方式,決定了頂層的外觀設計。

都市審議により容積などに変更が生じ、幾度となく建物高さや壁面の傾斜角が変更となるハプニングが生じた。基準階平面が各階異なる多面体のため、デザインと面積計算を効率よく行えるBIMを利用してデザインを進化させた。
最終的な審議の結果、クライアントと、①建物高さは風水的によい数字である272m、②リーシングを配慮して最上階のオフィスは奥行9.5m、③コストを配慮し、屋上のガラス工作物と塔屋の高さの差は10m、の3つで合意した。
高さは大きく減少し、合掌した手の「爪」に見立てた頂部の透明ガラスが縮小、浮遊感が激減した。全体のプロポーションを向上させるため、①頂部の幅を細く保つ、②中央と両先端の高さに差をつける、③ガラスボックスを妻面頂部に挿入して視線を集めることを、100を超えるスタディでデザインを決定していった。

Significant wind pressure due to Taipei 101

「台北101」帶來的強大風壓
「台北101」による大きな風圧

10/24 2013

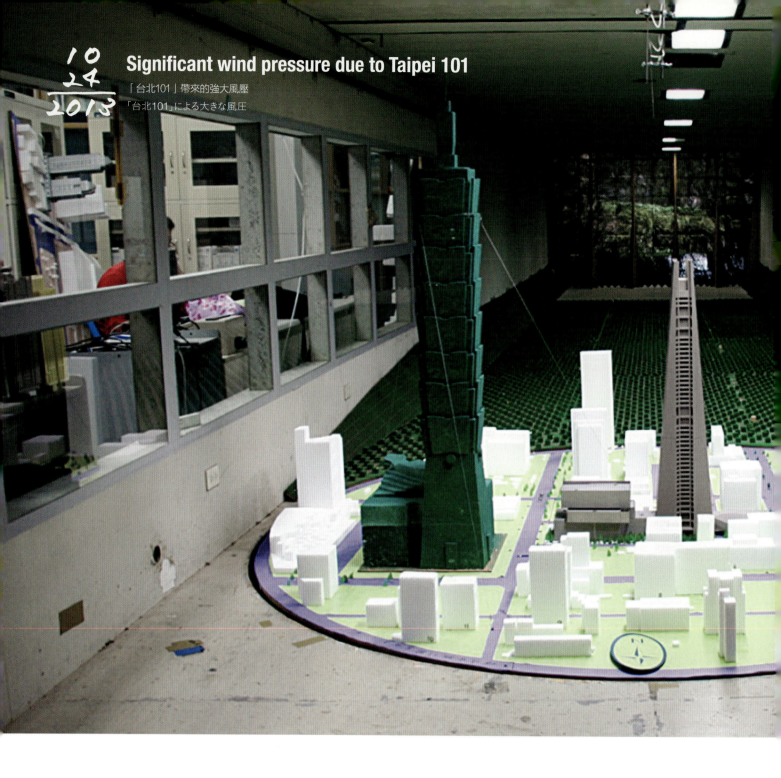

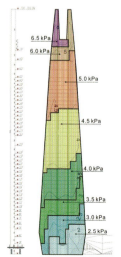
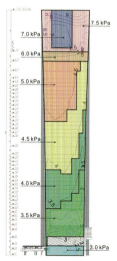
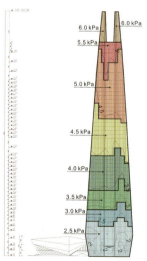
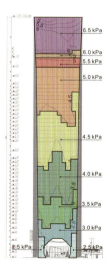

Figures for the wind pressure on each surface of the facade, obtained by conducting wind tunnel experiments (positive pressure).

Conducting wind tunnel experiments for the city council
When we conducted wind tunnel experiments, we discovered that the locally strong winds due to the presence of Taipei 101 reached a maximum wind pressure of 11.5kPa - a figure that was significantly higher than our initial projections. In order to withstand these winds, we amplified both the wall thickness and width of the cross section of the curtain wall to 1.5 times the usual figure, and increased the amount of aluminum used. As this entailed a dramatic increase in costs, we extruded the back mullions that are typically installed in the interior and integrated them with the environmental louvers in a design that sought to reduce costs.

為了都市設計審議所進行的風洞實驗
實施風洞實驗後得知「台北101」所帶來的風切效應比當初的預估值超出許多。最大的風壓高達11.5kPa。為了讓帷幕牆可以承受這個程度的風壓，不論是帷幕的厚度還是剖面，都加強到平時的1.5倍大，因此造成用鋁量倍增。因為成本大幅提高，我們改變設計，將原本設在內側的背襯材移至戶外，並與節能用的遮陽板結合，期能降低成本。

都市審議のため風洞実験を行う
風洞実験を行うと、「台北101」によるビル風で、当初の想定値よりもはるかに大きい、最大11.5kPaの風圧が発じることが分かった。これに耐えるために、カーテンウォールの肉厚も断面も通常の1.5倍程度に巨大化し、アルミ量が増大した。コストが大幅にアップするため、内側に設けるバックマリオンを外部に表出し、環境ルーバーと一体化することでコスト削減を図るデザインに変更した。

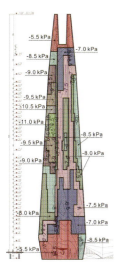 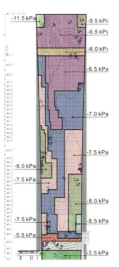 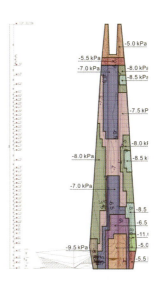 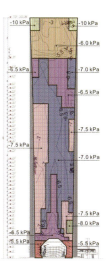

Figures for the wind pressure on each surface of the facade, obtained by conducting wind tunnel experiments (negative pressure).

11/27 2013

Schematic design is still ongoing | Dismantling the existing buildings, and starting the underground work

設計還只進行到基本設計｜拆除既有建物，地下工程開工
設計はまだ基本設計中｜既存建物解体、地下工事着工

Foundation piling. The cast-in-place piles directly beneath the tower are 40m at their longest, with a diameter of 3.0m at their widest. A total of some 243 piles were used across all three buildings.

Groundbreaking ceremony.

Construction site.

Underground piled column, 1,400mm × 2,000mm, with a length of 26.4m.

Piling
On November 27, 2013, after around a one-year design period, construction started on Taipei Nanshan Plaza. Due to the shortened construction period, an inverted construction method was adopted. On-site construction and the design of the details proceeded concurrently. The steel pillars on the first floor measured some 2×1.4m — big enough for a person to enter into.

基樁施工
2013年11月27日，設計進行約一年之後，「臺北南山廣場」終於動工。為縮短工期，工地採用逆打工法，現場工程與細部設計同時並進。一樓的鋼柱尺寸達2×1.4公尺，幾乎是人可以進入的大小。

杭工事
2013年11月27日、約1年の設計期間の後、「臺北南山廣場」は着工した。工期短縮のために逆打ち工法を採用したが、現場工事と詳細設計は並行して進む。1階の鉄骨柱は2×1.4mもあり、人が入れるほど大きい。

Reinforcement work for the pile

Creating a design for the top of the building with a sense of liveliness and transparency

創造熱鬧且具通透感的頂部設計
賑わいと透明感ある頂部デザインをつくる

Early study for the distribution and layout of beams at the top of the building.

A structural design that takes into account the view from the terrace

We studied efficient methods of creating a pleasant and comfortable outdoor space with a sense of transparency that would form a unified whole with the design of the top of the building and its structure. Sash windows were supported by steel back mullions about 30m high placed at an interval of 2m in order to enhance the views from the terrace and create a sensation of transparency that would be evident from both the inside and outside. A particular effort was made to eliminate cross ties as much as possible, as well as anything that would obstruct one's line of sight when looking up at Taipei 101 from the terrace.

從露臺眺望美景思考的結構設計

為讓頂部的設計與結構體一體化，我們研究了有效率的設計方式，打造讓使用者舒適且呈現通透感的頂樓戶外空間。為了讓使用者不論位於室內或室外皆能感受到通透感，並提高從露臺眺望景觀的視覺效果，我們採用間距2m，高度約30m，一支到底的鋼背撐來支撐玻璃外牆，盡量減少橫向連接構件，希望盡可能地避免從露臺眺望「台北101」時造成視覺阻礙的設計。

テラスからの眺望も考えた構造デザイン

頂部のデザインと構造体を一体として、透明感のある心地よい屋外空間を、効率よくつくる方法をスタディした。テラスからの眺望を高め、利用者が内外から透明感を感じられるように、2m間隔で高さ約30mの1本のスチールバックマリオンでサッシを支える。横繋を極力なくし、テラスから「台北101」を見上げた時に視界をさえぎるものが極力少なくなるよう工夫した。

01/08/2014

Diversity of greenery on the ground

各式各樣的綠意在腳邊蔓延

足元に広がる多種多様な緑

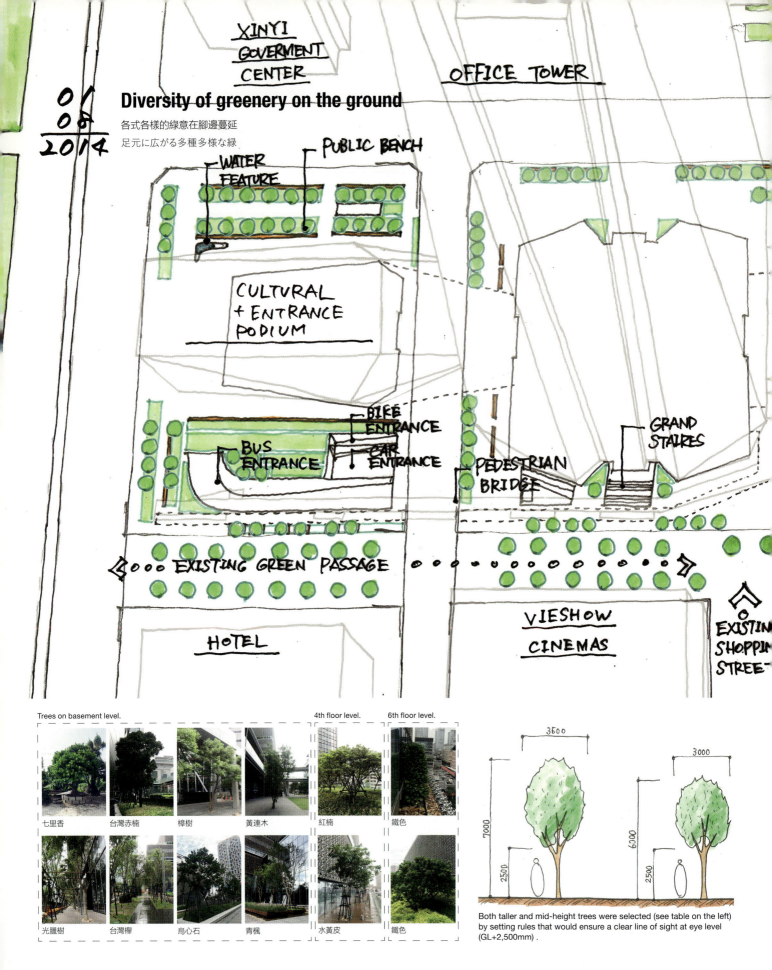

Both taller and mid-height trees were selected (see table on the left) by setting rules that would ensure a clear line of sight at eye level (GL+2,500mm).

Taiwan has a "green architecture" environmental performance assessment system similar to the LEED criteria. In order to fulfill the criteria for the "biodiversity index" that is one of the evaluation factors in landscape planning, 12 varieties of both tall and short trees and shrubs were planted, creating a design emphasizing diversity of vegetation in order to obtain diamond level "green architecture" certification. In addition to the environmental design of the exterior, drainage was improved on account of the frequent typhoons, and biotopes serving as a stopover for insects and birds, as well as areas of tree shade where people can stand were created.

台灣的環境性能評估制度中也有與LEED同樣基準的「綠建築標章」。景觀計畫中為滿足其評估項目之一「生物多樣性指標」的標準及取得鑽石級的認證，我們重視植物的多樣化，採用約12

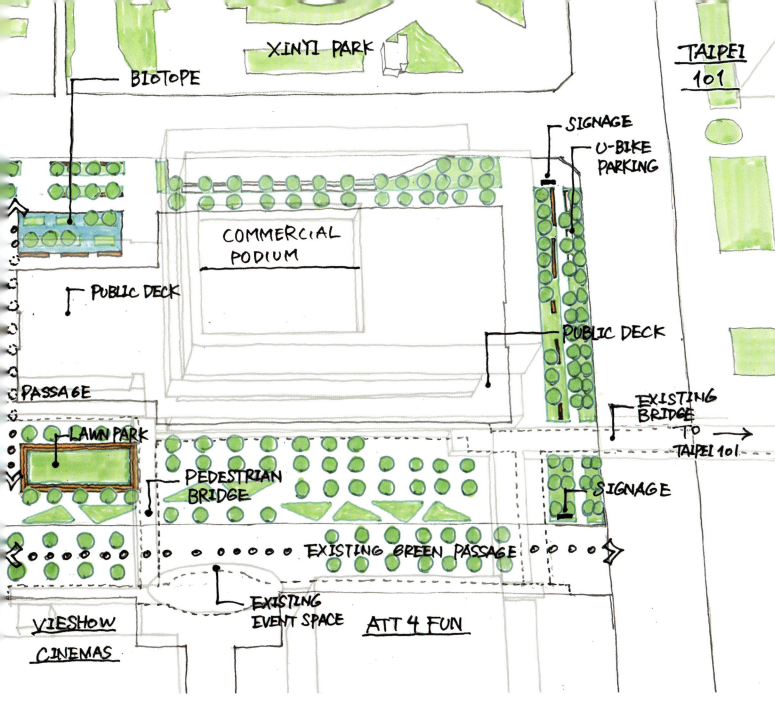

Plan for greenery.

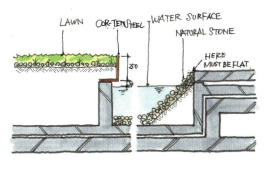

Biotope sectional detail (s:1/40)

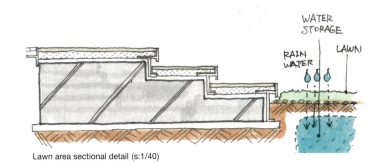

Lawn area sectional detail (s:1/40)

種大小喬木植栽混植的設計。除外觀等的節能設計外，因為颱風也很頻繁發生，我們同時規劃了完善的排水系統，還有可讓鳥類及蟲類棲息的生物棲地，和人們可以停駐休憩的綠蔭。

台湾の環境性能評価として、LEEDと同様の基準である「緑建築」がある。ランドスケープ計画では、その評価項目のひとつ「生物多様性指標」の基準を満たすため、大高木・小高木合わせて12種類の樹木を配置し、緑建築ダイヤモンドレベルを取得するために植物の多様性を重視した混植設計を行った。外装なども環境設計以外にも、台風が多いため水はけをよくし、鳥や虫の飛来地となるビオトープ、人がたたずむことのできる緑陰を創出した。

03/19/2014

Creating day and night cityscape
創造白天與夜晚的景緻
昼夜の風景をつくる

Lighting that harmonizes with the city of Taipei, and reducing the burden on the environment through various types of glass

What would a light-up that harmonizes with Taipei 101, the solitary tower that serves as a symbol of the city, look like? When one gazes upon the rooftop terrace from Taipei 101, what sort of lighting would help to project a space with a sense of originality? The office tower causes the contours to light up and emphasizes the vertical lines, while the aluminum frames of the curtain walls at the top also light up, throwing the entire "claw" shape into sharp relief. The silver stainless steel exterior walls of the commercial podium by day turn a golden hue at night thanks to warm lighting. Lighting for the external facade of the cultural + entrance podium, which is surrounded by high-end residences, was kept to a minimum, with only the contours and edges illuminated. Conversely, we devised a method of using the light that seeps down to the ground from the strong interior lighting to create an enticing atmosphere for people.

使用與台北街景諧和的燈光・不同規格的玻璃造就低碳環境

甚麼是可與台北地標，單棟大樓「台北101」諧和的夜間照明？從「台北101」眺望本案屋頂露台時，甚麼樣的照明可以創造出獨特的空間感？
辦公棟：我們透過照亮建築物的輪廓，強調垂直線條，並打亮頂部帷幕鋁框來凸顯「指甲」部分。商場棟：白天是銀色的不銹鋼外牆，到了夜晚則透過暖色系的燈光妝點轉變成金色。因周邊有高級住宅區的關係，故藝文入口棟的外牆盡量避免裝設燈光，僅讓建築物輪廓的光影顯現出來。為彌補這個部分，透過相較明亮的室內照明，由地面映透出來的光線吸引人群前來。

台北の街と調和するライティング

1棟単独のタワーである台北のシンボル「台北101」と調和するライトアップとは？「台北101」からルーフトップテラスを眺めた時、どのような照明がオリジナリティある空間と映るだろうか？高層棟は、輪郭を光らせて垂直なラインを強調し、頂部カーテンウォールのアルミ枠を光らせ「爪」全体を浮かび上がらせた。商業棟は、昼間はステンレスの銀色の外壁を、夜間は暖色系のライティングで金色に変

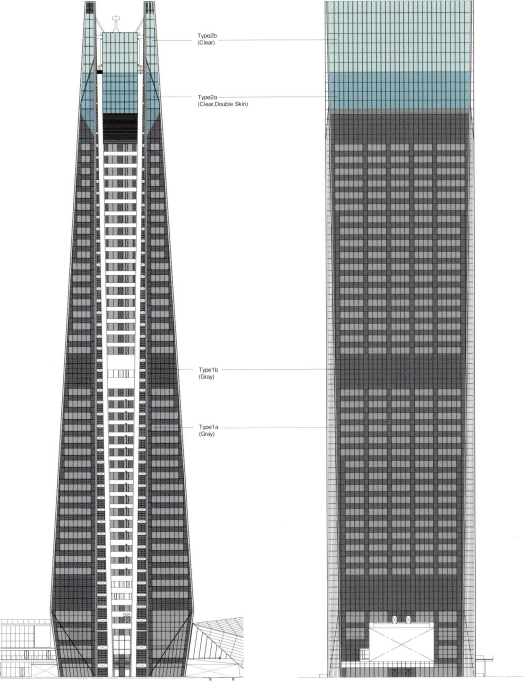

South elevation (s:1/1,500). Glass that met the requirements for "Green Architecture" in Taiwan was selected.

West elevation.

Type 2b:
Laminated Glass/ Clear

Type 2a:
Double Low-E Glass/ Clear

Type 1b:
Lanimated Low-E Glass/ Gray

Type 1a:
Double Low-E Glass/ Gray

える。周辺に高級レジデンスがある文化・入口棟は外装の照明を極力なくし、輪郭のみを照らした。その分、強い内部照明で地面に滲み出す光で人を誘う計画とした。

Glass performance and "Green Architecture"

During our studies for the facade design of the upper floors of the office block, we wanted to use black glass for everything except the transparent tip. This value in performance of using a variety of glass with an extremely high sun shielding performance with a shading coefficient (SC) of 0.23 was also something that was demanded by the environmental review board in order to obtain the diamond level "Green Architecture" certification. In Taiwan, the composite performance of features such as interior blinds and air conditioning systems are not added as functions for the performance of the exterior facade of buildings. Instead, they rely only on the sun shielding of louvers and the performance of the glass.

「綠建築」與玻璃的性能數值
檢討塔樓的外觀設計時，除頂部使用高透明度的玻璃外，其他部分都使用深色系的玻璃。因應業主希望能取得綠建築標章鑽石級認證的需求，按照試算結果，必須使用日照遮蔽性能極高，且遮蔽係數SC（Shading Coefficient）需達到0.23的玻璃規格。在綠建築評估上，室內捲簾和空調系統無法被納入外殼厚度視為複合外牆系統，可被視為節能設計的部份，僅有可遮蔽日照的遮陽板和玻璃性能而已。

「緑建築」とガラスの性能値

オフィス高層部のファサードデザインの検討にあたり、透明感のある頂部以外は黒色系ガラスとしたい。その性能値についても、緑建築ダイヤモンドレベルの取得にはSC（Shading Coefficient）値0.23という、きわめて日射遮蔽性能の高いガラスの使用が試算結果により求められた。緑建築審査上、内部ブラインドや空調システムの複合性能は外装ファサード性能として加味されず、あくまでルーバーによる日射遮蔽とガラス性能のみである。

04 / 10 / 2014 Underground work | Building the juncture between the underground beams and pile heads using inverted construction methods

地下工程｜逆打工法地樑及基樁頂部的接合點
地下工事｜逆打ち工法による地中梁と杭頭部の接合点

Cutting of the temporary support columns as part of the inverted construction method for the bus terminal.

Construction of the three underground stories. Inverted construction method. Mining for construction proceeds, and bottoming is completed. Steel bars being arranged for the foundation mat slabs. Underground piled columns and steel bars of the pile heads are visible at the front.

Inverted construction methods and underground construction

As the underground bus terminal directly beneath the cultural + entrance wing consisted of parking spaces and driveways, it was not possible to insert columns, and therefore necessary to skip the span. Accordingly, a Vierendeel truss frame to function as upper and lower chords for the one-storey space between the basement two and basement one floors was adopted. These columns were done away with only on the middle floor (basement two). As a result of using inverted construction methods, columns were continuously dropped in from the ground level. After the underground framework was laid, only the underground piled columns at the level of the bus terminal were cut open.

逆打工法及地下施工

藝文入口棟正下方的地下巴士轉運站因規劃為停車場及車道的關係不太能落柱，必須盡量將柱子跨距拉大，因此，地下二樓至地下一樓的大梁採用有上下弦構材的范倫第桁架結構，巴士轉運站的柱子僅落到地下三樓為止。因為逆打工法需從地上層連續降下配置柱子，所以在地下工程完成後，才將地下巴士轉運站當層的逆打鋼柱裁斷。

逆打ち工法と地下構築

文化・入口棟直下の地下バスターミナルは、駐車場と車路からなるために柱を入れられず、スパンを飛ばす必要がある。そのため、1階、地下2階の大梁をそれぞれ上下弦材とするフィーレンディールトラス架構を採用。バスターミナル内の柱は、地下3階のみなくなるが、逆打ち工法にあたり地上から連続して柱を落とし込むため、地下構築後にバスターミナル階のみ、構真柱を切断した。

2016　　　　　　2017　　　　　　2018

Essay

須部恭浩　株式会社三菱地所設計 首席建築師

Thoughts from the chief architect

首席建築師的想法
チーフアーキテクトの想い

Yasuhiro Sube | Mitsubishi Jisho Sekkei Chief Architect | Born in 1972 at Kanagawa, Japan / In 1995, graduated the department of architecture, Meiji university / In 1995~2001, Mitsubishi Jisho / In 2001~, Mitsubishi Jisho Sekkei / Adjunct professor of Meiji university

須部恭浩 | 三菱地所設計首席建築師 | 1972年出生於日本神奈川縣／1995年明治大學理工學院建築學系畢業／1995~2001任職三菱地所／2001年~任職三菱地所設計。明治大學兼任講師

須部恭浩 | 三菱地所設計チーフ・アーキテクト | 1972年神奈川県生まれ／1995年明治大学理工学部建築学科卒業／1995~2001年三菱地所／2001年~三菱地所設計。明治大学兼任講師

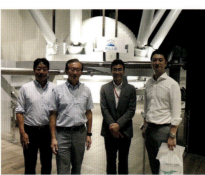

Taipei Nanshan Plaza, located on the southern edge of the central axis that runs through Xinyi Special District, is a development that adjoins Taipei 101, the tallest building in Taiwan. The client, Nan Shan Life Insurance, is currently leasing the site from the government on a fixed-term 50 year lease, and sought to build a project that would revitalize the neighborhood through offices and commercial activity.

When I first visited the site, I felt that the narrow site measuring some 270m east-west obstructed the flow of people, causing an interruption to the bustling vitality of the neighborhood. In order to attract and entice people and create a sense of liveliness, I thought it necessary to reconfigure the area on a more human scale, and create a new icon that would attract people even from a remote distance. More than anything else, I felt that it was important to have a tower that would, together with the adjoining Taipei 101, form a pair, so as to create a new skyline for Taipei.

The project consists of three blocks that connect the human bustle and traffic to the surrounding areas: a commercial podium, which resembles a stack of boxes covered in plum blossoms (the national flower of Taiwan) made of stainless steel processed by hand, and a cultural + entrance podium integrated with the cultural facility, each located on one side of the tower block. The terrace of the commercial block is integrated with the adjoining park in order to create a verdant, green environment, while the top of the tower features Taiwan's first ever rooftop terrace, which entices people towards the upper floors of the building.

Unlike Europe and the US, Japanese architects are not separated according to professional specializations. They are educated to think about various issues in a holistic way, from cities

「臺北南山廣場」開發案位於信義計畫區中心軸線的南端，鄰近台灣第一高樓「台北101」。業主南山人壽向政府承租50年地上權，在此地打造辦公大樓及商場，企能促進地區活化。

第一次造訪此地時，我感受到東西270m狹長的土地切斷了人流，同時也阻斷了商業活動的延續。我認為，要吸引人潮營造熱鬧的氛圍，必須以人性尺度重新建構街道配置。建立從遠處就可以吸引人群目光的新地標固然必要，但最重要的是，要創造出與鄰近的「台北101」並駕齊驅的台北新天際線。

另外，外觀由手工加工的不銹鋼管製作而成的梅花(台灣國花)牆包覆，宛如箱子疊砌的商場棟，和藝文設施一體化設計的藝文入口棟，分別配置於塔樓的兩側。設計三棟建築物的概念，是為了連結週邊商圈的人潮及商業活動。商場棟的露臺建構綠化環境，與緊鄰的公園相互呼應。尤其屋頂規劃了台灣第一座露天屋頂酒吧，希望吸引人群前往高樓層。

有別於歐美國家的建築師會將專業細分化，日本的建築師大多是接受了包括都市規劃、建築室內設計甚至到景觀的整體思考的教育，且也習慣整體規劃的設計方式。與日本相同，本案業主將窗口統整委託我

「臺北南山廣場」は、信義計画区中心軸の南端に位置し、台湾一の高さを誇る「台北101」に隣接した開発である。クライアントの南山人寿は政府から50年の定期借地としてここを借り受け、オフィスと商業により地域活性化の拠点をつくろうとしていた。

初めてここを訪れた時、東西270mもの細長い敷地が人の流れを断ち、街の賑わいを途切れさせていると感じた。そこで、人を引きつけ、賑わいをつくるため、ヒューマンスケールで街を再構築することと、遠方からも人を集める新たなアイコンの存在が必要だと考えた。何より、隣接する「台北101」と対になるタワーを置き、台北に新たなスカイラインを創出することが重要だと考えた。

また、手加工のステンレスで製作した梅の花（台湾の花）で覆われた箱を積み上げたような商業棟と、文化施設と一体化した文化・入口棟をタワー両側に配した3棟構成とし、周辺街区へ人の賑わいを繋げていく。商業棟のテラスは隣接する公園と一体で緑化環境を構築し、さらにタワー頂部には台湾初のルーフトップテラスを設け、上層へ人をいざなう場所とした。

日本の建築家は、欧米のように専門分化されておらず、都市から建築の内装、ランドスケープまで、一体的に考える教育を受け、その手法に慣れている。

to the interior furnishings of buildings, and landscaping, and are accordingly used to this method.

For this project, all liaising with the client with regard to design issues went through us, just as it would in Japan. We obtained positive feedback regarding the speed of operations as a result of this approach, and were also able to win the trust of the client. As a result of Japanese architects obtaining projects abroad, we feel that there is some potential in thoroughly exploring this Japanese approach to design.

On the other hand, I feel that Japanese architects lack the necessary skills to convey their thoughts directly. However, when it comes to creating cities and architecture, they are able to explain how they took their thinking and developed it into a design. In this book, we have depicted in chronological order what goes on in the mind of these architects, from urban scale to full-size scale, in relation to the process of creating and the communication that accompanies it.

Although I am even now extremely worried about how the building will be maintained after completion and whether its continued existence will have future value, the unique appeal of this project resided in how multiple trials at a range of scales were conducted simultaneously, using sketches, models, and computers, enabling us to take pleasure in creating something together with the client.

I look forward to the next opportunity to create something new with this team.

們進行一體化設計。這樣不但可以獲得業主高效率的好評，更可以累積信賴關係。我們感受到若是日本的建築師在國外拿到案子，徹底實踐這種日本方式的設計模式，應該可行性很高。

另一方面，我也感受到日本的建築師不太擅長傳達自己的想法。但是，規劃都市或建築，其實都是從傳遞自我的思想進而發展到設計。本書描繪了創作的過程還有溝通方式。從都市規劃尺度，到視覺模型的規模，建築師腦中早已用時間軸的方式，刻劃出完成時的模樣。建築物竣工後的維護，以及將來的存在價值等等，種種擔心至今仍未解除。我們使用了廣泛的尺度，同時以草圖、模型及電腦進行設計驗證。過程中與業主共同創作的樂趣，是此專案最令人吟味的地方。

我們非常期待未來還有機會和這個團隊共同創造新的價值。

今回も、日本での場合と同様、クライアントからの依頼を私たちに一本化して設計した。これによるスピード感が好評を得て、クライアントから信頼を得ることができた。日本の建築家が海外で仕事を獲得する上で、こうした日本式の設計スタイルを突き詰めていくことに可能性を感じた。

その一方、日本の建築家は思想を直接伝えることは不得意だと感じる。しかし、都市や建築をつくるにあたり、どのように思想を設計へと展開してきたかは伝えることができる。本誌では、つくることとそのコミュニケーションについて、都市スケールから原寸まで、建築家の頭の中を時系列にアウトプットする様子を描いた。

竣工後のメンテナンスや、将来存続し得るだけの価値があるのか、今でも心配は尽きないが、幅広いスケールで同時に検証し、スケッチと模型とコンピューターを駆使して、クライアントと共にものをつくる楽しさは、このプロジェクトの醍醐味であった。

またこのチームで新しいものづくりができることを楽しみにしている。

Drawings that straddle 2D and 3D

交付2D與3D設計圖
2Dと3Dを橋渡しする図面

04/10/2014

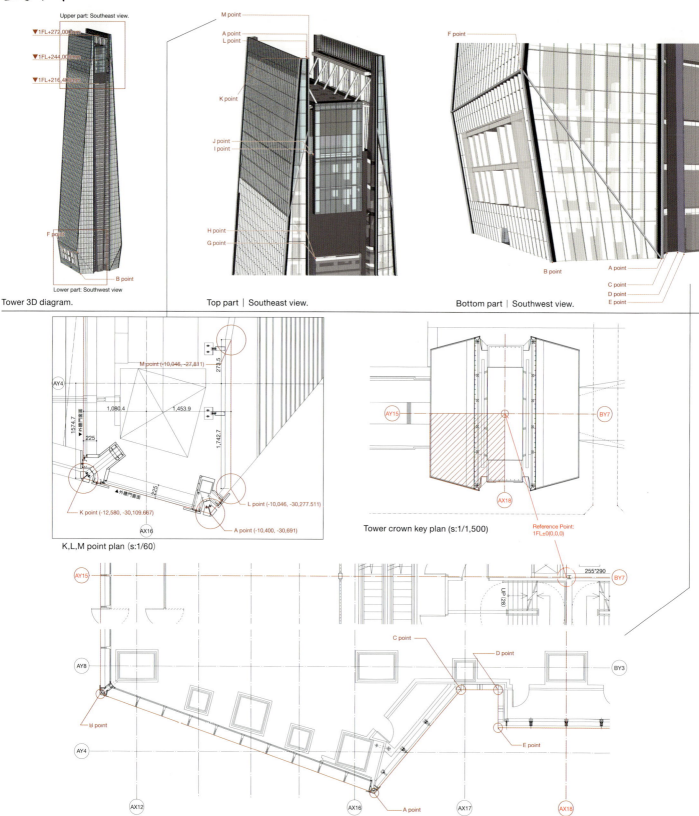

How to convey a complex form

During the construction of the polyhedral office tower and the cultural + entrance podium, it was necessary to convey forms to local architects and builders in an accurate manner. For this, we added the coordinates of the top of the building that would serve as a standard onto the SD drawings (schematic design drawings), so that they could move back and forth between the 2D drawings and the 3D models. By indicating the coordinates that would ensure the accuracy of the 3D renderings, this method of generating design drawings facilitated easy construction and supervision.

如何傳達複雜的型態

多面體的辦公棟及藝文入口棟施工時，必須傳達正確的形狀讓當地的建築師和施工廠商理解。因此，必須在SD（基本設計圖）上標註基準的頂點座標，在2D圖說和3D模型之間來回反覆確認。在2D圖上標示正確的3D座標的作圖方式，可以讓施工及監造更容易進行。

3D diagrams of the G Detail.

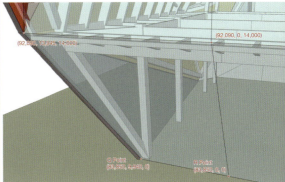

Cultural + entrance podium key plan (s:1/1,500)

3D diagram of the F Detail.

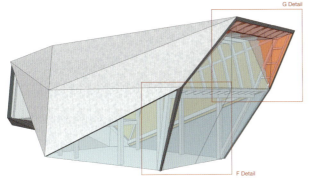

3D diagrams of the Southeast view.

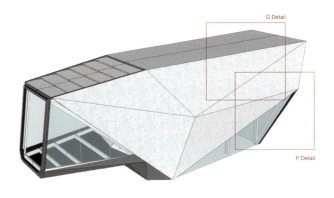

3D diagrams of the Southwest bird's eye view.

複雑な形態をどう伝えるか

多面体の高層棟や文化・入口棟の施工では、現地建築家や施工者に正確に形を伝える必要があった。そこで、SD図（基本設計図）上に、基準となる頂点の座標を書き加え、2D図面と3Dモデルを行き来できるようにした。3Dの正確さを担保する座標を示し、施工・監修しやすい作図方法とした。

Quality of drawings

In order to obtain the agreement of the client, local architects, and consultants for the floor plan and cross section of each floor, we prepared numerous drawings and made presentations. SD drawings (schematic design drawings) in Japan are about equivalent to DD drawings (design development drawings) abroad. For the purposes of construction in Taiwan, drawings were annotated in both Chinese and Japanese. Taiwanese building regulations are fairly close to the Building Standards Act in Japan. As restrictions on the structure of buildings are almost identical, we were able to draft the drawings at at equal level, with the resulting environment proving quite easy for Japanese architects to adapt to.

設計圖的質感

為了能與業主、本地建築師及顧問們，就各層平面和剖面圖的內容取得共識，我們製作了相當多量的設計圖說進行簡報。日本的SD（基本設計圖）的完成度很接近於國外的DD（細部設計圖）。因施工地點是在台灣，設計圖必須用中文及日文兩種語言並列標示，由於台灣的建築法規與日本建築法規也很類似，結構的限制也幾乎沒有太大差異，對日本的建築師而言，是能容易進入狀況並發揮專業能力的環境。

図面の質

クライアント、現地建築家、コンサルタントから各階平面や断面の合意を取るため、多くの図面を作成しプレゼンテーションを行った。日本のSD図（基本設計図）は、海外のDD図（実施設計図）に近い。台湾での施工にあたり、図面は中国語と日本語の二段表記とした。台湾の建築法規は日本の建築基準法に近い。構造の制約もほぼ変わらないため、ほぼ同等に作図でき、日本の建築家が親しみやすい環境にある。

Detail drawings related to the piled up exterior walls. The height exceeded 1m as of October 2014.

Sketches for the plum blossom concept by Samuel Yin.
2014/02

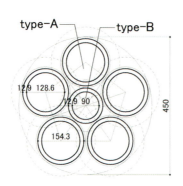
2014/03

2014/03

2014/03

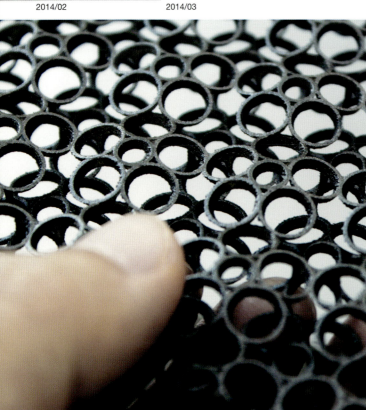
Models for the plum blossom façade, made using a 3D printer (s: 1/20).

Lighting study.

05 27 2014 — Using the plum blossom, Taiwan's symbolic flower, for the façade design of the commercial podium

以代表台灣的「梅花」裝飾商場棟的外牆

台湾の花「梅」を商業棟のファサードデザインに

Covering the facade with "plum" art

Initially, we wanted to clad the commercial podium with a simple exterior facade by covering the three boxes with bronze louvers. When we showed the client photos of the completed Otemon Gakuin University offices that had used cast aluminium to make cherry blossoms for its facade, they proposed using the plum blossom as a motif, which would be a symbol of Taiwan. A plan for covering "art boxes" with plum blossoms started to take shape, and trials using bent and cast aluminium began.

We decided that computer graphics would be unsuited to express this flower pattern on a small scale, so a 1:20 scale model was produced using a 3D printer. Further studies were made using actual samples.

用工藝點綴外牆

商場棟一開始是打算用青銅質感的百葉，包覆三座箱子的簡單外觀設計。但是，當我們向業主介紹其他設計作品，如日本「追手門學院大學」行政大樓的鑄鋁櫻花飾牆竣工照片時，業主向我們反應可以用象徵台灣的梅花作為設計主題，於是決定了用梅花來包覆呈現出「藝術寶盒」的方向性。我們以鋁材彎曲加工和鑄造方式開始試做構件。過程中發現小型的花朵圖案表現在透視圖上的效果並不理想，於是改用3D印表機製作1/20的模型，並以1比1大小的樣品等同步進行檢討。

ファサードを「梅」のアートで覆う

商業棟は、当初3つの箱をブロンズのルーバーで覆うシンプルな外装としていた。しかし、私たちが日本で設計した、アルミキャストの桜の花をファサードに用いた「追手門学院大学」オフィスの竣工写真をクライアントに紹介すると、彼らから台湾を象徴する梅の花をモチーフにする提案を得た。こうして「アートボックス」として梅の花で覆う方針がまとまり、アルミの曲げや鋳物での試作が始まった。

小スケールの花模様の表現にCGは不向きと判断し、3Dプリンターで1/20模型を製作、実物サンプルなどによる検討を進めた。

2014/04

2014.4

2014/04

2014/05

Models for the plum blossom façade. Three-dimensional version of the metal ribbon model. This model became the definitive version, and became the master design.

2014/05
Full size mock-up made of aluminium.

Interior of commercial podium.

Escalators laid out in an "8" pattern in the atrium of the commercial podium

The interior furnishings of the commercial podium were to be constructed by the tenants, so we undertook the design only for the common areas by making proposals regarding the lines of movement of visitors. Escalators in the central atrium were laid out as if to trace a figure "8", in order to enhance the navigability of the space.

商場棟挑空區以8字型配置電扶梯

因商場棟的室內裝修是屬於租戶工程，故僅針對公共區域和來客動線規劃等進行提案。而中央的挑空區，為了提高來客的回遊性，以8字型配置電扶梯。

商業棟吹き抜けの8の字配置エスカレータ

商業棟内装はテナント工事であるため、共用部のみを設計し、客動線などの提案を行った。中央の吹き抜けには8の字を描くようにエスカレータを配し、回遊性を高める計画とした。

Essay

藤貴彰　川岸昇　大﨑駿一　永澤一輝

Translating the forms using words and models

透過語言及模型來傳達設計
かたちを言葉や模型で伝える方法

Conveying the form of something: using presentations as a method

In order to convey the unique appeal of crafting something that emerges out of a relationship where the architect interfaces with client from the planning stage up until the completion of the building, we took models, full-size scale samples, and other materials from the initial stages along with us to the presentation, in addition to the perspective drawings, sketches, and computer graphics, so that the client would get a three-dimensional sense of the building and be able to verify details of the design while coming into contact with the real thing. In this way, we made sure to create a situation in which both client and architect could make progress on the creative process together.

For this project, things were decided not just by several key people, but by gathering all those involved in one place. As project managers gave presentations with the assistance of an interpreter, explanations were given in both Japanese and Chinese, and required double the time. In addition, differences in the nuances of particular words that occurred between the project managers and architects made it necessary to expect and assume the possibility of causing misunderstandings with the client.

Content that was inevitably going to be difficult was explained by laying out the theory behind it like a formula. Care was taken so that it would be easy to translate without causing misunderstandings. Although we typically use Powerpoint for presentations, ease of comprehension was demanded here, so we arrived at the solution of making a picture-story show with a single word or phrase per page. Despite the fact that this was a time-consuming task, it made the presentation flow smoothly by consolidating the story behind it.

At one point, the person in charge on the client side told us that "you are geniuses when it comes to making a presentation. Usually, it's very likely that the people at the top, who can be quite harsh when it comes to giving opinions, would give their approval."

A presentation with no deviations

The materials sometimes ran to 100 pages. Although Taiwan is basically a paperless culture, people sign off on the final plan on a single sheet of paper. These signatures are proof that the entire team is in agreement with each other, making it possible to reconfirm what was previously agreed upon at the next meeting — basically, an effective means of ensuring that that there are no deviations.

A presentation where speed is constantly demanded

This project was a continuous series of processes where discussions were held with the client on-site, ideas were brainstormed and developed, and everyone raced towards the goal while deepening one's understanding of each other. Simple models were generated using Google Sketchup and Rhinoceros, detailed sketches were drawn, samples were compared, and we sometimes returned to concepts on the scale of the city: preparations that would allow us to go back and forth between a 1:1,000 and 1:1 scale were always required. Presentations were usually

---

傳達設計　簡報手法

建築師從產品規劃階段到完工為止都必須對業主。為了充分地傳達作品的魅力，在進行簡報之際，除了透視圖、草圖及3D以外，我們還必須讓業主感受到建築的立體感。於是，從初期階段開始，我們將模型、實體樣品及建材等帶到台灣，讓業主實際觸摸同時進行設計確認。我們很重視透過這種方式，營造出隨時與業主及本地建築師一起進行創作的環境。

這個專案不會只侷限於幾位主事者，只要是專案的相關成員都會齊聚一堂共同決定細節。專案經理也會透過專業翻譯進行簡報，除日文及中文的來往翻譯需要雙倍時間外，專案經理與建築師們之間也可能產生言詞上細微的含意差異，故我們必須先預設與業主之間發生誤解的可能性。

對於比較難以理解的內容，我們會使用類似數學公式，有順序有理論作為佐證解釋，並用避免雙方誤解且容易翻譯的方式說明。簡報時除了使用PPT，為了讓資料更容易明瞭，我們每一頁皆用主題式說明，如同說故事般掌握重點切入內容，雖然準備較為費時費工，但透過完整的陳述，可以讓簡報更加流暢。

在某次簡報會後，業主方的專案窗口告訴我們：「貴公司的簡報手法簡直是爐火純青！」

而平時要求很嚴格的業主高層長官，的確在我們做完簡報後，認同我方提案的機率也變高了。真是沒有比這種稱讚更令人開心的事了！

精準明確的簡報

簡報的頁數有時多達100頁，台灣基本上是無紙化的模式，最後雙方的決定事項，則是歸納在一張紙上全體成員簽名。這個署名也代表全體成員達成共識的證明，下次會議時，也會重新確認前一次的決議事項。這樣的作法不會產生模糊地帶，是很有效的方式。

隨時追求速度感的簡報

本專案除了在當地與業主討論外，為發揮最大的創意，並朝著彼此可以理解的目標前進，上述的流程須一而再再而三反覆執行。我們經常在當場使用Google Sketch Up及Rhinoceros來建立簡易的模型，並且繪製細部收頭的草圖，同時比對樣品。因有時需要回歸都市尺度的概念重新檢視，故我們隨時準備，以因應設計在1/1,000及1/1比例之間來回討論。

かたちを伝える　プレゼンテーションの手法

企画から竣工までクライアントに向き合う建築家。そこで生まれるものづくりの魅力を伝えるため、プレゼンテーションの際は、パースやスケッチ、3Dの他にも、立体的に建築を感じられるように、初期段階から模型、原寸サンプル、素材を持ち込み、実物に触れてもらいながらデザインを確認できるようにした。これにより、常にクライアントと建築家が一緒にものづくりを進める環境をつくることを心がけた。このプロジェクトでは、数人のキーマンのみならず、あらゆる関係者が一堂に会して物事が決定された。プロジェクトマネージャーは、通訳を介してプレゼンテーションを行うため、説明には日本語と中国語で倍の時間を要する。また、プロジェクトマネージャーと建築家の間に生じる言葉のニュアンスの違いも、クライアントに誤解を生じさせる可能性を想定する必要がある。止むを得ず難しくなる内容は、数式のように順に理論立てて説明して、誤解なく翻訳しやすく配慮した。プレゼンテーションではパワーポイントを用いるが、分かりやすさを求めた結果、1ページにひと言の、紙芝居のようなプレゼンテーションにたどり着いた。時間のかかる作業だが、ストーリーを固めることで、プレゼンテーションは順調に流れる。ある時、クライアントの担当者から「あなたたちはプレゼンテーションの神様だ」と言われた。普段は厳しい意見もするクライアントの上層部がOKを出す確率が高いからだという。これ以上ない褒め言葉だった。

ぶれないプレゼンテーション

資料は、時に100ページに及ぶ。台湾は基本的にペーパーレスだが、最終方針では1枚の紙にサインをもらう。このサインはチーム全員の合意の証明であり、次の打ち合わせで前回の合意事項を再確認でき、ブレを生じさせない点で有効だった。

常にスピード感が求められるプレゼンテーション

本プロジェクトは、クライアントと現地で議論し、アイデアを膨らませ、互いに理解を深めながらゴールへと走る、というプロセスの連続だった。その場でGoogle Sketch UpやRhinocerosで簡易モデルを作成し、ディテールのスケッチを描き、サンプルを比較し、時には都市スケールのコンセプトに立ち戻るなど、常に1/1,000と1/1を往復できるよう準備することが求められた。プレゼンテーションは2

Takaaki Fuji | Born in 1982 in Hyogo, Japan / 2007 Master's degree, Waseda University / 2007~ Mitsubishi Jisho Sekkei | 藤貴彰 | 1982年出生於日本兵庫縣／2007早稻田大學建築研究所碩士／2007年～任職三菱地所設計 | 藤貴彰 | 1982年兵庫県生まれ／2007年早稲田大学大学院修士課程修了／2007年～三菱地所設計

Noboru Kawagishi | Born in 1981 in Ishikawa, Japan / 2006 Master's degree, Niigata University / 2007 MAS degree, ETH Zurich / 2013~ Mitsubishi Jisho Sekkei | 川岸昇 | 1981年出生於石川縣／2006年新潟大學建築研究所碩士／2007年瑞士蘇黎世聯邦理工學院都市設計學位學程畢業／2013年～任職三菱地所設計 | 川岸昇 | 1981年石川県生まれ／2006年新潟大学大学院博士前期課程修了／2007年スイス連邦工科大学チューリッヒ校MASUD修了／2013年～三菱地所設計

Shunichi Osaki | Born in 1990 in Tokyo, Japan / 2015 Master's degree, Waseda university / 2015~ Mitsubishi Jisho Sekkei | 大﨑駿一 | 1990年出生於東京都／2015年早稻田大學大學院碩士／2015年～任職三菱地所設計 | 大﨑駿一 | 1990年東京都生まれ／2015年早稲田大学大学院修士課程修了／2015年～三菱地所設計

Ikki Nagasawa | Born in 1984 in Gifu, Japan / 2011 Master's degree, Kyoto Institute of Technology / 2014~2017 Mitsubishi Jisho Sekkei (Project Architect) | 永澤一輝 | 1984年出生於岐阜縣／2011年京都工藝纖維大學建築研究所碩士／2014～2017年三菱地所設計臺北南山廣場專案設計複委託 | 永澤一輝 | 1984年岐阜県生まれ／2011年京都工芸繊維大学大学院修士課程修了／2014～2017年三菱地所設計臺北南山廣場プロジェクト委託

made during a three-day two-night business trip to Taiwan — discussions with the person in charge on the client side were held on the first day, after which we would return to the hotel to rework our plans, and staff members in Japan would modify the computer graphics. There were many occasions where the materials were reconsolidated so that we could give the presentation anew three days later. The process of crafting something with the person in charge on the client side was thoroughly enjoyable, and the way in which things were decided and logically considered in the absence of an ample timeframe was an extremely edifying experience for us.

Presentations with the aid of diagrams

For this project, Mitsubishi Jisho Sekkei drew the drawings in the phases of conceptual design, architectural schematic design 1 and 2, and public space interior design development and supervised the shop drawings. Although the drawings were annotated in both Japanese and Chinese, we tried as much as possible to reduce the amount of text and made ample use of symbols and legends, in view of the risk of subtle changes in meaning resulting from the translation process, and in order to shorten the working time required.

During the supervision of the construction drawings, details were decided by discussing with local staff and determining what techniques would be possible in Taiwan. As building regulations and the use of materials were almost the same as those in Japan, there were no difficulties with understanding each other. Where the design was concerned, however, if we tried to communicate verbally (through an interpreter), there was the possibility that meaning and context would drift off in a direction that was not intended. Explaining the matter at hand while making sketches made it easier to get the point across. In this way, we were able to have smooth discussions with the local builders.

Presentation to the city government

The materials for the urban design council, too, were prepared by dividing the labor: Mitsubishi Jisho Sekkei handled the logical parts, while local Taiwanese design firms handled the drawings. These materials for deliberation by council might also be called "explanatory analytic materials" — they are rather difficult to parse. The logical materials were prepared based on Mitsubishi Jisho Sekkei's wealth of experience in urban design in Asia and Japan.

A presentation as a gift

When we reached a milestone during this project, we presented the client with hanging scrolls of ink paintings made from the perspective drawings, picture scrolls that consisted of a chain of nearly 100 perspective drawings, and wooden toy bricks of the tower block. Rendering the building in the form of toys and pictures allowed the client to feel a sense of familiarity with regard to Taipei Nanshan Plaza. The sense of distance in the repeated conversations that unfolded between us, the client, and the local builders is directly connected to the quality of the final building.

停留台灣三天兩夜的出差行程中，通常第一天與業主的專案窗口先做初步討論，回到飯店進行修正工作，並要求在日本的同事協助CG修正，資料重新彙整，第二天再度進行修正簡報的過程數不勝數。這種與業主共同創作，且在有限的時間內，做出決定及邏輯性思考的方式，讓我們獲益良多。

使用圖面的簡報

本案之中三菱地所設計負責的業務包括：CD（概念設計）、建築的SD1．2（基本設計）、公區室內設計的DD1（前段細部設計）之圖面繪製與施工圖確認。圖面上雖然採日文及中文併列標示，但避免翻譯過程中因些許的語意差錯造成誤解，且為縮短作業時間，我們盡量減少文字敘述，多用符號及圖例說明。

關於施工圖的確認工作，我們是與當地的團隊成員們討論，並考量台灣可行性較高的技術後，決定細部收頭設計。因法規及建材的使用方式幾乎與日本相同，故溝通上沒有太大的困難。但是關於設計面（需透過翻譯），如果只是透過言詞溝通，很有可能在含義及前後文上偏移了本意，所以我們會一邊描繪草圖，一邊進行重點說明，這樣的方式較容易表達設計想法，且與當地施工業者之間的討論也更加順暢。

提送市政府的簡報

都市設計審議資料中有邏輯性的部分由三菱地所設計主導，設計圖面的部份，則與本地建築師事務所分工製作。都審的資料一般來說應是「具說明性的分析資料」，但並非很容易了解。三菱地所設計以在亞洲及日本的豐富都市設計經驗為基礎，製作了這份邏輯性資料。

作為贈禮的簡報

專案進行途中的各個里程碑，我們將透視圖用水墨畫的方式呈現製作成畫軸，也使用將近100張的透視連續圖做成畫卷，以及塔樓造型的積木，贈送給業主。將建築物以玩具及圖畫的方式呈現，是為了讓大家對「臺北南山廣場」產生親近感。執行專案的過程中，業主與施工業者及我們之間，透過反覆的對話縮短「距離感」，我們認為這種做法，最終反映了建築物的品質。

泊3日程の台湾出張の中で、初日にクライアントの担当者と議論を交わし、ホテルに戻って練り直し、日本にいるスタッフがCGを修正。資料をまとめ直し、2日目に再度プレゼンテーションを行うことも多々あった。クライアント担当者とのものづくりは楽しく、十分な時間はない中での物事の決め方、ロジカルな思考は大変勉強になった。

図面を介したプレゼンテーション

今回、三菱地所設計は、CD（基本計画）、建築のSD1・2（基本設計）、共用部内装のDD1（実施設計）までの図面作成、施工図の監修業務を行った。図中では日本語と中国語を併記したが、翻訳過程で意味が微妙に変わるリスクや作業時間の短縮のため、文字を極力減らし、記号や凡例を多用した。施工図監修では、現地スタッフと議論し台湾で可能な技術とすり合わせてディテールを決める。法規や素材の使い方が日本とほぼ同じであることから、意思疎通は難しくはなかった。しかし、デザインに関しては、（通訳を介して）言葉だけでコミュニケーションを図ると、意味や文脈が意図しない方向にずれる可能性があった。スケッチを描きながら説明すると要点を伝えやすくなる。このようにして、現地施工者とのスムーズな議論を実現した。

市政府へのプレゼンテーション

都市設計審議資料についてもロジカルな部分は三菱地所設計、図面部分は現地設計事務所と分担して作成した。審議の資料は一般に「説明的分析資料」とも言うべきもので、分かりやすさがない。三菱地所設計の豊富なアジアや日本でのアーバンデザイン実績を元に、ロジカルな資料を作成した。

贈り物としてのプレゼンテーション

プロジェクトの節目では、パースを水墨画風に仕上げた掛け軸、100枚近いパースが連なる絵巻物、タワー棟の木製積木などをつくって、クライアントに贈呈した。建物をおもちゃや絵にして、「臺北南山廣場」に親しみを感じてもらうことができた。プロジェクト全体にわたり、クライアントや現地の施工者と私たちの間の距離感が縮まり、最終的な建築のクオリティに直結すると考える。

07/27/2014 The facility plan befitting Taipei Nanshan Plaza

展現「臺北南山廣場」特質的設備計畫
建物配置や用途配置に合わせた特徴的な設備計画

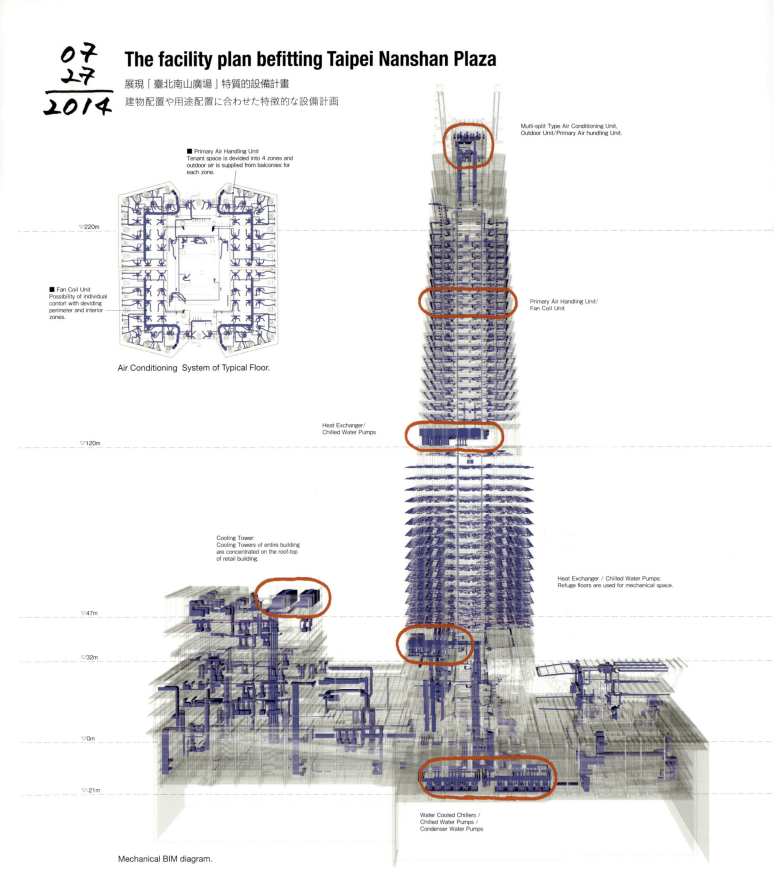

Mechanical BIM diagram.

High rise architecture and facility planning that would support mixed use

A heat source plan suited to each use case was drawn up by taking into account the overall energy used in the building. Optimal combinations of heat sources were considered by taking into account the state of the infrastructure in the area, and a highly efficient system was adopted. As it was not possible to install any machinery or equipment on the top of the office tower that would become the roof terrace, all of the machinery and equipment for Taipei Nanshan Plaza as a whole was placed on the upper levels of the commercial podium.

支持超高層建築及複合用途的設備計畫

全面性思考建物的能源使用，建構了適合各種用途的供熱設備計畫。我們從區域的基礎設施來檢討供熱設備的最佳組合，建立高效能的系統。因為無法在辦公棟頂部設置機器設備，所以將「臺北南山廣場」所有的機器設備聚集在商場棟的頂樓。

超高層建築と複合用途を支える設備計画

建物の使用エネルギーを総合的に考え、各用途に適した熱源計画を構築した。地域のインフラ状況から熱源のベストミックスを検討し、高効率システムとした。ルーフトップテラスとなる高層棟頂部には機械設備を設置できないため、商業棟の上部に「臺北南山廣場」全体の機械設備を集約した。

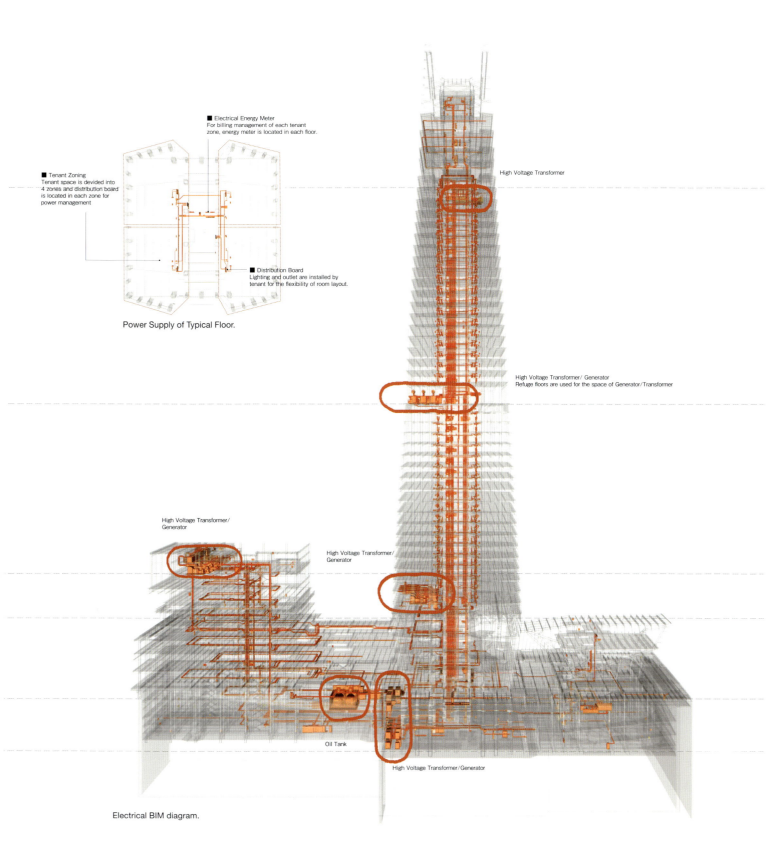

Power Supply of Typical Floor.

Electrical BIM diagram.

An efficient electrical plan that utilizes the truss floors in the office tower

By segregating the electrical rooms into lower, middle, and higher levels, and transmitting high voltage power to each electrical rooms, we were able to clarify how the electric power supply is sorted during periodic inspections, seek to reduce the transmission loss, and improve the serviceability and energy efficiency of the building. In order for the power supply to the whole building to continue when infrastructure is disrupted due to natural disasters, we installed the generators by spreading them out according to how the electric power supply is sorted, planning them so that they could still operate efficiently and deliver power even during a blackout.

利用辦公棟桁架層進行有效率的電源計畫

配電室分散於高、中、低各個樓層，為確保高壓電源可傳送到各配電室，我們必須考慮定期維修時作好明確的電源供給區分，及減少電力運輸時的損耗，並提升可維修性及節能性。另外，為了在發生災害基礎設施斷電時也能為整棟建築物供電，我們規畫依照電源供給使用區分分別設置發電機，即使停電也可有效率地啟動發電機輸送電源。

高層棟トラス階を利用した効率的な電源計画

電気室を低・中・高層に分散し、各電気室まで高圧送電して、定期点検時の電源供給区分の明確化や送電ロスの低減を図り、保守メンテナンス性や省エネ性を向上させた。また、インフラ途絶時にもビル全体へ電源供給できるように、電源供給区分ごとに発電機も分散配置して、停電時にも効率的に発電機を起動し、送電できる計画とした。

Full size mock-up of office tower.
Louvers: doing away with the horizontal joints.
Giving part of the slit a shadow.
Extending the horizontal fins up until the corner material.
Adjusting the color of the glass.

Verifying the color of the glass at actual size.
Verifying the shape of the corners in the office tower.

Verifying the design using full-size scale models

使用一比一視覺模型確認設計

原寸模型でデザインを確認する

Conducting reviews using mockups of the exterior
There have been times when we were surprised by the gap between the components that we envisioned using in Japan, and the actual local items that met cost and performance considerations. This issue was resolved by reviewing the components in question using mockups — a prime opportunity for everyone in the team to assess what is good or bad, since these are 1:1 scale models that can be seen and touched. In this way, we were able to communicate with each other about changing to a type of glass that was offered by a local supplier, modifying the layout of corners that were not built according to the sash drawings, and verifying the accuracy of colors.

外觀視覺模型檢討
我們在日本設定的建材，與為了符合當地成本及滿足性能的實際建材相比，有相當大的差異性。為了解決這種落差，我們透過視覺模型進行討論，直接目視、觸摸1/1比例的模型，所有團隊成員皆可判斷何謂好與何謂不好。會勘視覺模型時，我們接納了由本地提出的玻璃變更、未比照帷幕設計圖施作的轉角收頭的重新修正，以及顏色確認等。

外装モックアップによる検討
日本で想定した部材と、現地でコストや性能を満たした実物との差異に驚くことがある。これを解消するのがモックアップでの検討だ。1/1スケールで、見て、触れられるため、チーム全員が「何が悪く、何がよいか」を判断するよい機会となる。モックアップの検査で、現地で提案されたガラスの変更や、サッシ図通りになっていなかったコーナーの納まりの修正、色の確認などのコミュニケーションが行われた。

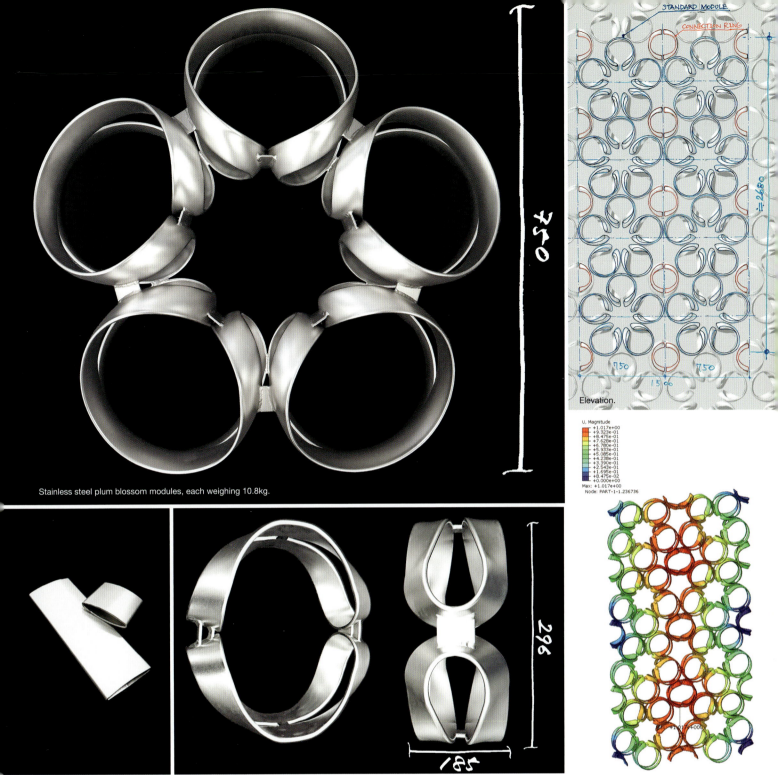

Stainless steel plum blossom modules, each weighing 10.8kg.

Cross section of a stainless steel tube.

Detail of part of a petal joint.

Elevation.

Study for distances between supporting points using FEM analysis.

Designing the plum blossom facade using stainless steel

After the shape of the plum blossoms for the exterior walls of the commercial podium was decided, the engineering trials began. The type of aluminium we envisioned using at the beginning was difficult to realize at a strength that would withstand the wind load. In addition, there were many issues related to how it would be installed and cleaned. With the support of the client, we sought out a manufacturer that could produce the flowers using stainless steel.

Stainless steel that can undergo passivation can be used in the foundation. Even if it is damaged, the base metal remains untouched. Trials to determine the strength and cost could also be carried out concurrently. Components that required strength were cast, while those that needed to be lightweight were produced by welding together hand-processed oblong cross-section tubes and turning them into panels, and then covering the three boxes seamlessly. The result was the world's first ever facade of silver stainless steel plum flowers blooming across the entire surface.

不銹鋼材質設計梅花飾牆

決定商場棟外牆的梅花造型後旋即開始討論工程面。最初設定的鋁材強度很難承受風荷載重，加上安裝及清潔面也有很多待決課題，最後透過業主的協助，找到了採用不銹鋼製作的製造商。經鈍化處理的不銹鋼材質可以直接使用製作，即使刮傷也不會損害基材。我們同時檢討強度及成本，需要強度的部分採用鑄造，而輕量化的部分則用手工加工的橢圓形中空管材焊接，做成板狀單元，幾乎是無縫地包覆商場棟的三個箱體。世界上第一座整面綻放銀色梅花的不銹鋼外牆就此誕生。

梅ファサードをステンレスでデザインする

商業棟外壁用の梅の花の形状決定後、エンジニアリングの検討が始まった。当初想定したアルミは風荷重に耐える強度の実現が難しく、取り付けや清掃面でも課題が多かったため、クライアントの協力でステンレスでつくれるメーカーを探し出した。不導体化処理できるステンレスは素地のままで使用でき、傷がついても母材が傷まない。強度やコスト検討も同時に進行できる。強度を要する部分はキャスト、軽量化を要する部分は楕円形断面のチューブの手加工品を、溶接してパネル化し、3つのボックスを継ぎ目なく覆う。一面にステンレスの銀の梅が開花する世界初のファサードが生まれた。

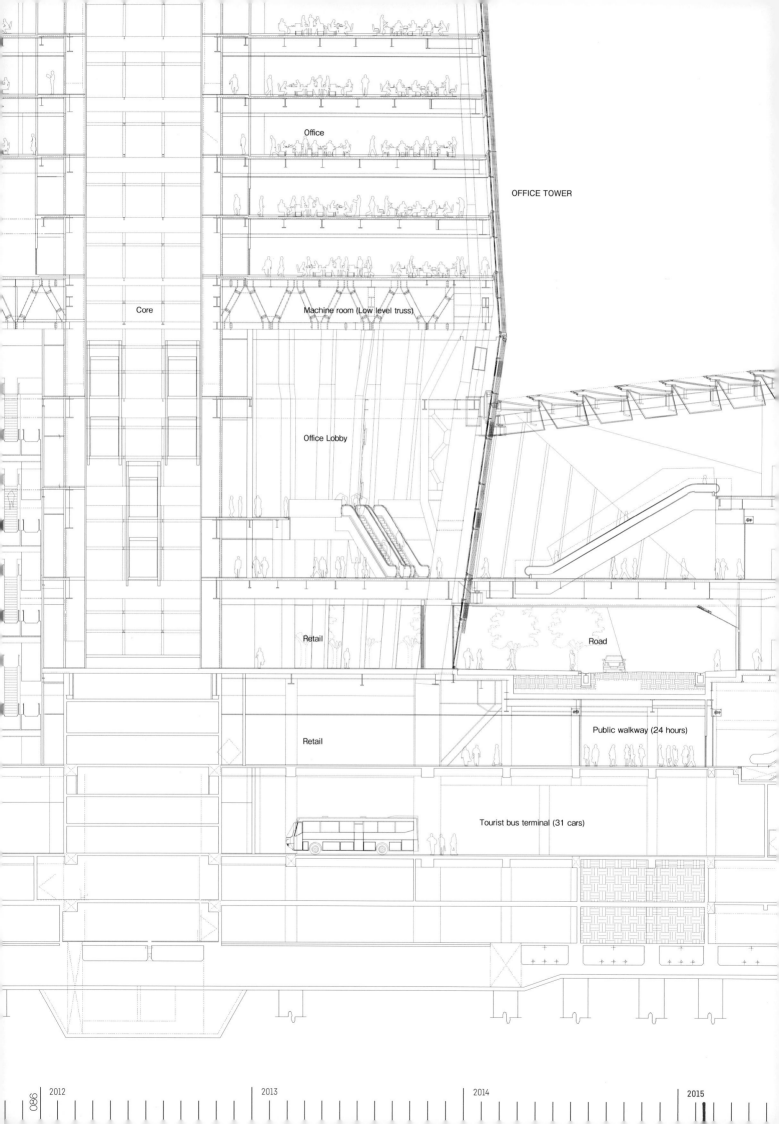

02/14/2015 Design development of the interior spaces begins

啟動室內空間的細部設計
内部空間の実施設計開始

A multilayered space for humans and vehicles

While we provided for an office lobby that approaches the upper floors from ground level, and a public walkway inside the building open 24 hours a day that allows people to access all areas of basement one from the ground level, all the car park spaces were placed underground in order to make a clear demarcation between foot and vehicular traffic. Visitors can ascend to the second floor via the cultural + entrance podium, and approach the office lobby on the second floor of the office tower. The space combining the approach to the second floor offices and the foyer was positioned on the road. Using escalators, we gave a dynamic expression to how people are sucked into the building, and flow through its spaces.

人流與車流的複層空間

我們規劃了引導人潮從地面層前往上方樓層的辦公大廳空間，和從地面層到地下一樓，由四面八方皆可進出的24小時室內公共通道。停車場全部配置於地下，明確地實踐人車分離。來訪者可經由藝文入口棟上到二樓到達辦公棟大廳。這條通道兼具辦公大廳及藝文中心前廳空間的機能。我們運用了電扶梯等設計，表現建築物吸引人潮入內及人潮穿梭其中的空間動態。

人と車の多層な空間

地上から上層階へアプローチするオフィスロビー空間と、地上から地下1階の四方にアプローチする24時間建物内公共通路を設ける一方、駐車スペースはすべて地下に配置し、明確な歩車分離を行った。来館者は文化・入口棟を経由して2階へ上り、高層棟のオフィスロビーにアプローチする。2階のオフィスアプローチとホワイエを兼ねる空間を道路上に設けた。建物に人が吸い込まれ、流れるような空間を、エスカレータなどを用いてダイナミックに表現した。

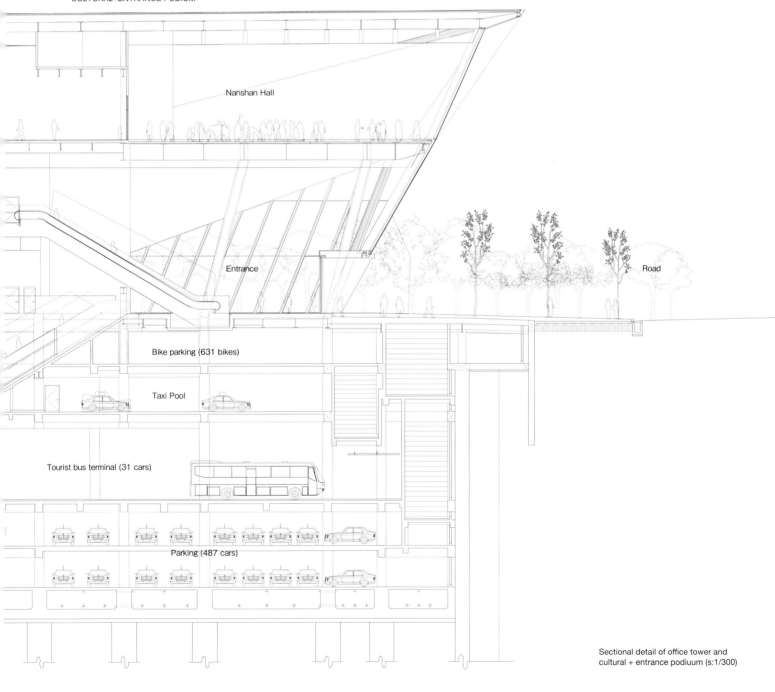

Sectional detail of office tower and cultural + entrance podiuum (s:1/300)

03/10/2015

The best way to experience an office lobby is through a model
模型最能實際感受辦公大廳空間
オフィスロビーを実感するには模型がいちばん

As one enters into the cultural + entrance podium from the front, the massive space of the lobby that forms the face of the offices appears. Having confirmed the width, depth, and height, how should we arrange the four ornamental elements: the illuminated counter, the art that mimics plum blossoms, a gigantic wall of greenery, and the escalators that resemble an artistic pictogram. We turned these into a model that reconstructs the interior view to facilitate communication with the client, and proceeded with the trials.

從正面進入藝文入口棟後，映入眼簾的是辦公室主要門面的寬廣大廳空間。確認空間的寬度、深度跟高度後，我們使用室內空間模型，與業主討論透光大廳櫃臺、藝術金屬簾、大型植生牆、藝術圖像化電扶梯等四個空間的規劃配置。並製作室內空間模型和業主共同研究討論。

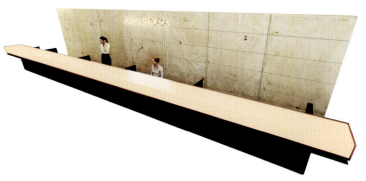

Reception | Lighting Counter

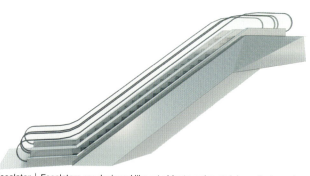

Escalator | Escalators are designed like art objects, using stainless steel panels.

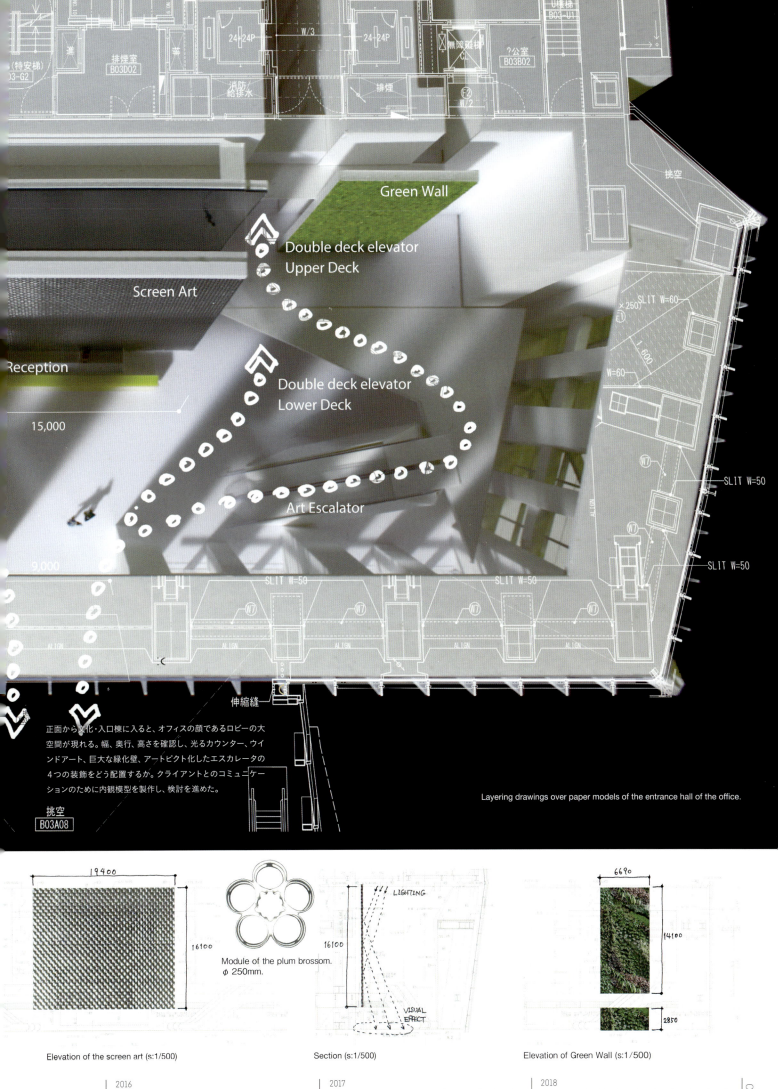

Layering drawings over paper models of the entrance hall of the office.

正面から文化・入口棟に入ると、オフィスの顔であるロビーの大空間が現れる。幅、奥行、高さを確認し、光るカウンター、ウインドアート、巨大な緑化壁、アートピクト化したエスカレータの4つの装飾をどう配置するか。クライアントとのコミュニケーションのために内観模型を製作し、検討を進めた。

Elevation of the screen art (s:1/500)

Module of the plum brossom. φ 250mm.

Section (s:1/500)

Elevation of Green Wall (s:1/500)

3rd floor Nanshan Hall foyer.

2nd~3rd floor office entrance.

05/15/2015 Elegant and refined interior spaces using natural materials

用天然素材建構高質感的室內空間
自然素材で上質な内部空間を構成

 Earth Material ▶ Metal Stone Soil Tree Water ▶   Steel/Stainless Granite Brick Wood Glass

From Imaginary to real materials

For this project, we worked on the principle of using natural materials. The colors of materials that are chemically processed tend to fade; conversely, they do not acquire an aged patina with the passage of time. Natural materials are necessary in order to create an elegant, tasteful space that becomes familiar and comfortable over time, and it is the touch, feel, and fragrance of these materials that imparts richness to a space. Even with the same material, the smooth portions cause light to be refracted, while the rough parts cause shadows to form. Even while working with a limited number of materials, we took pains to make the space look more varied, by juxtaposing these textures and creating a diversity within the material, for example.

從想像到選擇真實的建材

本專案原則上只使用天然建材。化學製成的建材雖然不會褪色，但經年累月後無法呈現建材本身的特色。高質感的空間，選用隨著時間流逝可融入空間的天然素材甚是必要。建材的觸感及氣味可以讓空間更豐富。即使是同樣建材，Smooth（光滑）可以反射光線，而Rough（粗糙）會產生陰影。以質地對比的建材呈現多樣化，即便使用少樣建材也可以創造多層次的空間感。

空想からリアルな素材へ

本プロジェクトでは自然の素材を使うことを原則とした。ケミカルな素材は色あせない一方、経年で味が出てこない。時間とともに空間に馴染む、高品質な空間には自然素材が必要だ。素材の手触りや香りは空間を豊かにする。同じ素材でもSmooth（ツル）は光を反射させ、Rough（ザラ）は陰影を生む。この肌理を対比させて素材に多様性をつくるなど、少ない素材でも、より多様な空間に見える工夫をした。

3rd floor office elevetor hall.　　　　　　　　　　　　　　　Typical floor corridor.

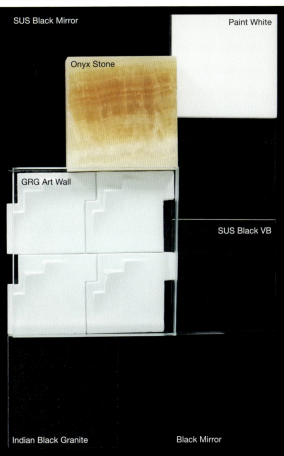

Reviewing the interior design by looking at samples of the materials.

3 images | A pattern resembling the corporate logo of the client was carved into glass fiber reinforced gypsum using a laser cutter. Study for turning this into a luminous wall with a sense of transparency.

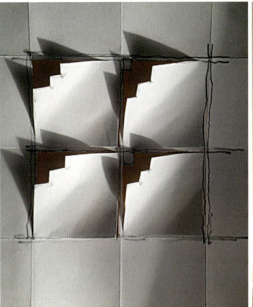

Vertical lines of movement that turn into a "pictogram"

圖像化設計的垂直動線

ピクトグラム化した垂直動線

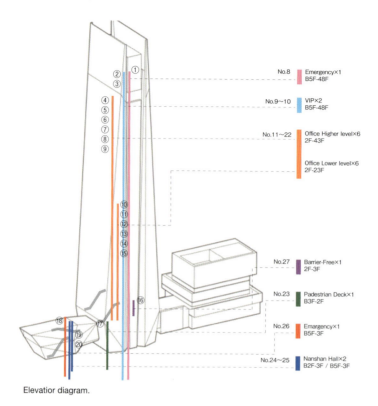

Elevatior diagram.

Elevator No.19.

Office entrance hall image.

Variations on elevator designs: 7 types × 20 elevators
High rise buildings typically have many elevators. If they all look the same, it becomes unclear where one is, and originality becomes lacking. In the same way, we made the use of natural materials one of the conditions for the color scheme of the interior, designing each individual elevator using light and glass art.

7種類×20部多樣化的電梯設計

超高層建築通常會設置很多部電梯。如果每一部電梯都是相同的話，不但不容易找到位置，且缺乏獨特性。我們比照與室內設計相同的建材配色，在使用天然建材的前提條件下，透過光線及玻璃工藝等手法設計了不同的電梯。

7種類×20台の多様なエレベータデザイン

超高層建築には、多くのエレベータがあり、どれも同じだと場所が不明瞭でオリジナリティがない。内装カラースキーム同様、自然の素材を使うことを条件とし、光やガラスアートで個々のエレベータをデザインした。

Elevator No.20.

Elevator No.9.

Elevator No.11~22.

Elevator No.11~22.

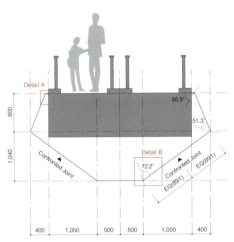
Escalator section(s:1/80)

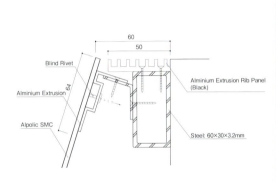
Escalator sectional detail A(s:1/3)

The inside of the elevators featured a combination of half mirrored glass and glass with holes bored into it. The repeated reflections of the plum blossoms impart a sense of depth to the space.

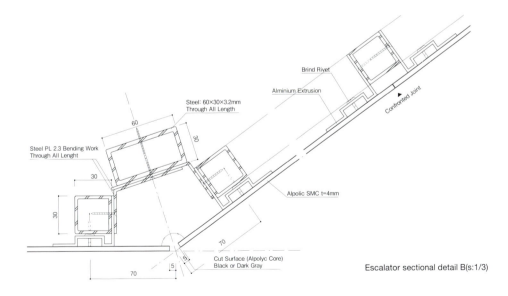
Escalator sectional detail B(s:1/3)

Polyhedral escalator design as a "pictogram"

Escalators are necessary to move up or down a large space. Here, we attempted to design the escalators in order to eliminate the inefficiency of spaces that require signage to make the escalators visible. Aluminium polyhedral surfaces were deployed, the base was removed, and the escalators themselves were transformed into a pictogram.

多面體電扶梯的圖像化設計

廣大的空間必須透過電扶梯上下移動。電扶梯就在可視之處，但卻需要另外設置指標的空間是沒有效率的。為了解決此事，我們嘗試做了電扶梯的外觀設計，將鋁板以每一面都是正面的多面體形式表現，讓電梯本身就是圖像化的指標。

多面体エスカレータのピクトデザイン

大空間の上下移動にはエスカレータが必要だ。エスカレータがそこに見えるのにサインを要する空間の非効率を解消するためのエスカレータのデザインを試みた。アルミの多面体化して底面をなくし、エスカレータそのものをピクトグラム化した。

Section of cultural + entrance podium. Installation positions of the "signages".

The reception counter and screen art sparkle and glimmer in an enticing manner.

Escalators leading to Nanshan Hall, designed so that the escalators themselves function as signage.

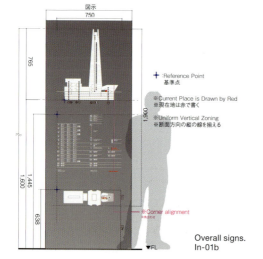
Overall signs.
In-01b

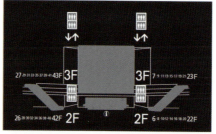
Signs leading visitors to the double deck elevator.
Lo-02a(Above) and Lo-01(Bottom).

Signage indicating directions.
In-01a

Signage that blends into the space while providing necessary information.

Wall surface of the core that welcomes visitors.

06
02
2015

Making a space itself as a "signage"

指標化設計的空間

空間自体をサイン化する

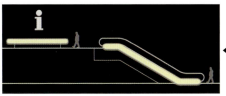
A particular effort was made with the writing so that the items would actually be recognized and interpreted as pictograms.

Pictogram.

Typically, universal signs are made up of directional indicators, pictograms, and text. For Taipei Nanshan Plaza, however, we transformed objects along its lines of movement into art pieces, illuminated it to enhance its visibility, and "pictogrammed" it. Human vision perceives bustling activity up to a distance of 30-50 m away, and evinces interest. We made a special effort to create situations where people would naturally drift towards, and to transform spaces themselves into signs.

一般來說，通用設計的指標是由方向標誌和圖像及文字組成。但是，「臺北南山廣場」則是將人行動線上視覺可及的空間藝術化，並輔以燈光提高辨識度，進行「圖像化」設計。人的視覺可以感知30～50公尺前方的熙攘狀況，並被吸引前往。我們特地使用空間本身就是指標的設計方式，讓人潮會自然舉步前來一探究竟。

一般的に、ユニバーサルサインは方向サインとピクトグラム、文字からなる。しかし、「臺北南山廣場」の動線上のアイテムをアート化、ライトアップして視認性を高め、「ピクト化」することとした。人の視覚は30～50m程度までは賑わいを判断し、興味を示す。人が自然に足を向けるようにし、空間そのものをサインにすることを心掛けた。

Column setting ceremony
06 08 2015
立柱式
立柱式

Steel frame construction
The columns that formed the main structure of the office tower were a maximum size of 2,000×1,400×70mm.

鋼構工程
辦公棟的主要柱子，最大尺寸到達2,000×1,400×70mm。

鉄骨工事
高層棟のメインとなる柱は、最大のもので2,000×1,400×70mmのサイ

10/11/2015

Manufacturing of the stainless steel façade for commercial podium started

開始製作商場棟不銹鋼外牆
商業棟の外装ステンレスを製作開始

Steel casting.

Wax decoration.

Ceramic coating.

Molding.

Surface quality control.

Manufacturing that realizes the "plum" facade
With the tie-up with the manufacturer, We could study the fine design while creating the sample. In manufacturing this exterior, we applied a technique for manufacturing the parts of yacht. The method of attaching the parts was examined by alternately comparing the detailed drawing and the 3D model.

實現梅花飾牆的精工製造
透過與製造商的合作，做了樣品來研究設計的細節。為了實現這面梅花飾牆，應用了遊艇零件製造的技術。安裝方法也以細部設計圖和3D模型雙方交互比對進行研究。

梅のファサードを実現するものづくり
メーカーとのタイアップにより、サンプルを作成しながら細かなデザインの検討を行った。梅の花の外装の実現にあたっては、ヨットの部品製作の技術を応用した。取り付け方も詳細図面と3Dモデルを突き合わせながら検討した。

Surface grinding.

Stainless steel pipe before bending.

Pipe bending.

Petal welding.

Passivation.

Essay

張瑞娟　株式会社三菱地所設計　國際業務企劃部

Role of the project manager

專案經理的職責
プロジェクトマネジャーの役割

Samuel Yin (left) and Beckie Tiunn (right).

Working together with the architects on the team, I played an intermediary role between the Taiwanese and Japanese teams to successfully create a building in Taiwan. Using both Japanese and Chinese, I connected members from both sides together.

Taiwanese clients seek out quality proposals from foreign architects that cannot be found in the architecture of their own country. To that end, we repeatedly held discussions and conducted research with the project team. We committed our fullest efforts to devising a way of enhancing the value of the client's company through this building, and conveying this in an approachable way. At times, there were many things that could not be realized due to the environment, culture, or regulations of a foreign country. However, we made an attempt to turn this "could not" into a "how can we make it happen," and seek out a different way of doing things. These accumulated efforts yielded positive results. By deepening our relationship of trust with numerous parties, we sought cooperation and progress with an eye on the goal. The most fulfilling aspect of this job was being able to be involved with the core of this process.

Beckie Tiunn | Mitsubishi Jisho Sekkei, Overseas Operations Planning Department

I joined the team from the building stage as an on-site supervisor. From the design and details to the realization of the construction methods and cost control issues, there was no end to the challenges we faced. Although there were numerous situations where an agreement could not be reached, both Mitsubishi Jisho Sekkei and the local Taiwanese parties boldly stuck to their guns, proactively voicing their own particular concerns in a bid to resolve any issues, and were able to talk things through successfully.

Lyoyd Lin | Mitsubishi Jisho Sekkei, Project Manager Cooperator

Voices from the creative team that collaborated with us

Archasia Design Group, an architectural design firm that has won the overwhelming trust of the client, is extremely honored to have been able to play a role in the development and construction of Taipei Nanshan Plaza, the second tallest skyscraper in Taiwan. We were suitably impressed by their seriousness in relation to the design proposed by Mitsubishi Jisho Sekkei, which developed the project jointly, and their meticulous attention to various details. In the future, we hope to continue to transcend national borders, put together a global team of stellar talent, and create sustainable architecture and cities together. Drawing on the extraordinary experiences gleaned from this project, our team hopes to be able to widen our horizons even further, and work towards creating spectacular buildings with a long-term perspective.

Stan H. H. Lo | General Partner of Archasia Design Group, a local Taiwanese architectural design firm

---

為了和團隊中的建築師們一起在台灣成功地設計出建築物，我的角色是扮演台日團隊的橋樑。使用台日兩國語言，進行雙方團隊成員的溝通和磨合。

台灣的業主，會多半希望可以從國外建築師獲得超越自己國家的高水準提案。為此，我們反覆地與專案團隊成員進行討論及研究，思考了如何透過設計手法，讓這座建築物提升業主的企業價值。並盡最大努力，用容易理解的方式將設計內容傳達給各位。有時候因為國情、文化及法規等的不同，無法落實設計的狀況也不勝枚舉。但是，我們盡可能將「做不到」的思維轉換成「用甚麼方法可以做到？」，不斷地嘗試各種不同方法，一點一滴的累積，創造了美好的成果。我們與許多的參與人員建立了深厚的信賴關係，朝向完工目標合力邁進。對我來說，可以進入到專業團隊的核心擔任協調角色是這份工作最大的價值。

張瑞娟 | 三菱地所設計　國際業務企劃部

我參與了從施工階段到現場監造顧問的過程。不論在設計、細部收頭、工法施作及成本調整上都充滿了各式各樣的挑戰。雖也曾經有過好幾次僵持不下的場面，朝著解決問題的方向，三菱地所設計與台灣當地的相關人員積極地溝通，雖有各自所堅持的部分，最後還是達成圓滿的共識。

林宣宇 | 三菱地所設計　特約專案副理

共同參與創作的團隊成員的心得

瀚亞建築事務所很榮幸受到業主完全的信任與委託，全程參與北台灣第二高樓「臺北南山廣場」的開發與建設工程。合作過程充見識到日本三菱地所設計，對建築物各項設計細節的認真與堅持。未來是打破國界與區域限制，全球人才流通合作，共同開創永續家園的時代。透過這次愉快的合作，瀚亞團隊將以更開闊的胸襟與更長遠的視野，去繼續促成每一個優秀建築的誕生。

羅興華 | 瀚亞國際設計　主持建築師　台灣本地建築師設計事務所

私は、チームの建築家とともに、台湾で建物をつくることを成功させるための台日の懸け橋としての役割を担った。日本語と中国語を使い、双方のメンバーを繋ぎ合わせていった。

台湾のクライアントは海外の建築家に対して、自国の建築にはない優れた提案を求める。そのためにプロジェクトチームと議論とリサーチを繰り返した。この建物でクライアントの会社そのものの価値を高める手法を考え、これを分かりやすく伝えることに尽力した。時には、異国の環境・文化・法令により実現できないことも多く発生した。しかし、こうした「できないこと」を「どうしたらできるのか？」に変換し、違う方法を試していく。その積み重ねがよい結果を生んだ。多くの関係者と信頼関係を深め、完成を目指して協力し、邁進する。その中心に関わることができたのが、この仕事の最大の醍醐味であった。

張瑞娟 | 三菱地所設計　海外業務企画部

施工段階から現場の監修でチームに参画したが、意匠やディテール、工法の実現やコストの調整において、チャレンジは尽きなかった。合意に至らない場面は何度もあったが、問題解決に向け、三菱地所設計と台湾現地の関係者の双方が、果敢に自らの「こだわり」を前向きにぶつけ、話し合うことができた。

林宣宇 | 三菱地所設計　プロジェクトマネジャー協力

私たちと共にモノづくりをしてきたチームの声

瀚亞建築師事務所は、クライアントから絶大な信頼を頂き、北台湾第二の高さを誇る超高層ビル「臺北南山廣場」の開発と建設工事に参加できたことを光栄に思っている。プロジェクトを共同で進めた三菱地所設計の設計に対する真剣さ、諸々のディテールへのこだわりを十分に感じることもできた。これからは国を越え、世界中から優秀な人材が集まり、一緒に持続可能な建築、街をつくっていく時代となるだろう。今回の素晴らしい経験を生かし、私たちのチームは今後より広く心を開き、長期的な視野で素晴らしい建物の誕生に携わっていきたいと考えている。

羅興華 | 瀚亞國際設計　ジェネラル・パートナー、台湾現地建築設計事務所

Beckie Tiunn | Mitsubishi Jisho Sekkei, Project Manager | Born in 1979 at Chiayi, Taiwan / In 2002, graduated the department of architecture, Tamkang university / In 2006, Completed the master's degree at the Kyoto university / In 2006~2011, Da-Ju Architects and Associates / In 2011~, Mitsubishi Jisho Sekkei

張瑞娟 | 三菱地所設計 Project Manager | 1979年出生於嘉義／2002年淡江大學工學院建築學系畢業／2006年京都大學建築研究所碩士／2006~2011年台灣大矩聯合建築師事務所／2011年〜三菱地所設計

ベッキー・テュン | 三菱地所設計 プロジェクトマネジャー | 1979年台湾嘉義生まれ／2002年淡江大学工学部建築学科卒業／2006年京都大学大学院建築学専攻修士課程修了／2006~2011年大矩聯合建築師事務所／2011年〜三菱地所設計

Foundation laying ceremony, attended by the client, designers, and builders.

In order to realize the design as Mitsubishi Jisho Sekkei envisioned it, we negotiated with the relevant administrative bodies and construction teams, and proposed various solutions that would bring the greatest profit to the client, such as the configuration of the driveways and the introduction of double-deck elevators. In Taiwan, a project of this scale typically requires more time to complete. In addition to these types of proposals, the challenge for us was to apply for the relevant permissions and devise ways of shortening the construction period, so that we could complete the project within the period stipulated by the client.

Liefeng Chen | Architecture Lead, Archasia Design Group

What left an impression on me was how structural engineer Hiroshi Kawamura from Mitsubishi Jisho Sekkei, which has a wealth of experience in designing many skyscrapers in Japan, submitted a proposal for the structural frame soon after a draft of the design was decided on. In response to a demand for a high-ceilinged atrium at the main entrance to the tower, we realized an atrium with a height of 15m, after making repeated studies and trials with them. Small trusses were used within the columns as auxiliary components. The experience of considering the structure together with the design in an integrated manner was an extremely interesting one.

Hsi-ying Kan | Evergreen Consulting Engineering, Structural Engineer

The memories that stayed with me strongly were of the wind tunnel experiment for the curtain wall mockup, and working together with the construction team to install the back mullions measuring some 30m at a height of 272m, in order to realize our transparent design for the top of the tower. Another valuable experience was my involvement in the exterior facade, where the entire surface of the exterior walls of the commercial block was processed to make it look like it had a three-dimensional curve to it, after which it was covered by cast ornamental plum blossoms.

Amy Chiang | H & K Associates, Exterior Consultant

The most pressing question for this project in terms of landscape design was how to achieve a sense of three-dimensional layering while also creating organic links to the surrounding neighborhood. Over the course of the landscape design process, which stretched over three years, I felt a keen sense of the utmost importance of the link to the architecture itself in creating a holistic sense of place. The selection of paving materials, in particular, demonstrated how it was possible to realize something utterly unique through repeated discussions and the use of handmade tiles from Japan.

Joyce Lin | Landscape Consultant

我們為了能落實三菱地所設計的原始設計方案，協商了行政單位、施工團隊，以及車道配置、雙層車廂電梯的導入等，最後我們終於完成對業主最有利的提案。一般來說，在台灣這種規模的專案需要耗費很多的時間，我們面臨的挑戰就是執行設計發展的同時，需進行申請建照及尋找縮短工期的方法，並在業主要求的期限內完成。

陳列峯 | 瀚亞國際設計　建築窗口、台灣本地建築設計事務所

令我印象最深刻的是建築設計草案方才定案，擁有日本多座超高樓建築設計經驗的三菱地所設計結構工程師川村浩先生，立刻提出了結構構架的方案。像是建築師希望在塔樓主要大廳做挑高設計，經過我們結構團隊反覆地研究，最後實現了高度15米的挑高空間。我們在柱子內設置小型桁架作為輔助構材，對於結構與建築設計合為一體的討論方式，是非常有趣的經驗。

甘錫瀅 | 永峻工程顧問公司　結構工程師

對我而言最難忘的是，帷幕牆視覺模型的風雨試驗和為了營造塔樓頂部的穿透感，我們和施工團隊共同討論，在高度272米的空中設置了長度30米的鋼背擋。另外，商場棟的整片外牆採用3D立體彎曲加工的不銹鋼製作成梅花的模樣裝飾，這個部分也成為我們團隊很寶貴的經驗。

江玉如 | 康普工程顧問　帷幕顧問

本專案景觀設計的最大課題，是如何襯托立體的疊箱建築量體，以及要能融入周邊商圈與綠化環境整合。在執行將近三年的景觀設計中，我深刻地感受到景觀細部設計與建築的融合，是提升整體氛圍很重要的部份。尤其在選擇鋪面材質上，我們反覆地討論，最後使用日本製造的手工磁磚，呈現獨樹一格的特色。

Joyce Lin | 景觀設計顧問

私たちは、三菱地所設計によるデザインをイメージ通り実現できるよう、行政や施工チームと調整し、また車路の配置やダブルデッキエレベータの導入など、クライアントが最大の利益を得るための提案を行った。台湾では一般的にこの規模のプロジェクトにはより多くの時間を要する。私たちの挑戦は、こうした提案と同時に、許可申請や工期を短縮する方法を考え、クライアントが求める期間で竣工させることだった。

陳列峯 | 瀚亞國際設計　建築担当、台湾現地建築設計事所

印象に残っているのは、デザイン草案が決まるとすぐに、日本で多くの超高層ビルの設計経験を持つ三菱地所設計の構造エンジニア川村浩氏から構造フレームの提案があったことだ。高層棟のメインエントランスに高い吹き抜けを設けたいという要望には、彼らと検討を繰り返して、高さ15mの吹き抜けを実現した。柱には補助部材として小型トラスを設けることになったが、構造とデザインの一体的な検討は興味深い経験になった。

甘錫瀅 | 永峻工程顧問公司　構造エンジニア

強く残る思い出は、カーテンウォールのモックアップの風洞実験や、タワー頂部の透明感のあるデザインを実現するために、高さ272mの上空に、長さ30mものバックマリオンの設置を施工チームとともに実現できたことである。また、商業棟の外壁全体を三次元曲げ加工を施したキャストでつくった梅の装飾で覆う外装に関われたのは貴重な経験となった。

江玉如 | 康普工程顧問　外装コンサルタント

立体的な積層と周辺街区との有機的な繋がりの両立は本計画のランドスケープデザインの最大の課題であった。3年に及ぶランドスケープの設計の中で、建築との納まりが、全体の雰囲気をつくる上できわめて重要だとしみじみ感じた。特に、舗装の素材選定ではディスカッションを繰り返し、日本製のハンドメイドタイルにより、ここにしかない特徴的なものが実現したと思う。

ジョイス・リン | ランドスケープコンサルタント

2016/01/14
View from Humble House Taipei
(work place in Taipei).

2016/06/21
View from Mt. Elephant (象山).

02 / 18 / 2016   Cultural + entrance podium | steel frame construction

藝文入口棟｜鋼構工程
文化・入口棟｜鉄骨工事

Cultural + entrance podium | Inverted triangular truss walls measuring 70m wide and 25m high, which allowed us to realize a massive interior space.

03/2016 Commercial podium | steel frame and exterior façade construction
商場棟｜鋼構＋外牆工程
商業棟｜鉄骨＋外装工事

Installing the plum blossom panels. The cantilevers extended to 10m at their longest.

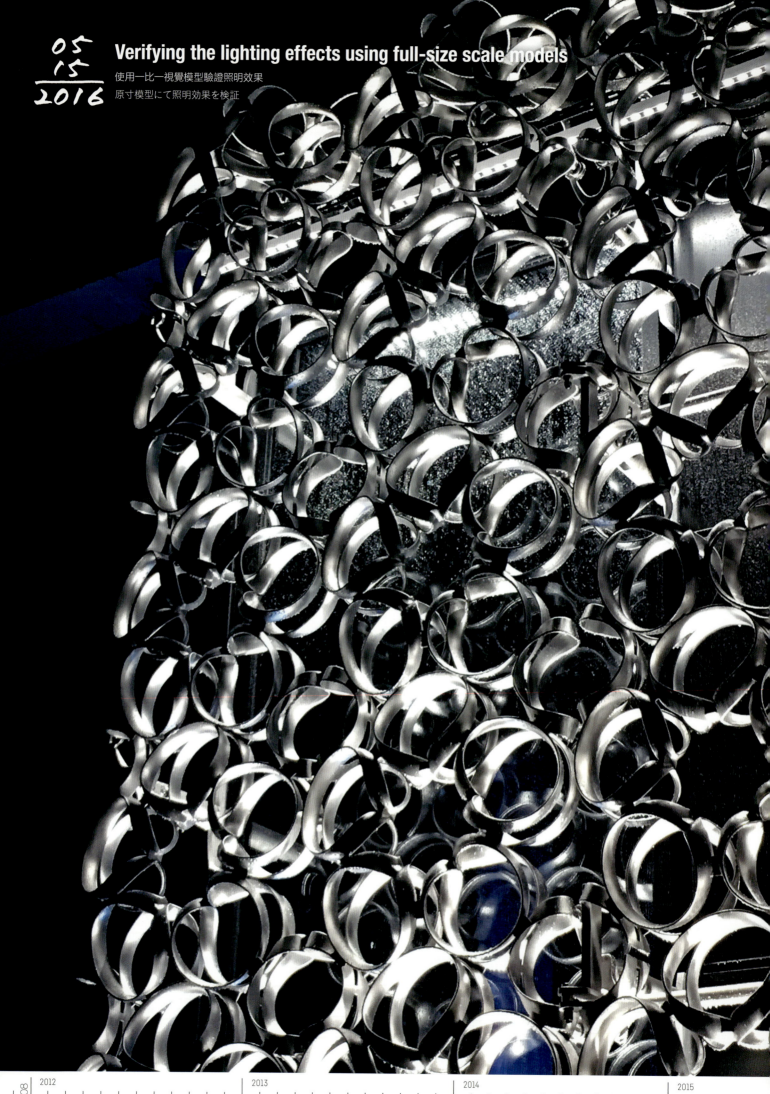

05/15/2016 Verifying the lighting effects using full-size scale models
使用一比一視覺模型驗證照明效果
原寸模型にて照明効果を検証

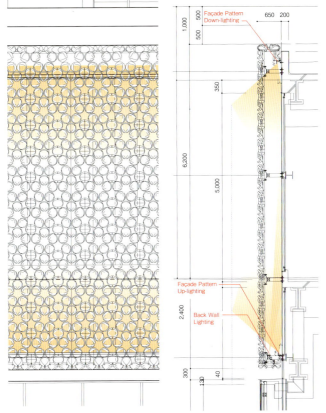

Lighting plan for the facade of the commercial podium. Elevation and section (s:1/100). Illumination from the back makes the plum blossoms appear to float.

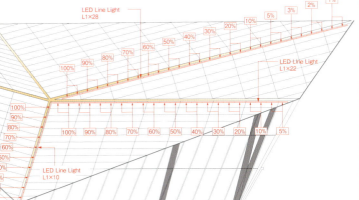

Lighting plan for the cultural + entrance podium, south elevation (s:1/500). The design emphasizes the five "lines" of the titanium exterior wall.

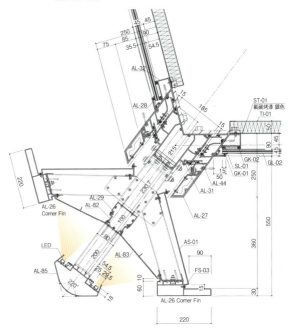

Detail of the corner fin of the office tower (s:1/50). In order to make the silhouette of the tower stand out, these fins were designed to be integrated with the lighting.

Reviewing the lighting design
In Japan, lighting with warm colors is considered to have a relaxing effect on people. In Taiwan, however, this kind of color is generally associated with the sodium vapor lamps used in factories and expressways: instead, a slightly lower color temperature of around 3,000K is considered elegant and refined. Whereas many colors are used for the illuminated buildings and neon signs in the surrounding area, we adopted a uniform color temperature of 3,000K for Taipei Nanshan Plaza.

檢討照明設計
在日本,為了讓人們可以放鬆,大多使用暖色系的燈光。但在台灣這類燈光大多令人聯想到工廠或高速公路上常見的鈉燈。所以我們認為採用比一般鈉燈色溫稍低的3,000K的設定,較能呈現高尚的質感。 相對於週邊建築物的夜間燈光與霓虹燈招牌,大多使用很多種顏色的模式,「臺北南山廣場」則是全棟統一使用3,000K色溫的照明。

ライティングデザインの検討
日本では人をリラックスさせるとされる暖色系のライティングだが、台湾では工場や高速道路に使われるナトリウム球のイメージが定着しており、色温度が少し低い3,000K程度が上品だと考えられている。周辺建物のライトアップやネオンサインには多くの色が使われているのに対し、「臺北南山廣場」では3,000Kに統一した色温度の照明を採用した。

Topping out ceremony

08/01/2016

上樑典禮
上棟式

08/15/2016 A diversity of landscape items that produce a sense of originality

創造獨特性且多樣化的景觀巧思
個性を生み出す 多様なランドスケープアイテム

North side of the office tower. Transparent shafts that increase the visibility of the moving elevators were used.

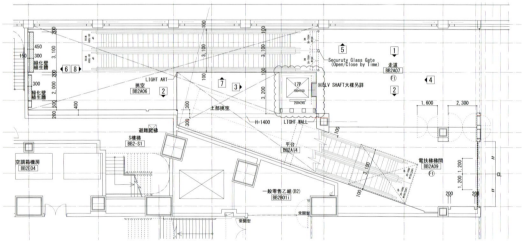

(Left) 2nd basement floor. (Right) 3rd basement floor. Underground passage linking the bus terminal with the ground level. Stoneware tiles were used to give the feeling of being inside a rock formation.

2nd basement floor plan (s: 1/250)

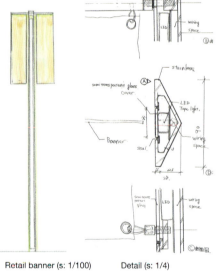

Retail banner (s: 1/100)   Detail (s: 1/4)

Interspersing various items that attract people

The two-dimensional form and design of the pedestrian deck that forms a network on foot for Xinyi District, its elevators, benches, varieties of plants and trees and the intervals at which they are planted, the lighting — all of this is subject to regulations set by the city council. The biotopes and *feng shui* pond in the cultural + entrance podium, which serve as a stopover for insects and birds, are also items that are particularly Taiwanese.

The pedestrian deck, which we were required to install according to the urban planning regulations of Xinyi Special District, was connected to the other decks that had already been installed in the area. A location that would allow for the organic creation of human flows was chosen. As one of the rules stipulated that columns must be installed on the same axis as the planters on the ground, we opted for V-shaped columns that would reduce the extent of the supporting surface —— a design that was inspired by the form of chopsticks.

分散配置吸引人潮的裝置

信義區的行人步行網絡的空橋及電梯、休憩長椅、樹木種類、種植間距及照明等的平面形狀和設計準則，皆在都市審議中有清楚規範。生物棲地、藝文入口棟旁的風水池等，作為鳥類及蟲類棲息地的設計，也是很相當具有台灣道地風格的空間。

信義計畫區的都市計畫規定必須設置空橋。我們規劃新設的空橋，不僅要延續其他既有的空橋系統，並將它安排在能有機地創造人流的位置。因都審要求空橋的落柱，需與地面層的樹木對齊於同一個軸線上，我們將空橋柱子設計為V形柱，盡量縮小柱子的接地範圍，其設計靈感是來自東方飲食文化中的「筷子」。

人を誘引するアイテムをちりばめる

信義地区の歩行者ネットワークであるペデストリアンデッキとそのエレベータ、ベンチ、樹木の種類とその間隔、照明などはすべて都市審議で平面形状やデザインが規定される。ビオトープ、文化・入口棟横の風水池も、鳥や虫の飛来地として台湾らしいアイテムである。信義計画区の都市計画で設置が義務付けられているペデストリアンデッキは、すでにエリアに設置されたデッキと接続し、有機的に人の流れをつくることができる位置に計画した。地上部の植栽と同じ軸線上に柱を落とすルールがあり、V字柱として柱の接地面を減らした。東洋の食文化である箸からインスピレーションを得たデザイン。

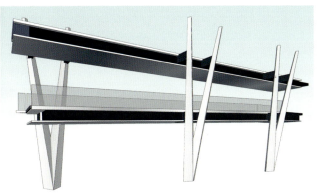

Pedestrian deck concept image. The V-shaped piers of the pillars feature a chopstick motif. They are configured in such a way as to reduce vibrations.

Section (s:1/50)

Sectional detail (s:1/5)

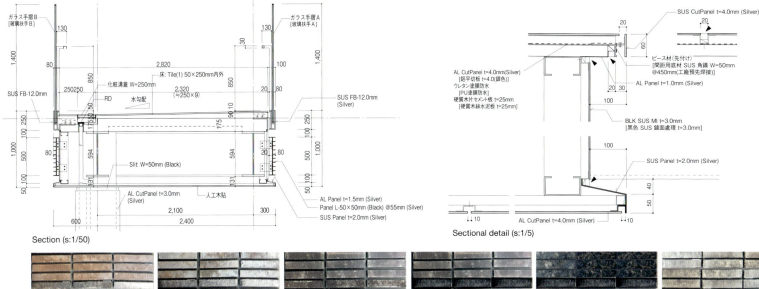

Gradation of pavement tiles.

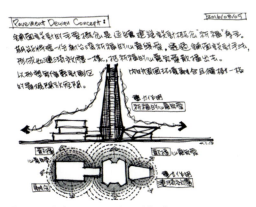

Pavement design concept note and drawing.

Landscape on the south side of the cultural + entrance podium. Benches that were required to be installed by the planning and zoning commission (left), and benches with an attached basin, the installation and shape of which was dictated by *feng shui* considerations.

Section (s:1/100)

10/02/2016 Steel flaming of the tower top
頂部鋼構
頂部鉄骨建方

In order to impart a sense of transparency to the exterior of the top of the tower, the structural materials were set back, so that only the sash windows and back mullions were visible on the outer layer.

Construction elevators on the north side of the office tower. Typically, this elevator is installed in the openings on the floors inside the building. As the floor plan of each floor of the office tower has a different shape, however, the elevator in this case was installed on the exterior of the south-north facade, so that it would not be affected by the shape of the floors.

Looking up at the top of the office tower from the north.

10/15/2016

One for Taipei 101, two for Taipei Nanshan Plaza
「台北101」1組、「臺北南山廣場」2組
「台北101」は1個、「臺北南山廣場」は2個

Tuned mass dampers (TMD). Iron plates are stacked onsite to form a spherical shape.

Iron plates are suspended one at a time from the beams above in order to stack them onsite.

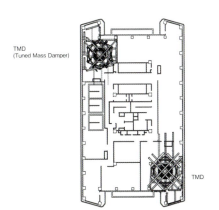

44th floor plan (s:1/120)

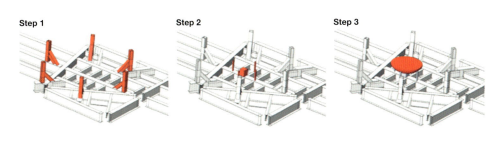

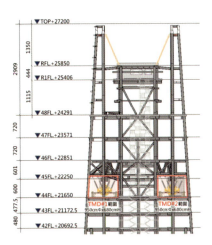

Section of the top of the office tower.

TMD installation process.

The key player that brought the vibrations of the building under control

A tuned mass damper (TMD), which consists of steel plates stacked in a spherical formation and suspended by wires, is a device that suppresses mechanical vibrations in buildings by vibrating in the opposite phase to any vibrations in the building that may occur due to wind pressure or earthquakes.

As the office tower of Taipei Nanshan Plaza has a long north-south two-dimensional form, two TMDs were installed in a diagonal formation. Their total weight is about 3% of the gross weight of the tower. Taipei 101, which has a square two-dimensional form, was designed with only one TMD.

抑止建築物搖晃的立功者

以鐵板堆疊成球狀，用纜索吊掛的調諧質量阻尼器TMD（Tuned Mass Damper），它的主要機制是因強風及地震產生振動時，透過反方向的擺動來吸收能量的同時，也可以抑制建物的振動。因辦公棟的平面是南北向較長的形狀，故在對角線上各安裝了一組阻尼，其重量為塔樓總重量的3%。而「台北101」因為是正方形平面的關係, TMD僅需設置一組即可。

建物の揺れを抑える立役者

鉄板を球状に積層し、ワイヤーで宙吊りになっているTMD (Tuned Mass Damper) は、風圧や地震で建物に振動が生じると、それぞれが逆位相に振れることで建物の振動を抑える仕組みである。「臺北南山廣場」の高層棟は南北に長い平面形状のため、2基が対角線上に設置された。合計重量は、タワー総重量の3%に相当する。隣に建つ「台北101」は正方形平面のため、TMDは1個で計画されている。

11/03/2016

Massive alminium sash that can withstand the winds in Taipei

可承受台北高風壓的巨大窗框

台北の風に耐える巨大アルミサッシ

A delicate design for massive sash windows
In order to withstand the high wind pressure of the environment adjacent to Taipei 101, the cross section of the aluminium sash windows becomes extremely thick. These windows are more than twice as heavy, 1.5 times as thick, and 1.5 times as deep as the typical curtain walls in Japan. In order not to make them too rugged looking, we opted to have environmental louvers with vertical fins threaded through as round pipes to reduce their visual impact,

將巨大窗框細緻設計

為承受因鄰接「台北101」所造成的高風壓，本案鋁窗框的橫切面非常地厚實，與日本一般使用的帷幕相比，超過兩倍以上的重量，而厚度和深度都是一般的1.5倍左右。為了避免看起來太過笨重，我們使用圓管做成鏤空的垂直遮陽板，弱化窗框的份量並具有節能功效。

巨大なアルミサッシを繊細にデザインする

「台北101」に隣接する環境の高い風圧に耐えるため、アルミサッシの断面はとても肉厚である。これは、日本で一般的に使用されるカーテンウォールの約2倍強の重量、約1.5倍の肉厚、見込みは約1.5倍ある。無骨にならないよう、縦フィンを丸パイプとして透過させ、存在感を減らした環境ルーバーとした。

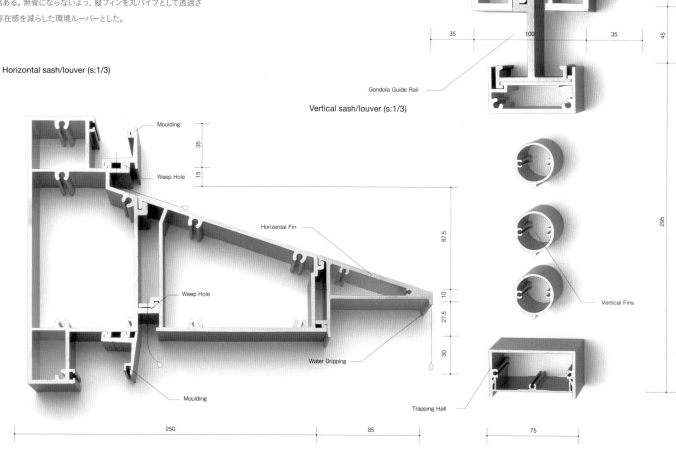

Horizontal sash/louver (s:1/3)

Vertical sash/louver (s:1/3)

In order to make the Taipei Nanshan Plaza the leading building in Taiwan in terms of thermal environment performance, louvers with a vertical height of 590mm and a horizontal length of 335mm were used. Round pipe louvers were used for the vertical fins in order to give the exterior a sense of transparency.

12/08/2016 — The top of the 272m structure is completed
完成272m的頂部
272mの頂部ができ上がる

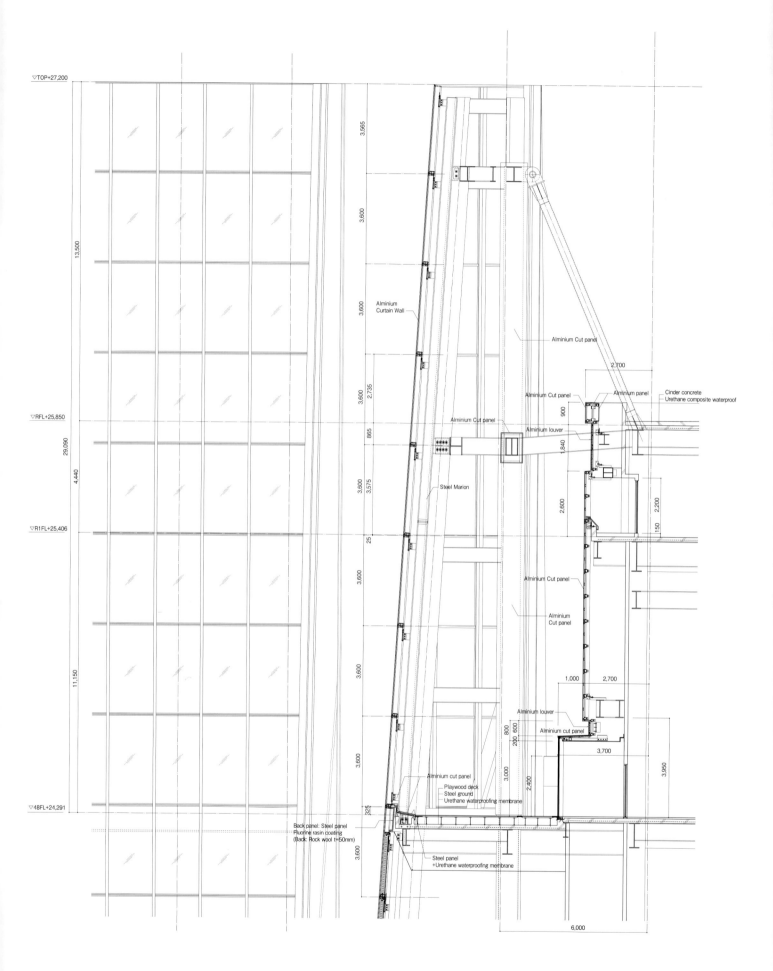

Details of elevation and section of the top of the office tower (s: 1/150). The first roof-top terrace for a skyscraper in Taiwan.

Installation of the curtain wall at the top of the office tower.

02/17/2017 Construction of the crown of the tower I

辦公棟頂部施工 I

高層棟頂部施工 I

Articulating the "nail" that forms the key motif of the design

The transparent curtain wall at the top of the tower involved the installation of massive back mullions with a height of some 30m that we obsessed over the most as architects, even as it caused a bottleneck for the construction. The mullions were assembled at ground level on-site before being welded together, after which a crane lifted them up one by one to install them. As no crosspieces were used in between the mullions, we were able to create a transparent facade with the sky visible even if one looks upwards.

設計的關鍵在於「指甲」的呈現

在頂部展現具有穿透感的帷幕，是建築師最為堅持的部份。但為了實現這個設計，必須設置高度30公尺的巨大鋼背擋，相對也是施工上最為窒礙難行的部分。必須在工地的地面層先將鋼背擋進行組裝和焊接，再用塔吊一支一支的吊至頂樓安裝。因鋼背擋之間沒有橫向連接的構件，從下往上仰視時可直達天空的富有穿透感的外觀真的實現了！

デザインの鍵となる「爪」を表現する

頂部の透明感あるカーテンウォールは、建築家として最もこだわった。施工上のネックとなった高さ30mもの巨大なバックマリオンの設置は、現場の地上でマリオンを組み立てて溶接し、クレーンで1本ずつ吊り上げ、据え付けた。マリオン間の横材をなくし、下から見上げても空が抜けて透明感のあるファサードを実現した。

Construction of the crown of the tower II

办公栋顶部施工-II
高层栋顶部施工

Installation of curtain wall. Construction was carried out by installing a small crane on the horizontal trusses at the top.

Installation of sash windows at the top of the 272m tower.

Installation of the back mullions at the very top, on the 48th floor. The back mullions are welded to a length of 30m at ground level before being lifted up to the 48th floor.

Exterior walls of the commercial podium. The stainless steel casts of the plum blossoms were affixed to the water sealing exterior wall panels.

03/09/2017

Commercial podium | Construction of the exterior façade and installation of the interior escalators

商場棟｜外牆工程＋設置室內電扶梯
商業棟｜外装工事＋内部エスカレータ設置

Escalator voids. The design was for guests to migrate to shopping.

11/08 2017 Continuing to convey to construction team what is depicted in the drawings
將圖面內容持續傳達給工地人員
図面に描いたものを現場に伝え続ける

Similar to how on-site supervision is conducted in Japan, in Taiwan we supervised the construction drawings in addition to visiting the actual site to ensure a level of craft that was equal, or superior, to what was laid out in the design drawings. Without Ling-Chen Chen on-site, our design not have been adequately conveyed to the builders and the teams of craftsmen from the manufacturers. In this way, all members of the team worked together in order to realize an extremely delicate design.

如同在日本工地進行監造一般，在台灣，我們也進行了施工圖說的審閱，且頻繁地前往工地，希望建築物能夠實現與設計圖相同，甚至更好的施工成果。如果沒有工地統籌陳玲瑱經理的協助，我們的設計應該很難傳達給施工者及製造商團隊。所有的團隊成員，一起朝著同樣方向前進，並實現了複雜的建築細部收頭設計。

日本の現場監理と同様に台湾でも施工図の監修を行い、設計図と同等以上のものづくりができるように現場にも足しげく通った。現場の陳玲瑱氏なくしては、私たちの設計は施行者やメーカーのものづくりのチームに伝わらなかっただろう。こうしてチーム全員が同じ方向を向き、繊細なディテールが実現した。

12/10/2017 Taipei's best-in-class office specifications

台北最高等級的辦公大樓規格
台北一のグレードとなったオフィススペック

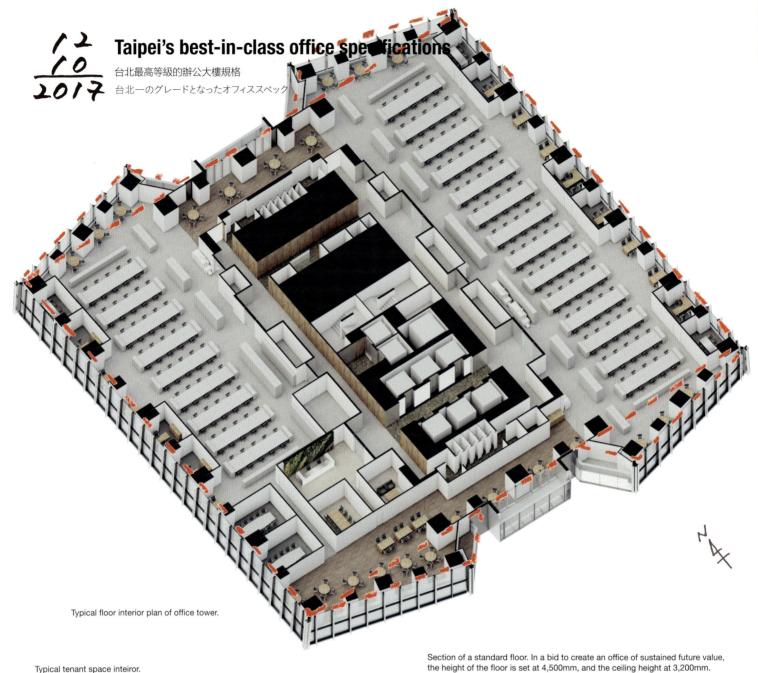

Typical floor interior plan of office tower.

Typical tenant space inteiror.

Section of a standard floor. In a bid to create an office of sustained future value, the height of the floor is set at 4,500mm, and the ceiling height at 3,200mm.

How to create competitive offices

The typical floors (7th-46th) of the octagonal tower, with a standard floor height of 4.8m and a ceiling height of 3.2m, house offices with the highest ceilings in Taiwan. The higher the floor, the shorter the distance from the windows — which is 9.5m at its shortest. Balconies that can house outdoor units for individually controlled air conditioners were installed on the south-north facade of the office zone.

The shape of the floor, which was based on regularly shaped floor plates, was designed with a view towards ease of use. Some portions that overhang the south-north facade were designed to be used as spaces for rest and relaxation, or meetings. Various amenities that are important to the offices were also provided for within the tenant zone.

Elevator halls on standard floors feature a ceiling height of 3.4m and paved stone flooring. There are no standard elevator buttons: the system is configured to allow users to stop and alight at floors that have been registered in advance on their individual security cards. Users tap their cards on the LCD monitor, enter their destination, and wait for the elevator to arrive.

In addition to restrooms with washlets, kitchenettes equipped with hot water, and garbage areas, the common areas feature nursing rooms for breastfeeding mothers that are unique to Taiwan, shower rooms, and elevators reserved for VIP guests. As floor area ratios can be relaxed in common areas, anterooms were provided at the entrances and exits of offices, thereby giving a distinctive character to the shape of the corridors.

實現具有競爭力的辦公大樓

八角形的辦公棟標準層（7~46樓）以樓高4.8米，天花淨高3.2米為標準規格，是全台灣天花淨高最高的辦公大樓。越高的樓層，距離窗戶的進深越短，但最小仍保有9.5米。辦公室專有區域的南北兩側也設計了陽台，提供作為租戶安裝個別空調用的室外機

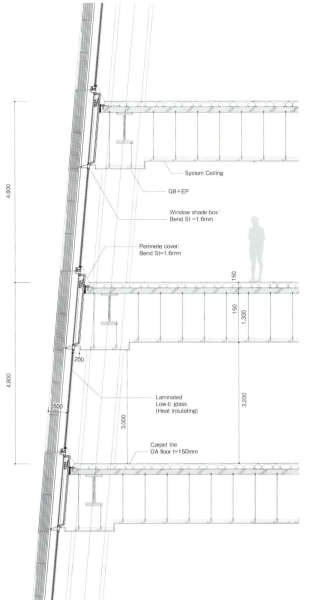

Office tower typical floor section (s:1/100)

Typical floor core plan of office tower (s:1/120)

Typical floor corridor.　　Typical floor elevator lobby.　　Women's restroom.　　Men's restroom.

空間。

平面形狀規劃方整的樓板，主要考量使用上的便利性。對於南北向局部有突出的部分，則設想作為人們放鬆小憩與進行會議的空間，這是租戶區域內展現辦公室重要價值的設施。

標準層梯廳的天花淨高為3.4米，地坪為石材。沒有一般的電梯按鈕，個人的門禁卡事先登錄要前往的樓層，使用時感應門禁卡，並在液晶螢幕上輸入目的地樓層後，等待電梯到來。

公共區域除有裝設免治馬桶的廁所、茶水間、垃圾暫存室之外，還有台灣獨有的集乳室、淋浴間、VIP專用電梯等。因為公共區域可免計入容積，所以各辦公室的出入口還規劃了一處小玄關，凹凸有序的走廊形狀也成為特色之一。

競争力あるオフィスを実現する仕掛け

八角形の高層棟基準階（7〜46階）は、階高4.8m、天井高さ3.2mを基準とする台湾一の天井高さのオフィスである。上層階になるほどオフィス奥行が浅くなり、最小9.5mとした。オフィス専有部の南北面には、個別空調対応用屋外機設置スペースとしてバルコニーを設けた。

平面形は、整形なフロアプレートをベースとした、使いやすさに配慮した計画。一部、南北面に張り出した箇所は、リフレッシュやミーティングのスペースとしての利用を想定した。テナント区画内にも、オフィスの重要な価値となるアメニティが設けられた。

基準階エレベータホールは天井高さ3.4mで床は石貼り。通常のエレベータボタンはなく、個人のセキュリティカードに事前に登録した階に停止するよう設定され、液晶モニターにカードをかざして行き先を入力、エレベータが来るのを待つ。

共用部にはウォシュレット付きトイレ、給湯室、ゴミ庫以外に、台湾特有の搾乳室、シャワールーム、VIP専用エレベータがある。共用部は容積対象緩和があるため、オフィス出入口に前室をとり、廊下形状に特徴を持たせた。

Stationary observation
定點觀測
定点観測

2015/08/14

2015/11/24

2016/01/11

2016/03/07

2016/04/26

Annual fireworks display held every year on January 1st.

2016/06/21　　　2016/10/17　　　2016/12/26　　　2017/03/21　　　2017/04/25

F&B outlets that offer guests a view will be tenants in the portion of the building with transparent glass measuring some 50m high, from the 46th through 48th floors.

The twin structures of Taipei Nanshan Plaza and Taipei 101. The skyline formed by these two buildings approaching completion.

Interview

杜英宗　南山人壽保險股份有限公司 董事長

Giving Back to the Taiwanese Community with Great Architecture

回饋台灣社會的高質感建築
台湾社会に貢献する高品位な建築

——Let's begin with a brief history of Nan Shan Life Insurance and the significance of Taipei Nanshan Plaza.

Originally, Nan Shan Life Insurance was a subsidiary of U. S. life insurance giant American International Group (AIG). In 2011, we left AIG to become an independent Taiwan-based life insurance company. Our goal at the time was to become a business with deep and enduring roots in Taiwan and a familiar presence in the Taiwanese community. Currently, Nan Shan Life Insurance has life insurance agreements with around 6.3 million people throughout Taiwan. That works out to about half of the typical households in Taiwan as customers of Nan Shan Life Insurance. There is a saying in Taiwan that goes something like, "Repay society for the things that society has given to you." This is truly the creed of a life insurance company. Taipei Nan Shan Plaza is our way of giving back to the Taiwanese community. The building will stand for a long time. We hope that in future generations our grandchildren will see this building and understand what Nan Shan Life Insurance stands for.

——What was the Xinyi District like before Taipei Nanshan Plaza was built?

I have lived in the Xinyi District since 1992, and back then there were vacant lots everywhere. Xinyi is a district in the center of Taipei, Taiwan's capital. After extensive development, the last piece that remained to be developed in the Xinyi District was the outstanding site where the Taipei Nanshan Plaza now stands. It cost 26,888,000,000 Taiwan dollars (about 900 million US dollars) to acquire the land rights to this site. We set a goal to create a symbol for Xinyi District by building a landmark building of international quality containing offices and commercial facilities that would represent Nan Shan Life Insurance.

The occupancy rate for tenant office space is currently around 80 percent. While most of the tenants are foreign enterprises, consulates and embassies of various countries are also in the building. This means that the development has an excellent reputation overseas. It is expected that some 12,000 people will work there and that around 20,000 people will visit the commercial facilities every day. We intend to do more of this kind of socially beneficial real estate development in the future as well.

——What did you envision for this project in the beginning?

When the site was acquired in 2011, Ruentex Group president Samuel Yin, Nan Shan Life Insurance's largest stockholder, and I were absolutely determined to build the greatest building in Taiwan. Nan Shan Life Insurance set up a new real estate division for this development, which was also helped along by the outstanding design of Mitsubishi Jisho Sekkei.

——首先，我想瞭解一下，南山人壽的企業沿革及「臺北南山廣場」這專案的意義。

南山人壽保險公司原本是美國著名保險公司AIG(American International Group)的臺灣分公司。2011年從AIG獨立，成為臺灣本土保險公司。當時我們的目標在於成立在臺灣紮根源遠流長的企業，並且融入臺灣社會。目前，在壽險商品上，全臺灣的保單契約數量已經達到大約630萬人。這計算下來大約等於說臺灣一般家庭中約有一半都成為了南山人壽保險的客戶。有一句話說「取之於社會、用之於社會」，這正是人壽保險公司的信念。「南山廣場」是我們對臺灣社會感恩回饋的象徵。建築物會一直存在，我們希望後代子孫看到南山廣場時，就能夠認識南山人壽的企業理念。

——「南山廣場」的所在地信義區，原來是怎麼樣的地方？

我本身在1992年就住在信義區，當時到處都是空地。信義區處於臺灣的首都，臺北的中心地區。進行開發和發展至今，南山廣場的基地可說是信義區的最後一塊拼圖，地理位置非常有利。雖然當時取得土地所有權花了268億8,800萬新臺幣，但我們的使命在於在信義區打造辦公大樓及商業據點，建造象徵南山人壽的國際品質建築標的，使其成為信義區新的特色地標。

目前辦公樓層的入住率大約8成左右。進駐的大多數是外商企業，其中也包括各國領事館或大使館，獲得國際人士的高度評價。未來在「南山廣場」的辦公大樓，預計每天大約有一萬兩千名員工在此上班，商場的訪客也估計有兩萬人左右。像這樣對社會很有意義的不動產開發，我們希望今後也能夠繼續推展。

——當本案最初開始時，您有什麼樣的願景？

2011年，取得這塊土地時，我與南山人壽最大股東潤泰集團的尹衍樑總裁兩個人下定決心，無論如何，都要建造全臺灣最頂級的建築物。南山人壽為了這開發案新成立了不動產部門，另外三菱地所設計的優秀設計團隊也幫忙我們很多。當時與尹總裁下的決心，到目前為止從來也沒有動搖過。

——まず、南山人寿という企業の沿革と、「臺北南山広場」の意義をお伺いします。

2011年、米国の保険大手AIG (American International Group) の子会社であった南山人寿は、AIGの手を離れ、台湾本土の保険会社となりました。ここ台湾に根ざした息の長い事業者となるべく、台湾社会に馴染むことを当時の目標としました。現在、生命保険事業において、南山人寿は台湾全土で約630万人の契約件数があります。台湾の一般家庭の約半分が南山人寿のお客様である計算です。台湾のことわざのひとつに「社会から貰ったものを、社会に恩返しする（取之於社會、用之於社會）」というものがあります。これはまさに生命保険会社の信念です。「南山廣場」は、私たちの台湾社会に対する恩返しの印です。建物はずっと存在します。後代の子孫も、建物を見て、この南山人寿の信念を理解してもらえたらと思います。

——もともと、この「南山廣場」が建つ信義区はどのような場所だったのですか？

私は1992年から信義区に住んでいますが、当時は空き地だらけでした。台湾の首都、台北の中心に信義区があります。開発・発展した現在、信義区のラスト1ピースとして、すばらしいロケーションを誇るのが「南山廣場」の敷地です。今回の土地の権利取得には268億8,800万台湾ドルがかかりましたが、そこに南山人寿を代表するオフィス・商業拠点として国際クオリティの建築ランドマークを建てることで、信義区を特徴付ける役割を担うことを目標にしました。

賃貸オフィスの入居契約率は、現在8割程度です。入居者の多くは外資系企業ですが、諸外国の領事館、大使館も入居し、海外から高く評価されています。「南山廣場」のオフィスでは、毎日約1万2千人が就業し、商業棟は約2万人が訪れると予測されています。こうした、社会にとって有意義な不動産開発を、私たちは今後も継続していきたいと思っています。

——プロジェクトスタート時、どのような夢を思い描いていましたか？

2011年、この土地を取得した時に、南山人寿の最大の株主である潤泰集團・尹衍樑総裁とふたりで何があっても台湾で一番の建物を建てようと強く決心しました。南山人寿はこの開発のために新しく不動産部を設置し、また、三菱地所設計の優れた設計にも助けられました。尹総裁との決意は一度も揺らいだことはありません。

Y. T. Tu | Chairman, Nan Shan Life Insurance | Born in 1947 at Changhua, Taiwan / MBA, National Cheng Chi University / In 1990, Executive Director and Head of Taiwan Investment Banking Services, Goldman Sachs (Asia) L.L.C., HK / In 2000, Chairman, Citigroup Global Markets Taiwan / In 2011, Vice Chairman, Nan Shan Life Insurance / In 2015~, Chairman

杜英宗 | 南山人壽保險股份有限公司董事長 | 1947年生於臺灣彰化縣 / 國立政治大學企管研究所碩士 / 1990年、高盛證券駐台代表兼香港分公司執行董事 / 2000年、台灣花旗環球財務管理顧問股份有限公司董事長 / 2011年、南山人壽保險股份有限公司副董事長 / 2015年起出任董事長

ドゥ・インツォン | 南山人寿保険会社董事長 | 1947年台湾彰化生まれ / 国立政治大学大学院経営管理学科修士過程修了 / 1990年ゴールドマンサックス証券台湾支店長兼香港支店執行役員 / 2000年シティグループ・グローバル・マーケッツ台湾支社董事長 / 2011年南山人寿副董事長 / 2015年より現職

Even before it was completed, the media reported that office rents in Nanshan Plaza would be the highest in Taiwan.

The commitment we made with Mr. Yin has not wavered in the least.
——**You saw Mitsubishi Jisho Sekkei apply the Japanese creative process firsthand during this project. Please give us your impression of their work process.**
We are interested in Japanese-style corporate management as well as Japan's economy, and every year around 2000 of our employees visit Japan for training and other activities. Mitsubishi Jisho Sekkei's design is extremely meticulous and thorough. If, for example, Taipei were to experience a very strong earthquake, the safest place where one should evacuate to would most likely be Taipei Nan Shan Plaza. The building's huge pillars and splendid structural frame are the gift of superior structural engineering. I was also moved by the beautiful and sensitive interior detailing, such as the interior design of the Mitsubishi Electric elevator cars installed in the building, to take just one example. Like the interior design of the Palace Hotel where I lodge when in Tokyo (also designed by Mitsubishi Jisho Sekkei), it has a luxuriant and warm ambience.
——**What has been Taipei's response to the new building?**
Even before it opened for business, the building was applauded by people both here and abroad for an especially beautiful exterior and for the tower's crown, especially, which is unlike any other building. Once operation begins, I want many people to enjoy its interior as well. One client was amazed by how different the building is compared to the typical Taipei building, such as the Plaza's carefully designed public space as well as the lactation rooms, shower rooms and the like on every floor. After all, until now the typical Taipei office building has not had this much public space. Thanks to the design, tenants agree to leases mostly in the amount that Nan Shan Life Insurance is asking for. Right now, there are still a few vacancies on upper floors, but we are aiming for even higher rents for these spaces. So, it is a "sell when the price is right" situation, as we say in Chinese.
The New York Times profiled this project as one that will transform Taipei's skyline. I went to Tokyo on business recently, and all I was asked about was Taipei Nanshan Plaza. It is well-known not only in Taipei but overseas as well. I value this project not in monetary terms but for the intangible value it brings to the people of Taiwan. Taipei 101 was built by means of a multi-company merger, but Taipei Nanshan Plaza was built by our company alone, which is very rare in Taiwan. That is why it succeeds in fulfilling our vision of making a social contribution. We hope that this building will stand as a powerful symbol of the Nan Shan Life Insurance corporate philosophy of sustainable management.

(February 27, 2018 at Nan Shan Life Insurance, Responsibility for the wording: Shinkenchiku-sha)

——這次您與三菱地所設計合作並接觸了日本建築師的發展設計，過程中，有什麼特別的感受嗎？
我們對日本的企業經營和經濟很感興趣，每年大約有二千名同仁透過研修訪問日本。我認為三菱地所設計的設計非常細緻、完成度也非常高。比如說，如果現在臺灣發生大地震，考慮應該逃到哪裏時，我會說逃到「南山廣場」是最安全的。巨大的柱子和出色的框架結構是優秀的結構設計的成果。此外，這次引進的電梯（三菱電機製造）車廂內設計的每一個細節都很美、很精緻，讓我們非常感動。與我曾在日本住過的東京皇宮酒店（PALACE HOTEL TOKYO）（設計：三菱地所設計）的設計一樣，讓人感到高級的質感及溫馨的氣氛。
——對於南山廣場，臺北市民的反應如何呢？
雖然還沒開幕，但已經深受國內外人士的眾多好評，譬如外觀非常特別，尤其是大樓頂部的設計很獨特，在其它大樓從來沒有看過等。我希望在開始營業後，能有更多人來參觀體驗。曾經有一位顧客很驚訝地說，「南山廣場」的公共設施考慮得非常周到，每個樓層都有女性專用的集乳室和淋浴間等，配套設施如此完善，與臺北的一般建築物有很大的不同。一般在臺北的辦公大樓的公設比沒有這麼高。這樣設計出來的結果，在我們與企業簽訂租賃合約時，租戶幾乎都能接受南山人壽提出的租賃金額。現在，雖然目前高樓層部分還有些空屋，但是我們的目標是簽訂更高的租賃金額，正如處於「待價而沽」的狀態。這個案子在《紐約時報》中被報導為改變臺北的天際線的建築物。前陣子我因工作去東京，大家都詢問我南山廣場的事情。南山廣場不僅是在臺灣，在國外的知名度也很高。我認為，這個專案的價值並不是金錢，而是能夠為臺灣的民眾帶來無形價值。臺北101是由多家企業合資建造的，而「南山廣場」是我們一家公司單獨出資建造，是一個在臺灣很少見的開發案例。正因為如此，我們能夠實現我們的理想來回饋社會。我希望今後能夠透過這棟建築物來發揚「南山人壽」這家公司的永續經營理念。

（2018年2月27日、於南山人壽總公司／撰文：本誌編輯部）

——今回、三菱地所設計の日本式のものづくりに触れ、その過程をどう感じましたか？
私たちは日本の企業経営や経済に興味を持っており、毎年約2,000人の同僚が研修などで日本を訪れています。三菱地所設計の設計は非常に緻密で完成度も高いです。例えば今、台北で大きな地震が起こったとしましょう。どこに逃げるべきか考えると、おそらく「南山廣場」が最も安全だと思います。巨大な柱や立派な構造のフレームは優れた構造設計のたまものです。また、今回導入されたエレベータ（三菱電機）のカゴの内装デザインひとつ取っても、ディテールが美しく、繊細で感動しました。日本で宿泊したパレスホテル東京（設計：三菱地所設計）のデザイン同様、高級感のあるあたたかい雰囲気があります。
——台北での反応はいかがですか？
開業前ながら、国内外の方から外観が実に美しい、特に頭頂部のデザインは他のビルには見られない、という好評を数多くいただいています。開業した後には、ぜひたくさんの方々に中も見てほしいものです。あるお客さまからは、「南山廣場」の共用部は配慮が行き届いており、各階に女性の搾乳室やシャワールームなどの設備が整っているなど、台北の一般的な建物とは大きく違うと驚かれました。通常、台北のオフィスビルでは、共用部の割合はここまで高くはないでしょう。こうした設計の結果、テナントとのリース契約において、ほとんど南山人寿の提示額を受け入れてくれています。現在、高層階に多少の空室がありますが、更に高い賃料を目指しているところです、まさに、「待價而沽」（より高く売るために、現在は待つ、という意味）のような状態ですね。
このプロジェクトは、『ニューヨーク・タイムズ』でも台北のスカイラインを変えるプロジェクトとして紹介されました。先日、仕事で東京に行きましたが、「南山廣場」のことばかり聞かれました。台湾のみならず、海外でも認知度が高いのです。私は、このプロジェクトの価値は金銭的なものではなく、台湾の人びとに無形の価値をもたらすことができるだと思います。台北101は複数企業による合弁会社によって建てられましたが、「南山廣場」は、われわれ1社が単独で建てた台湾では珍しいプロジェクトです。だからこそ、私たちの考える社会貢献が実現できます。これからこの建物によって、南山人寿企業理念である持続可能な経営を強くアピールして行きたいと思います。

（2018年2月27日、南山人寿本社にて／文責：本誌編集部）

Looking at the three podia from the south of the site.

View from Xinyi Road, which lies to the southeast of the building.

View from Chung-shan Park.

View from across Xinyi Park, situated southwest of the building. Intersection of Songzhi Park and Xinyi Road.

View from the northeast.

View from Songren Road, which lies to the east.

Cultural + entrance podium. The exterior is covered with titanium honeycomb panels with a thickness of 215mm. The podium is connected to the office tower by a bridge. The pedestrian walkway and driveway at the bottom of the bridge connects the areas in the south-north area of the site.

Entrance to the cultural + entrance podium. The eaves, which are integrated into the facade, are also used by people waiting for the bus in rainy Taipei.

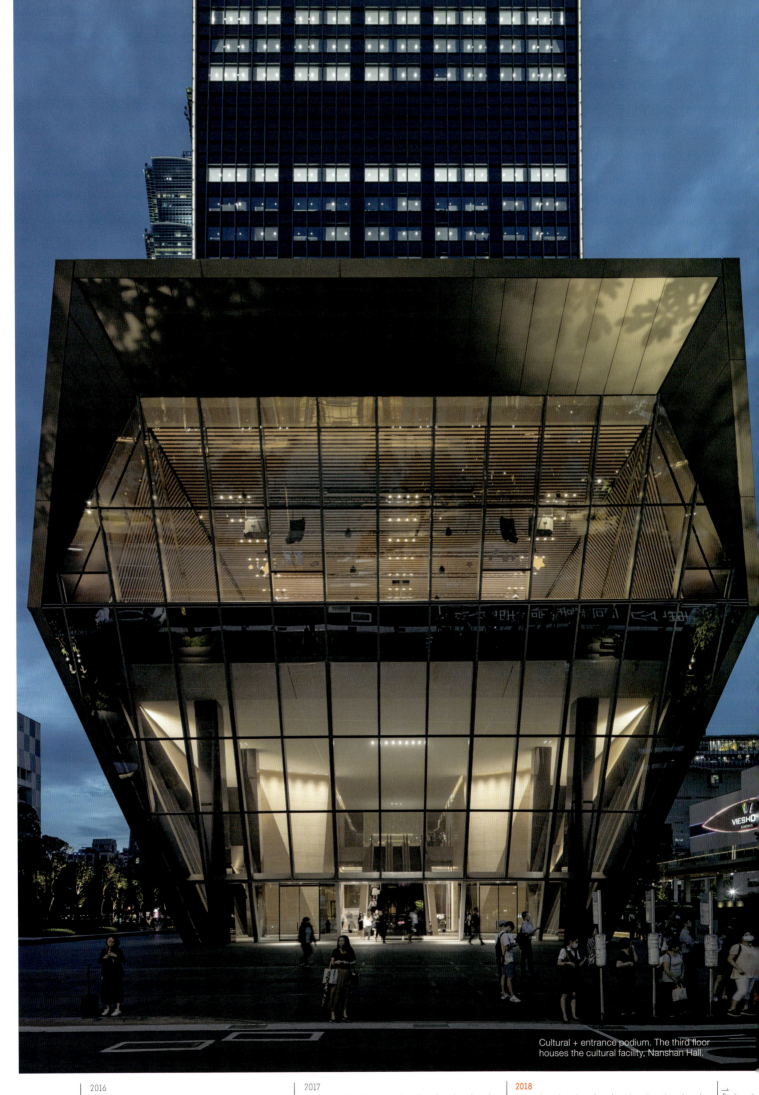

Cultural + entrance podium. The third floor houses the cultural facility, Nanshan Hall.

View of the cultural + entrance podium from the southeast.

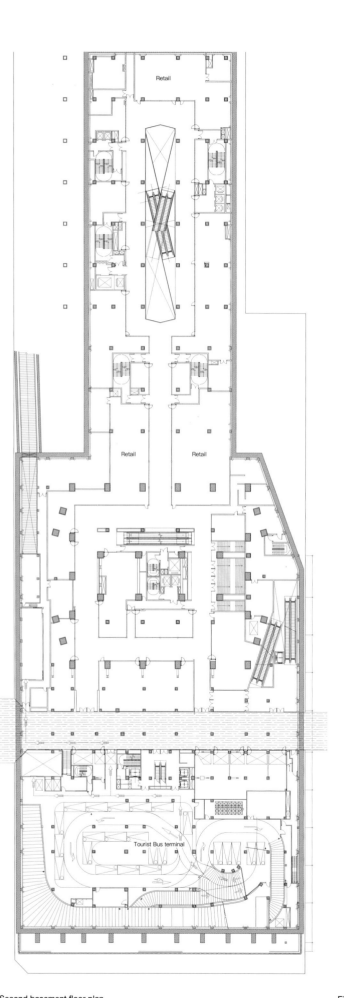

Second basement floor plan

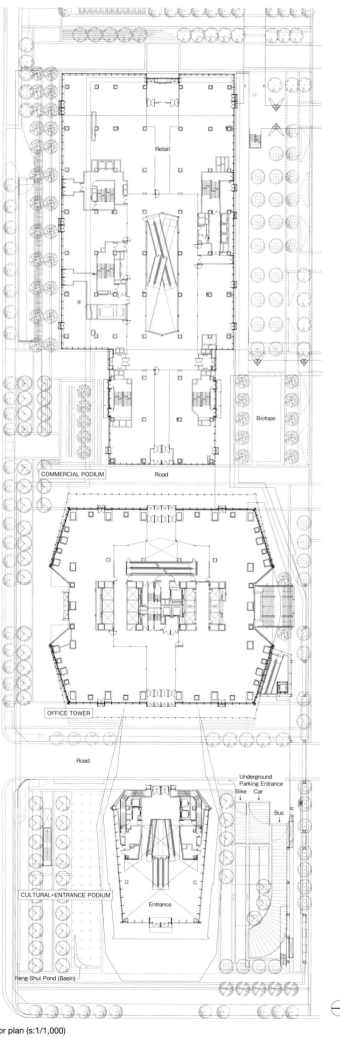

First floor plan (s:1/1,000)

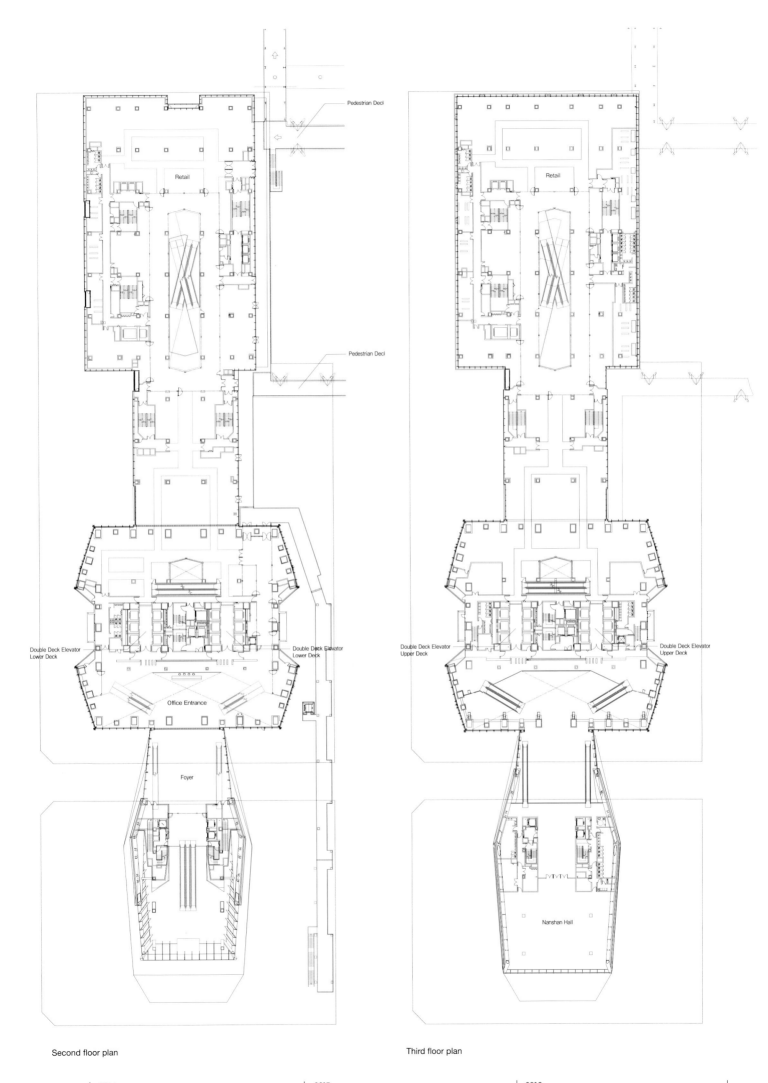

Second floor plan

Third floor plan

Entrance of cultural + entrance podium.

View of the entrance to the office tower from the second floor foyer of the cultural + entrance podium. The front features a screen art made up of stainless steel casts of plum blossoms.

Second floor entrance to the office tower. Double deck elevators with a destination oriented allocation system were used. The elevator lobby spans two floors.

Office entrance, green wall, and screen art. At the far end is the elevator hall for the office tower.

Entrance to the office tower, which can be approached from the cultural + entrance podium on the right.

40th floor of the office tower. The depth of the floor varies from 9 to 19.5m according to the incline of the exterior wall.

Elevator lobby and corridor on the 11th floor of office tower. The width of the corridor is 2m.

Balcony for storing equipment for the use of tenants.

Tenant office interior (6th floor).

Women's restroom. Specifications are laid out using high-grade offices in Japan as a benchmark, and include washlets and toothbrush stands.

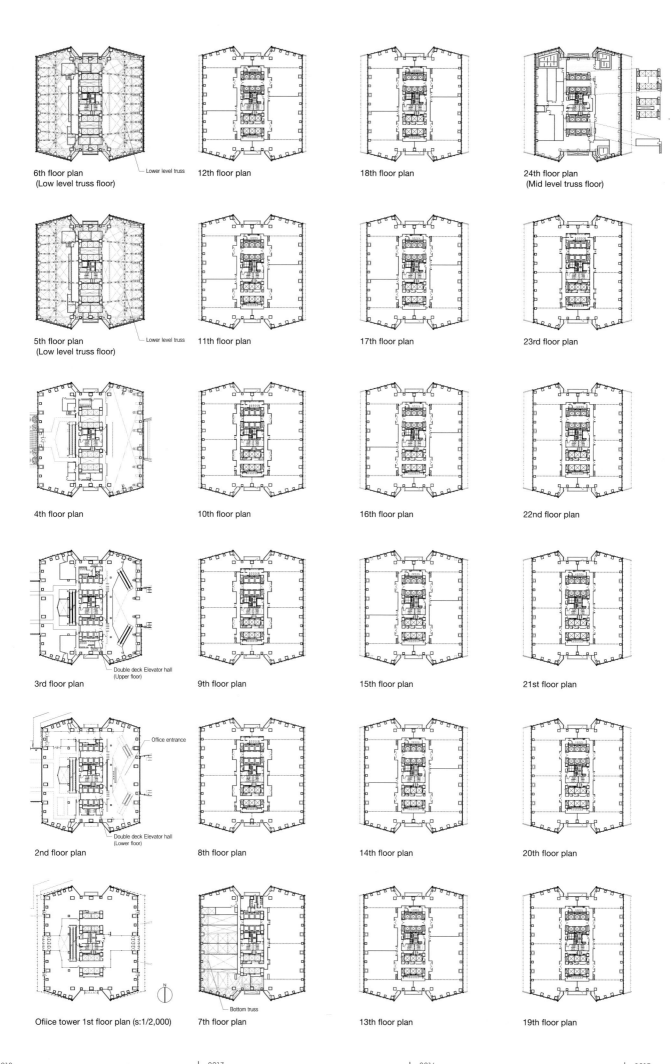

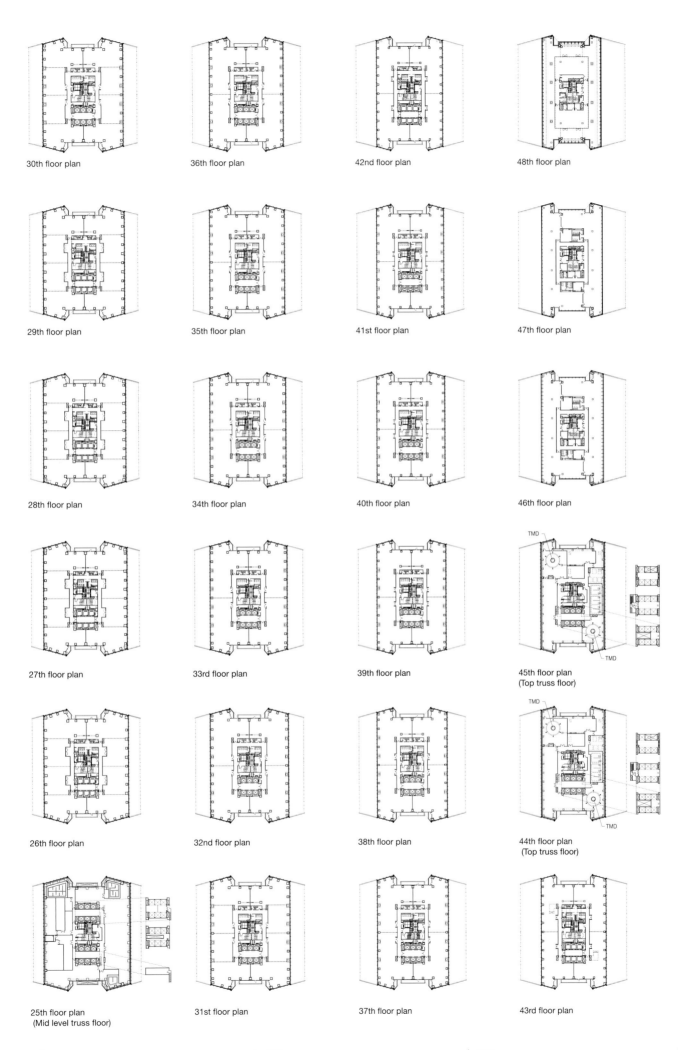

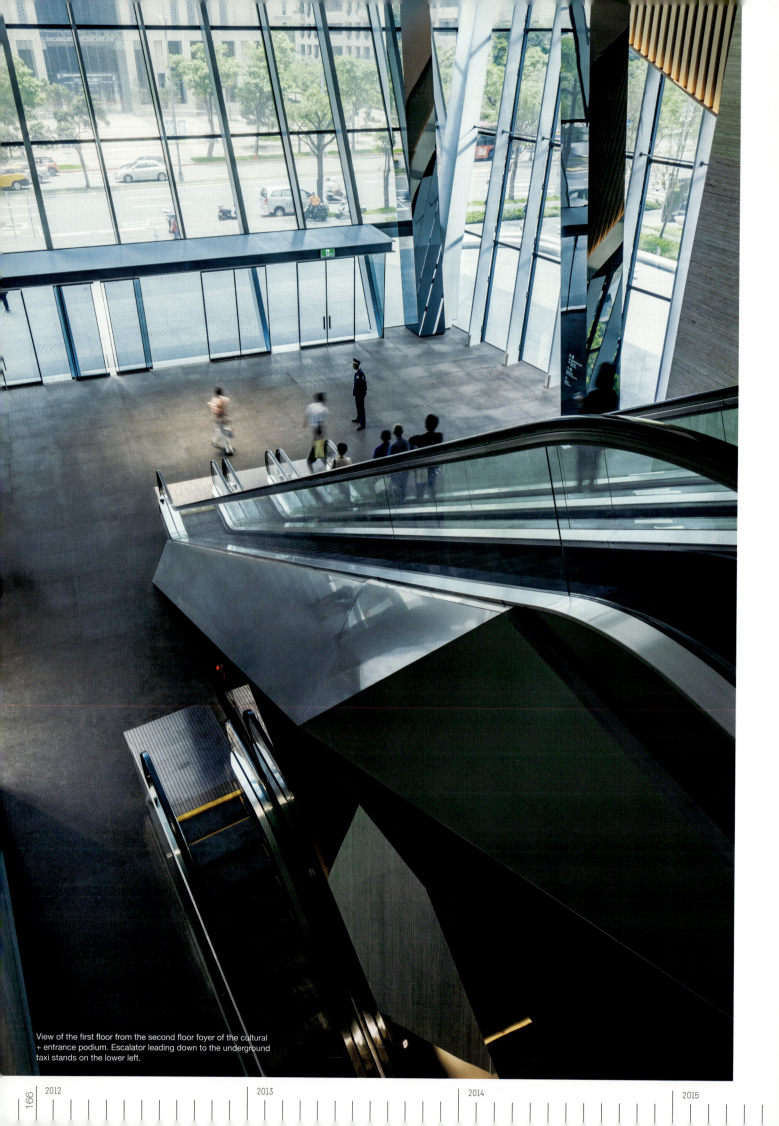

View of the first floor from the second floor foyer of the cultural + entrance podium. Escalator leading down to the underground taxi stands on the lower left.

Cafeteria on the north side of the second floor entrance to the office tower. The cultural + entrance podium is visible outside the window.

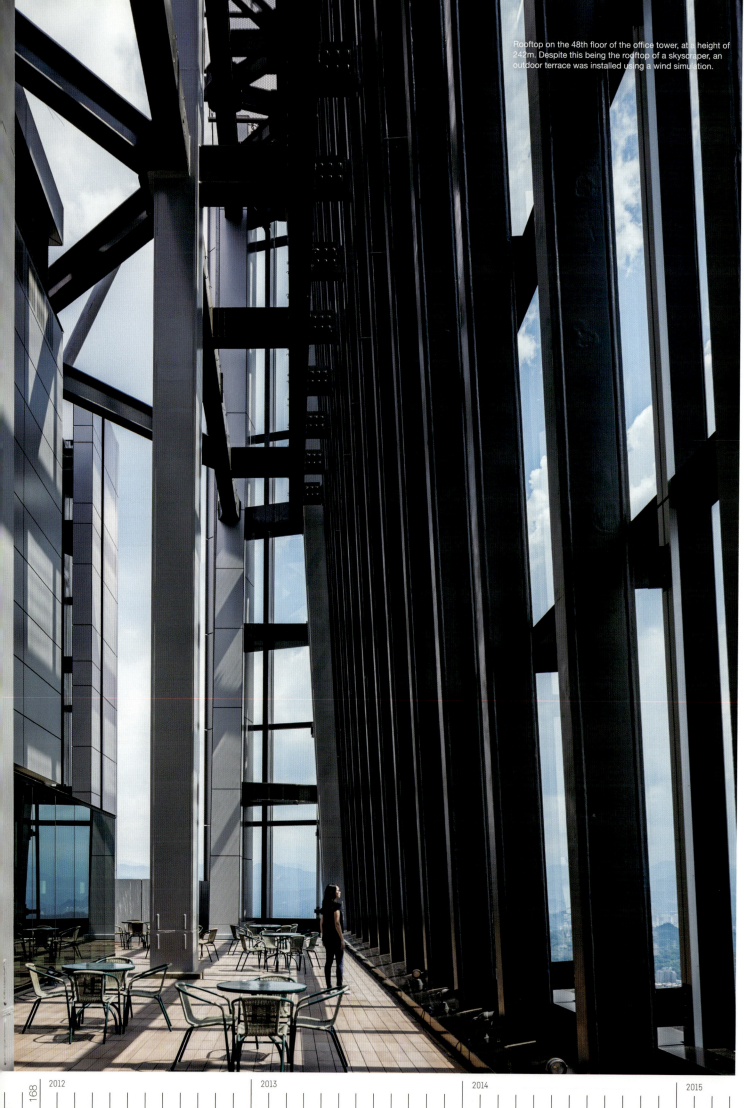

Rooftop on the 48th floor of the office tower, at a height of 242m. Despite this being the rooftop of a skyscraper, an outdoor terrace was installed using a wind simulation.

View of the west side from the 48th floor rooftop.

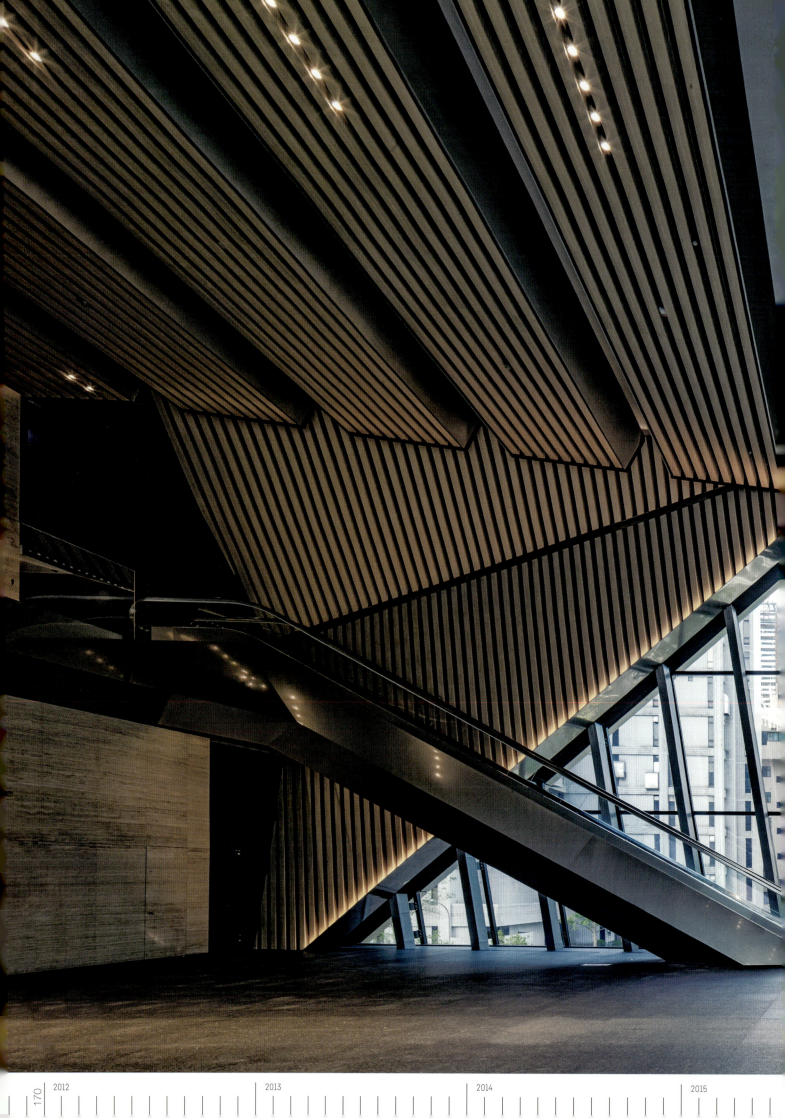

Second floor foyer of the cultural + entrance podium, situated along the pedestrian walkway and driveway that connects the south and north of the site.

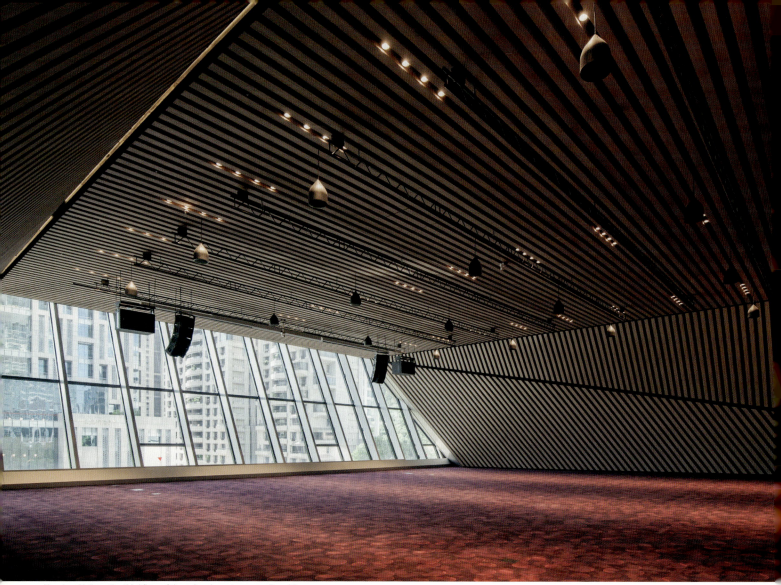

Nanshan Hall, on the third floor of the cultural + entrance podium. View of offices and residences along Songren Road through the window.

B2 level of cultural + entrance podium, entrance on the passageway side.

Taxi stands at B2 level of the cultural + entrance podium. Pick-up and drop-off areas in Taiwan are often situated underground.

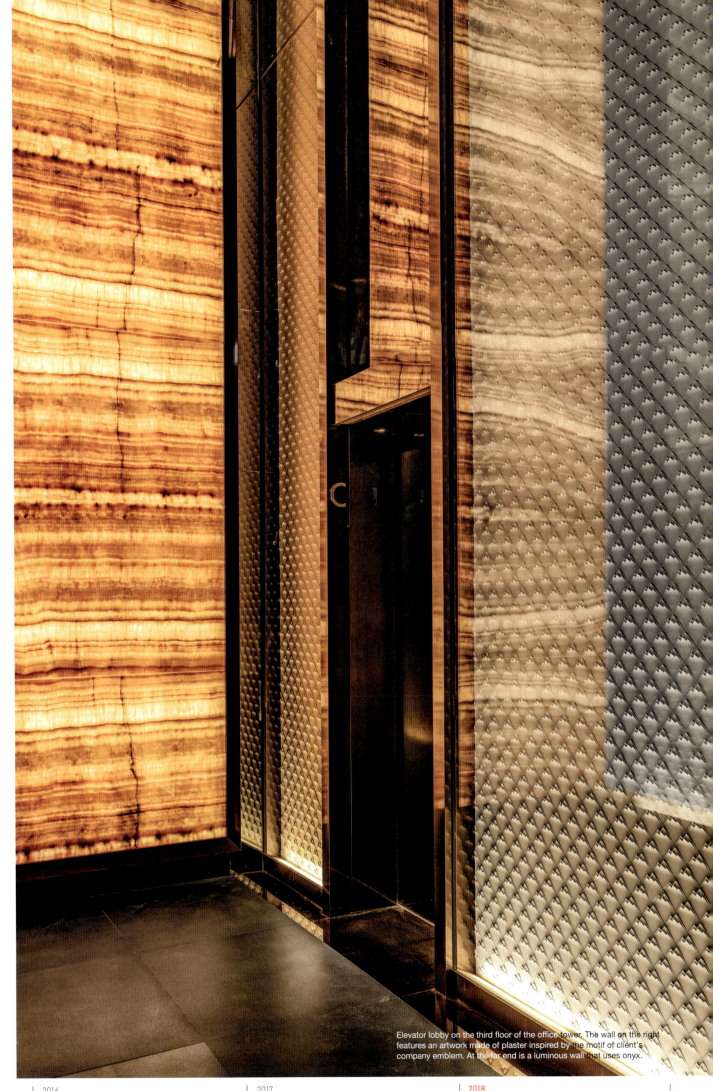

Elevator lobby on the third floor of the office tower. The wall on the right features an artwork made of plaster inspired by the motif of client's company emblem. At the far end is a luminous wall that uses onyx.

View of the cultural + entrance podium, looking across the second floor entrance to the office tower and the screen art.

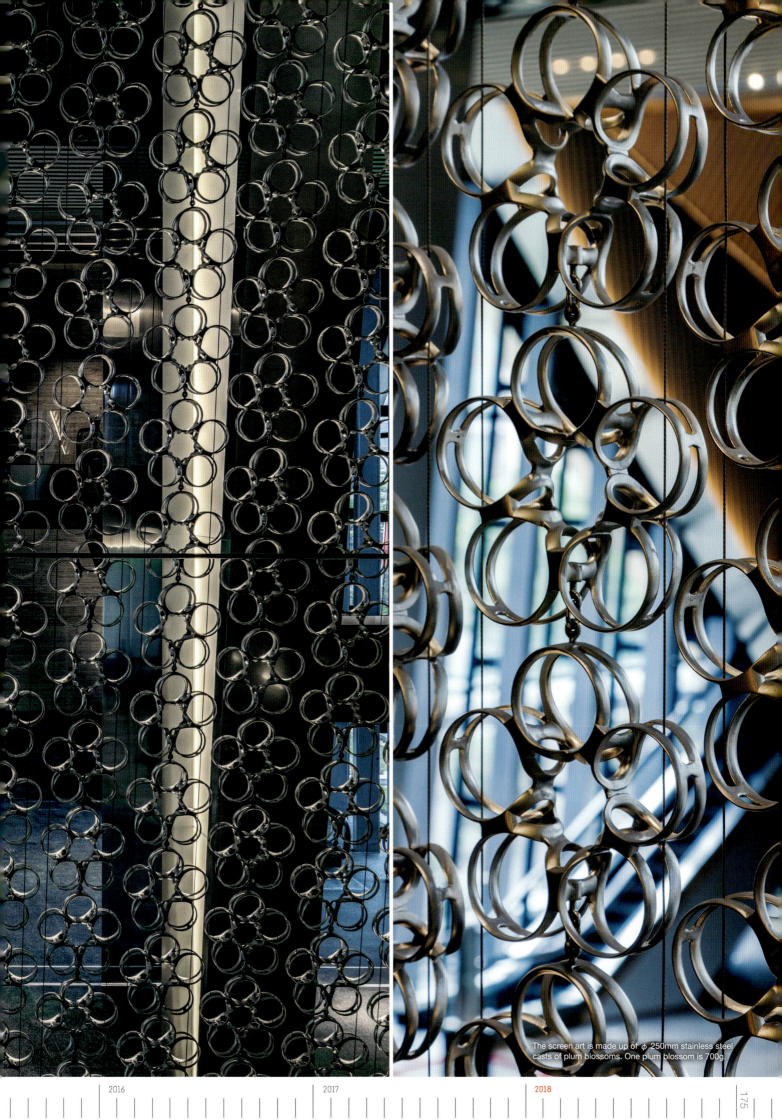

The screen art is made up of ϕ 250mm stainless steel casts of plum blossoms. One plum blossom is 700g.

Night view of the southeast. The lighting in the corner fins of the office tower emphasize the contours of the tower.

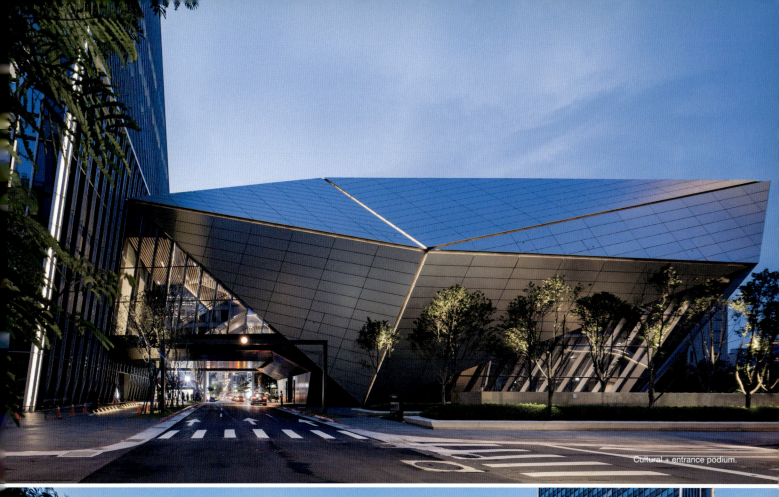

Cultural + entrance podium.

Commercial podium.

View from the west (Songzhi Road).

Biotope on the south side of the commercial podium, installed as required by the planning and zoning commission.

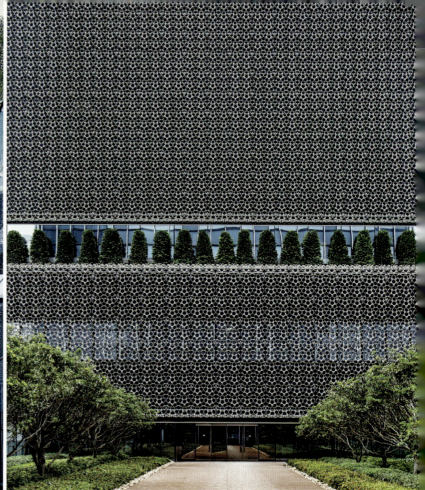

Terrace connecting the office tower and commercial podium, a public space accessible 24 hours a day.

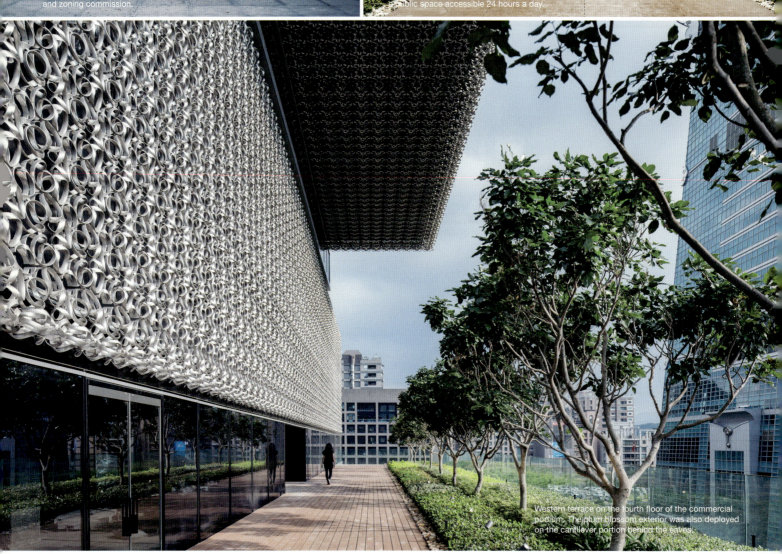

Western terrace on the fourth floor of the commercial podium. The plum blossom exterior was also deployed on the cantilever portion behind the eaves.

View from the south. Greenery was added to the terrace of the commercial podium, which was also connected to the adjacent park (Xinyi Park).

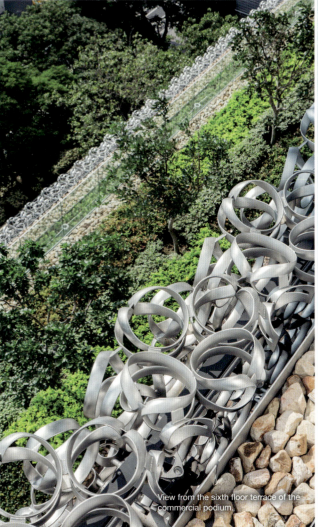

View from the sixth floor terrace of the commercial podium.

Exterior featuring plum blossom forms. The standard module is made of stainless steel —— a choice that was made because the rings that connect one blossom to another required a certain level of strength.

View from the Taipei City Hall Public Square on the northwest side.

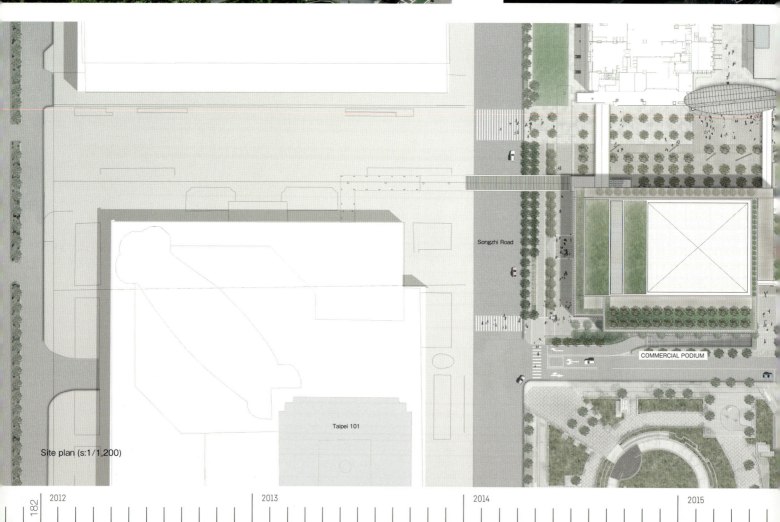

Site plan (s:1/1,200)

Public space on the north side of the commercial podium, which is encircled by the pedestrian deck at the second-floor level.

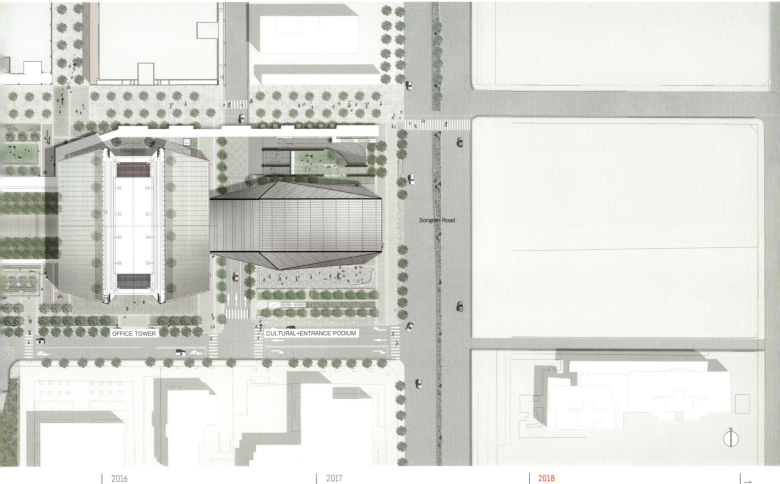

West side of the commercial podium. The lower portion of the box-shaped frame is made of glazing with two-sided support on the top and bottom, creating a floor that connects to the terrace.

View from Southeast.

Pedestrian-only passageway and pedestrian deck on the north side of the office tower. The piers feature a chopstick motif.

Second-floor pedestrian deck on the north side of the office tower.

First floor of the north side of the commercial podium.

North side of the commercial podium. The pedestrian deck at the second-floor level connects to the surrounding facilities.

Public space on the north side of the commercial podium. The triangular greenery objects create a gentle division between the site and the pedestrian-only passageway.

View from South.

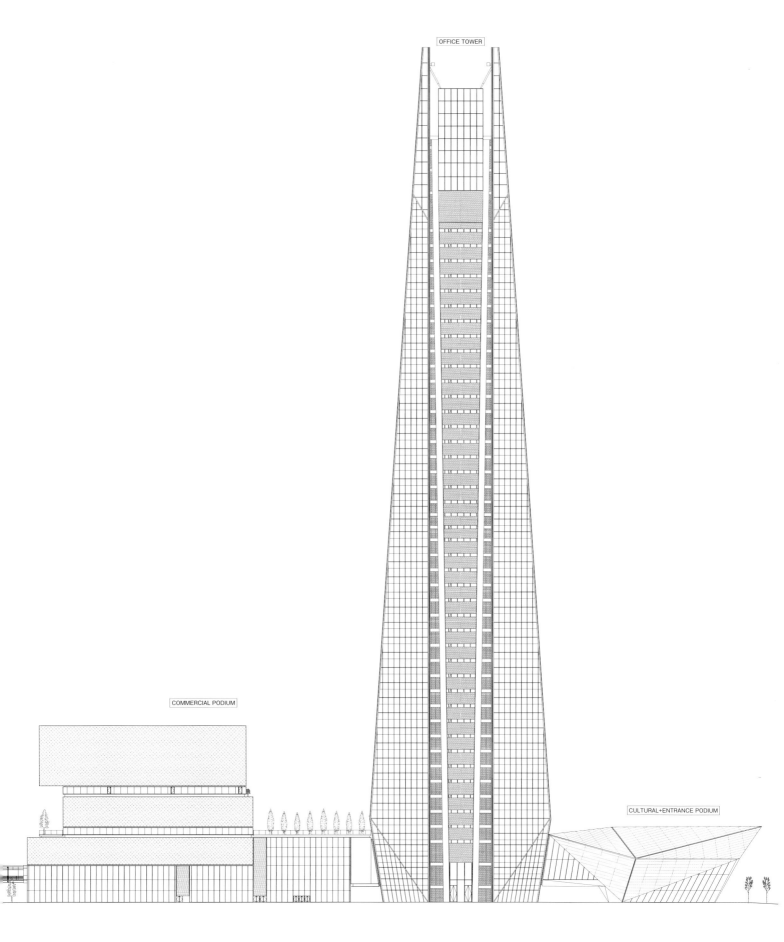

South elevation (s:1/1200)

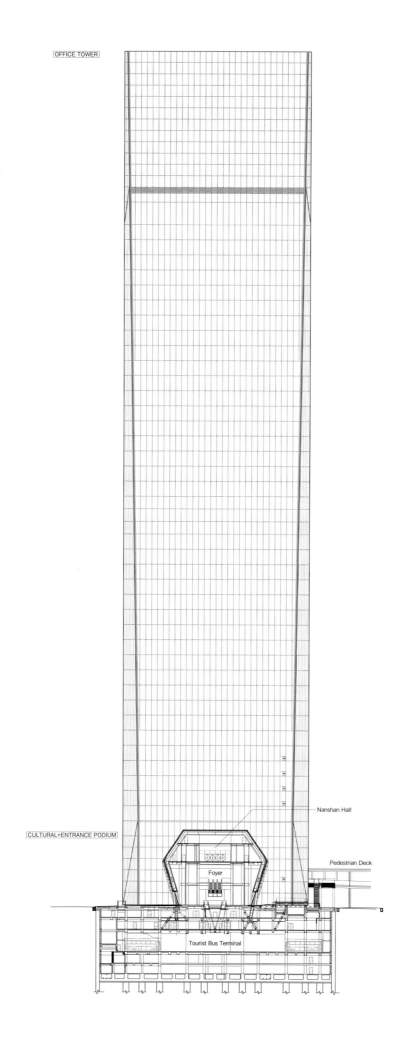

North-south section (s:1/1,200)

West-east Section (s:1/1,200)

Bird's eye View from the Southwest.

View from the neighborhood on the southeast.

View from the neighborhood on the southwest.

Article

藤森照信　東京大学名誉教授

Taipei Nanshan Plaza and its Context | A Realization of Urban Planning-Oriented Architecture

「臺北南山廣場」與其背景 | 從都市計畫來看建築的成立

「臺北南山廣場」とその背景 | 都市計画的建築の成立

Ties Between Taipei's and Tokyo's Urban Planning

Two sites famous among foreign visitors to Taiwan are the National Palace Museum, the great center of cultural heritage, and Taipei 101, the soaring architectural landmark. A few years ago, treasures from the former were exhibited at the Tokyo National Museum in the special exhibition Treasured Masterpieces from the National Palace Museum, Taipei (2014), which drew swarms of art enthusiasts, and the latter is also an object of interest for many Japanese. In addition to visitors to Taipei, people involved in architecture in some way have seen the building in photographs, but I believe a lot of them were not quite sure what to think of it. It more than fulfills its duty as an icon of a major city, but when I use the qualifier "more than," I speak of the bizarreness of its form. When I first saw it, I thought it seemed inspired by a Hindu pagoda, and on a recent visit to Taiwan I was struck again by its un-office-building-like structure, with each section protruding at an inverted incline, and a pinnacle also resembling that of a Buddhist's pagoda. The building is apparently modeled after a stalk of bamboo, but was that actually its original inspiration?

I also noticed the symbolic shapes mounted on the sides at the narrowest point of the hourglass-shaped lower part. They represent a traditional Chinese qian coin (which was the prototype for the Japanese sen coin in the Edo Period [1603-1868]). An economic sensibility is indispensable for urban business, and as architectural design elements, these coins make quite an impact.

This Xinyi District, where Taipei's iconic building stands, has developed as a sub-city center of since the 1990s, the equivalent of the Shinjuku fukutoshin (sub-metropolitan center) or the waterside areas by Tokyo Bay (Toyosu, Ariake and so forth) in Tokyo. And in fact, there was a man involved in Xinyi's development, Morin Kaku (1920-2012), with deep connections to Tokyo. After graduating from Taipei High School of Technology (present-day National Taipei University of Technology) in 1940, Kaku studied at the University of Tokyo Department of Architecture under Hideto Kishida (1899-1966) and had close ties with Eika Takayama (1910-99), Kenzo Tange (1913-2005), Yasumi Yoshitake (1916-2003), Atsushi Shimokobe (1923-2016), and other leading figures in postwar Japanese architecture, urban planning and land development, paving the way for his own career. The work that heralded his arrival as a major architect was the Kasumigaseki Building (1968). Commissioned by the client, Mitsui Fudosan, he organized KMG (the Kasumigaseki Mitsui Group) and dealt with people in diverse fields and balanced

結合台北與東京兩地的都市計畫

如同有文化遺產美譽的「國立故宮博物院」，在到訪台灣的外國人觀光客之間非常知名，建築地標最為聞名的則是「台北101」。前者許多珍藏品曾於幾年前在東京國立博物館巡迴展出（特別展「台北國立故宮博物院 神品至寶」2014年），吸引眾多的藝術愛好者前往觀賞，當然後者也有不少日本民眾對它感興趣。除了已去過台北101的人之外，因為看到照片而想親眼目睹的建築相關從業者也不在少數，但要怎麼評論它呢？應該大多數人都說不上來。我認為作為城市的地標它絕綽有餘，但所謂的「有餘」，大概就是它那不可思議的形狀吧。第一次看到它的時候，感覺是印度教佛塔般的印象，這次再度造訪台北，眺望著台北101，發現每隔幾個樓層，斜著突出的外觀與辦公大樓不太搭調，還有頂部如寶塔般的造型，據說是來自竹子的形狀轉化，原始概念到底是甚麼呢？

我發現高樓層與低樓層的銜接，正巧位在腰身的位置，有個象徵性的造型。回朔歷史，這是中國傳統的古錢（也是江戶時代日本錢幣的原型）。因商業城市必須與經濟連結，故此建築設計令人留下難以忘懷的印象。

擁有台北第一地標的信義區，在1990年代以後，被定義為台北副都心，陸續進行開發。以東京而言，相當於新宿副都心，及東京灣的灣岸區域（豐洲、有明等）。

在這裡必須介紹一位與東京緣分深厚的人物—郭茂林先生（1920～2012年）。

郭先生於1940年台北高等工業學校（現・台北科技大學）畢業後，進入東京大學建築學系學習，師承岸田日出刀（1899～1966年）、高山英華（1910～99年）、丹下健三（1913～2005年）、吉武泰水（1916～2003年）、下河辺淳（1923～2016年）等人。他主導戰後日本建築及都市計畫與國土計畫的這些前輩十分友好熟稔，也建立了日後活躍的基礎。郭先生的名聲開始在建築界廣為人知的契機是「霞關大廈」（1968年）的建設。他接受三井不動產的委託，創立了KMG（霞關三井集團）事務所，與相關單位磨合，並協調相互利害關係，終於實現了日本第一座超高層大廈。完成「霞關大廈」的建設之後，郭先生繼續致力於多項日本超高層建築的建設。再者，對台灣的都市計劃及國土計畫，也扮演了關鍵性的角色。

1988年，李登輝先生（1923年～）就任台灣總統，為了諮詢台灣未來發展方向，招聘了兩位旅日台灣人，分別是立教大學教授歷史學者戴國煇先生（1931～2001年）與郭茂林先生。幸運地是我早耳聞兩位大名，這兩位都是在異國綻放光彩且擁有實際功績的大人物。國土計畫上，接受戴先生與郭先生的建議，台灣興建了第二條南北縱貫道路，另外還有台北站前的都市更新計畫，以及副都心・信義區的規劃案。可

台北と東京の都市計画を結ぶもの

台湾を訪れる外国人の間では、その文化的遺産としては「国立故宮博物院」、建築的アイコンとしては「台北101」が広く知られる。前者は数年前、東京国立博物館で秘蔵の品々が展示され（特別展「台北 国立故宮博物院 神品至宝」、2014年）多くの美術ファンが詰めかけたが、後者もまた日本人の興味を引く。訪れた人はもちろん、写真などで目にした建築関係者も多いと思うが、何をどう評していいのか面食らう人の方が多いだろう。都市の求めるアイコンとして十二分の役は果たして余りあるが、その余りが不思議なかたちで溢れ出しているようにも思える。初めて目にした時は、ヒンズー教の塔のイメージをベースにしているように見えたが、今回、改めて台北を訪れて眺めてみると、各階が数階ごとに斜めに迫り出すというオフィスビルらしからぬ姿といい、頂部の宝塔状の造形といい、これは竹を模したものであるというが、元ネタは何だろうか。

気づいたのは、上層と下層との間の、ちょうどクビレの位置にシンボリックに取り付けられたひとつの造形だ。これは中国の伝統的な銭（江戸時代の日本の銭型の原型となった）をかたどっている。都市でのビジネスに経済的感覚は不可欠だが、建築デザインとして忘れ難い印象を残す。

この台北の強烈なアイコンが建つ信義区とは、1990年代以後、台北市の副都心として開発され、東京で言えば、新宿副都心や東京湾の湾岸地域（豊洲、有明など）に相当する場所である。

そしてここは、あるひとりの人物を介して東京と縁が深い。

郭茂林（1920～2012年）である。

郭は、1940年、台北の高等工業学校（現・台北科学技大学）を卒業後、東京大学建築学科に学び、師の岸田日出刀（1899～1966年）のもと、高山英華（1910～99年）、丹下健三（1913～2005年）、吉武泰水（1916～2003年）、下河辺淳（1923～2016年）ら、戦後の日本の建築と都市計画と国土計画をリードする面々と親しく交わり、活躍の基礎を築いている。郭の名を建築界に知らしめたのは、かの「霞が関ビル」（1968年）の建設である。建築主である三井不動産の依頼を受けてKMG（霞が関三井グループ）を組織し、日本初の超高層ビルの建設に向けて、関係諸方面に働きかけ、利害を調整し、これを実現している。「霞が関ビル」建設以後の郭の活動は今では忘れられがちだが、その後、数々の日本の超高層ビルの実現にも力を尽くし、さらに、台湾の都市計画と国土計画に対しても決定的な働きをしている。

1988年、李登輝（1923年～）が台湾総統に就くと、台湾のこれからのあり方を諮問すべく、ふたりの在日台湾人を招いている。立教大学教授の歴史家、戴国煇（1931～2001年）と郭茂林である。私は幸い両人とも知って

Terunobu Fujimori | Born in 1946 in Nagano, Japan / In 1978, Graduate from Post-graduate School of the University of Tokyo / In 1998~2010, Professor, Institute of Industrial Science, The University of Tokyo / In 2010~2014, Professor, Kogakuin University / In 2010~, Emeritus professor, The University of Tokyo / Director of the Tokyo Metropolitan Edo-Tokyo Museum

藤森照信｜1946年出生於長野縣／1978年東京大學建築研究所碩士／1998~2010年東京大學教授／2010~2014年工學院大學教授／2010年~東京大學名譽教授／現任，江戶東京博物館館長

藤森照信｜1946年長野県生まれ／1978年東京大学大学院修了／1998~2010年東京大学教授／2010~14年工学院大学教授／2010年~東京大学名誉教授／現在、江戸東京博物館館長

various interests so as to build Japan's first skyscraper. Although much of Kaku's career after the Kasumigaseki Building tends to be forgotten today, he went on to dedicate himself to construction of numerous skyscrapers in Japan, and played a decisive role in formulating Taiwan's urban planning and land development strategy.

In 1988, Teng-hui Lee (1923-) became President of Taiwan, and to assist in determining Taiwan's way forward, he invited two Taiwanese residents of Japan as advisers. One was the historian and Rikkyo University Professor Guohui Dai (1931-2001), and the other Morin Kaku. I was lucky enough to know both of them, and both men had the great strength of character you would expect of someone who achieves great things in a country not their own. In response to their homeland's request for advice, Dai and Kaku devised plans for construction of two major north-south roads, the redevelopment of the area in front of Taipei Station, and construction of the Xinyi District as a sub-metropolitan center. Of course, it was not Dai but Kaku who led the urban planning.

An urban planning-oriented approach to architecture

Next to Taipei 101, the centerpiece of the Xinyi District, is the newly completed Taipei Nanshan Plaza, centered on a high-rise office building, commissioned by Nan Shan Life Insurance and designed by Mitsubishi Jisho Sekkei.

Let us take a closer look at Morin Kaku's urban plan. After World War II the Xinyi District, where much open space remained, was assigned the role of city center, and was connected to the old city center around Taipei Station via Taipei City Hall Station (Taipei Metro Bannan Line) opened in 1999. Taipei 101/World Trade Center Station (Taipei Metro Tamsui-Xinyi line), also connected to Taipei Station, opened in 2013. These two stations are connected not only by roads but also by a pedestrian deck. At the time of Taipei 101's construction, pedestrian deck linkage in the district was not yet complete, but now the network has been expanded and Morin Kaku's vision has been realized.

Resolving the crucial paradox of vehicle and pedestrian coexistence has been a central theme in post-World War II urban planning around the world. All kinds of ideas have been tried both in the US and in Japan, and one effective approach is to have separate levels altogether, the ground surface exclusively for cars and a deck for pedestrians only. Mitsubishi Jisho handled the development and design of the Marunouchi area near Tokyo Station, and I have spoken with Masanori Sugiyama, who served as chief engineer soon after the war, about the design of

想而知，都市計畫並非戴先生，而是由有建築背景的郭先生進行主導。

「都市計畫思維的建築規劃」的手法

受到南山人壽公司的委託，三菱地所設計在比鄰於信義區地標台北101的鄰側，設計了以超高層辦公大樓為主體的「臺北南山廣場」。

首先，我們來確認郭茂林先生所主導的都市計畫內容。他將戰後存留廣大土地的信義區定位為心都，透過1999年新建的市政府站（台北捷運、板南線），與位於舊城區的台北車站連接。接著，2013年同樣可通往台北車站的台北101/世貿站（台北捷運、淡水信義線）也開通，這兩站之間的地區交通不僅是靠道路，還透過空橋連結。興建「台北101」的當時，區內的空橋系統尚未完成，現在空橋網絡已完整擴張，可說是實現了郭茂林先生的願望。

戰後，全世界都市計畫的主要課題，是解決汽車與行人共存這種宿命般的矛盾。美國與日本也提出各式各樣的提案，其中最有效的是地面層為汽車專用，空橋為行人專用的人車分離規劃手法。三菱地所長年著手開發及設計東京站前的特區丸之內，區內中心軸線的仲街，也是規劃往下挖一個樓層，地上為行人專用道，地下一樓則為汽車專用道。我曾聽戰後擔任三菱地所技師長的杉山雅則先生說過，丸之內也有過類似空橋化的計畫。

但是，實際上實施上下樓層的人車分離後，人的步行模式會產生不自然的現象（與天橋相同道理，人們大多不想往上多爬一層樓）。目前，於地面層提供汽車與行人雙方使用，但加強行人專用道的設置是一般常見的作法。如設置天橋，則僅是作為輔助功能，而信義區的空橋系統也是採用這種方式。

介由地上通道與空橋，可以到達「南山廣場」的用地，可以清楚看出基地的規劃方式與比鄰而立的台北101截然不同。台北101是單一街廓的單棟大樓，而「南山廣場」，則是將三個街廓整體化規劃。話雖如此，其實是地面層三個街廓區塊各自分開（街廓之間仍有道路經過），只有二樓的部分才合為一體。讓來自車站的空橋可以直接連通過三塊街廓，雖說目前信義區內只有這裡如此規劃，但以在城市導入空橋，圖求人車分離的意義而言，算是實現成真的首例。

以都市計畫思維來作建築計劃，將城市中的三塊街廓一體化的規劃方式十分少見。具體來說，要怎麼整合？三塊街廓雖於視覺上整合為一體，但依其機能共分為三種，從東側開始依序為藝文入口棟、辦公

いるが、異国でしかるべき実績を挙げるだけの大きな人柄であった。戴と郭が国土計画において諮問に答えて実現したのは2本目の南北縦貫道路の建設であり、都市計画では、台北駅前の再開発と、そして副都心・信義区の計画であった。もちろん、都市計画は戴ではなく郭の主導である。

「都市計画的建築計画」の手法

この信義区に建つイコンの隣に、このたび南山人寿（「人寿」とは生命保険の意）の依頼により、三菱地所設計が超高層オフィスビルを中心とする「臺北南山廣場」を設計した。

まず、近づいて郭茂林による都市計画の内容を確かめる。戦後、広い土地が残されていた信義区は副都心として位置付けられ、旧来の都心部である台北駅とは1999年に設けられた市政府駅（台北捷運、板南線）を介して接続された。さらに2013年には、同じく台北駅に繋がる台北101/世貿駅（台北捷運、淡水信義線）が開業。この2駅間の地区は、道路だけでなくペデストリアンデッキでも繋がられている。「台北101」の建設当時は、地区内のデッキによる接続は完全ではなかったが、現在ではネットワークが拡充し、郭茂林の念願が実現していると言える。

戦後、世界中の都市計画において、自動車と歩行者の共存という宿命的な矛盾をどう解決するかはその中心的テーマとなった。アメリカでも日本でもさまざまな提案がなされたが、その有力な手法が、地上を自動車専用、デッキを歩行者専用に分離することだった。三菱地所が開発と設計を手がけてきた、東京駅前を丸の内地区という。その中心軸である仲通りでも、通りを1階分掘り下げ、地上を歩行者専用道、地下1階を自動車専用道とする、デッキ化に近い計画を立てたことがあると、戦後すぐに三菱地所の技師長を勤めた杉山雅則氏から聞いたことがある。

しかし、歩車の上下分離を実際にやってみると、人の歩行に不自然が生じる（歩道橋の場合同様、人は地上から1階分上がって歩きたがらない）ものだ。現在は地上を自動車と歩行者の双方に供しつつも歩行者用の部分を充実させるのが一般的であり、デッキを設ける場合には、その補助として使うようになっている。この信義区のデッキもまさにそのようなつくりとなっている。

地上とデッキの両方を介して近づくと、「南山廣場」の敷地の使い方は、その後ろ隣りに建つイコンのそれとはまるで違うことが分かる。イコンの方は1区画にひとつの孤立したビルである一方、「南山廣場」は3つの区画を一体化して用いている。といっても、地上では3区画はそのまま分け（その間を2本の道が通る）、2階で一体化している。その結果、駅からのペデストリアンデッキが、3つの区画に直結することとなり、3区画だけではあるけれど、都市にデッキを導入して歩車分離を図る、というその意義が初めて実現する。

the district's central axis, Naka-dori. The plan is similar to the pedestrian deck model, as the vehicle roadway was buried so that the subterranean level is exclusively for cars and the street level for pedestrians.

In practice, however, actually trying to keep vehicles and pedestrians separate tends to disrupt pedestrians' natural behavior patterns (take pedestrian bridges, unpopular because people do not want to walk up and down flights of stairs). Today, it is more common to have vehicles and pedestrians share the same level, and use the decks for the enhancements to aid the flow of pedestrian traffic, and this is precisely the role of decks in the Xinyi District.

When approaching on either the ground or the deck level, it is evident that the usage of the Taipei Nanshan Plaza site is quite different from that of the neighboring icon Taipei 101. While the latter is an isolated building occupying a single zone, the former utilizes three integrated zones. On the ground level, Taipei Nanshan Plaza is divided into three zones (with two roads separating them), but it is all connected on the second-floor level. This means the pedestrian deck directly connects the station to all three zones. Although this strategy is confined to this area, it is significant as the first introduction into the city of a deck that keeps vehicles and pedestrians separate.

What does this unusual urban planning-style approach to architecture, with three zones of the city integrated, look like? The three zones are visually integrated but functionally divided into the cultural + entrance podium, the office tower, and commercial podium (in order from east to west). The Marunouchi office district is a long-established one, with a history going back to 1894 when Mitsubishi Ichigokan was built as Japan's first modern office building, but in recent years it has been overhauled with a new focus on culture and commerce. The lessons of this transition were incorporated into Mitsubishi Jisho Sekkei's design from the beginning here in Taipei.

Though not widely known, the problem of skyscrapers' first floors is one that has continually plagued modern architecture. While super-high-rise buildings have come to dominate our city skylines, on the ground level where pedestrians come and go they are bleak and alienating, showing us only blank glass walls and lobbies empty except for security guards and banks of elevators. I have worked at Kogakuin University, Japan's first university housed in a skyscraper, and I recall the first floor of the building next door as spacious yet deserted, with nothing to charm the eye but the lights of a Seattle-based coffee shop facing the Keio Plaza Hotel (1971). This problem also afflicts Taipei's architectural centerpiece, which seems to get more devoid of people the closer you get to it. I hope that the addition of new shopping area will contribute to resolution of this "skyscraper first-floor problem."

Asserting a new presence in the city

Let us look at the zones in order starting with the cultural + entrance podium, which you reach first on your way from the station. The low-rise building, with an undulating array of irregular triangles, resembles a turtle's shell. When entering from the front, you are guided via escalators to the upper floors, where there are galleries and a large space for cultural events such as conferences. While the building resembles a turtle sitting atop piloti, piloti are not actually used, and people entering at the ground level are immediately taken up to the second floor. When I asked Yasuhiro Sube of Mitsubishi Jisho Sekkei about this approach, uncommon both in Japan and elsewhere in the world, he explained that "the Taiwanese like this kind of entry sequences," and indeed it can be seen in various other large Taiwanese buildings. The monumental frontal quality of the building and the gradually rising approach, a spatial ordering reminiscent of the film The Last Emperor (1987), may have a deep-rooted appeal for the people of Taiwan.

After the cultural + entrance podium you arrive at the Office tower. When I visited on February 28, 2018 interior was still in progress, and unlike in Japan, in Taiwan the practice is to remove

棟、商場棟。以丸之內的辦公商圈為例，1894年日本第一座現代化辦公大樓三菱一號館建設完成後，長期以來此區域都是辦公專用區，近幾年則加入「文化」和「商業」的元素使其耳目一新。在本案規劃最初也是引進這樣的經驗。

現代建築界中存在著不為眾人所知的「超高層大廈的一樓課題」。雖然超高層是城市中表現突出的主角，但是，通常面對人群往來的人行道的一樓會設置玻璃牆，而前方就是入口大廳。這樣規劃的結果，走近時人影會變稀疏，警衛跟電梯的標示也顯得相當空洞。我第一次參與超高層大廈的經驗，是任職於工學院大學時的案子，隔壁大樓的一樓是寬敞卻空泛無比的地坪，位在對街的西雅圖咖啡的照明倒映進「京王廣場飯店」(1971年)的景象是我眼睛唯一的救贖。地標型大廈大都面臨相同的問題，一走近後人影看起來很稀疏。所以我也期待本案增加商場購物區塊的份量，以解決「超高層大廈的一樓課題」。

創造都市的新存在感

就從步出車站最先映入眼簾的藝文入口棟依序來看吧：低層樓建築物的外觀，是不規則的三角形凹凸起伏，構成龜殼般的形態，從正面進入後，搭乘電扶梯往上一個樓層，其上方是提供展示或集會等藝文活動使用的寬廣空間。雖然外觀像是底層挑空上方乘坐烏龜般的形式，但一樓挑空空間其實並未使用。為什麼要從入口處搭乘電扶梯，一口氣直達二樓？這樣的規劃方式無論在日本或全世界都是首例。為我導覽建築物的三菱地所設計須部恭浩說明：「台灣人喜歡這樣的規劃方式」。確實其它台灣大型的商辦大樓也有類似的設計方式。考量建築物的門戶特性，面向正前方逐漸往上升的移動方式，就如同電影「末代皇帝」(1987年)中所呈現的空間秩序感，是否也意味著台灣人頑強的生存模式。

穿過藝文入口棟後，抵達辦公棟。我參訪本案的時間正巧在進行室內裝修的施工(2018年2月28日)，因台灣的規定是將部份已經完成的裝修全部拆下，露出內部的結構及設備接受檢查。這是日本的竣工勘驗沒有的規定，故我並不很了解室內裝修的完成狀況，因此這個部分在本文就不提及。

辦公棟的重點，比起室內外觀更值得一提。越往上方樓層越來越瘦長的形態並非罕見。但變細的部分如雙手合十祈求的設計，我倒是第一次看到。而更吸引我目光的，則是支撐窗戶的框架的厚度和強勁的姿態。近幾年，多數的大樓都如比鄰的台北101，外牆全面採用玻璃，而本案則是強調連接窗框之間的水平構材。再者，轉角斜材也一路貫穿至低樓層，造型顯得相當明確。這絕對是罕見的設計方式。更往前走，商場棟的亮點也在於外觀，小型環狀的外皮包覆四角形塊體，琳瑯滿目精雕細緻。據說設計的概念，是來自象徵台灣的梅花。

都市の中の3区画を一体化して使うという珍しい都市計画的な建築計画は、具体的にどんな姿でまとめられたのだろう。3区画は視覚的には一体化しているものの機能的には3つに分かれ、東から順に、文化施設も入る文化・入口棟、高層棟、商業棟からなる。丸の内のオフィス街の場合、1894年に、日本初の近代的オフィスビルとなる三菱一号館が建設されて以来、長きにわたりオフィス専用地区であったが、近年は「文化」と「ショッピング」が要素として加わり、面目を一新している。その経験がここでは最初から組み込まれている。

あまり知られていないが、現代の建築界には「超高層ビル1階問題」がある。超高層が都市の主役に躍り出たのに、人の行き来する歩道に面した1階にはガラスの壁が立ち、その向こうに入口ホールはあるものの、人影は薄く、ガードマンとエレベータの表示が淋しくあるばかり。私は初の超高層ビル大学たる工学院大学に勤めた経験を持つが、隣のビルの1階は、床が広々とあるもののガランとし、「京王プラザホテル」(1971年)に面して入るシアトル系カフェの明かりだけが目の救いだった。イコンもまた、同様にこの問題を抱え、近づくにつれて人影が薄くなってしまっているように見えた。ここでは、ショッピングの区画を加えたことで、「超高層ビル1階問題」の解決を願いたい。

都市に新しい存在感をつくり出す

駅から歩いて最初に出会う文化・入口棟から順に見てみよう。外見は、不規則な三角形が凸凹してつくる亀の背のような低層の建物だ。正面から入るとエスカレータで上階へと導かれ、上階にはギャラリーと、集会などの文化的事業のための大きな空間が広がる。ピロティの上に亀が乗ったような姿をしながらピロティを使わず、どうして入口からエレベータで一気に2階に到るという日本でも世界でもあまり例のないアプローチをしたかについて、案内してくれた三菱地所設計の須部恭浩は、「台湾の人はこうしたアプローチが好きなのです」と説明してくれたが、他の大型ビルを見ても確かにそう。施設の正面性と、正面に向って少しずつ上昇しながらアプローチするという、映画「ラストエンペラー」(1987年)的な空間秩序感は、台湾の人びとには抜きがたく生き続けているということか。

文化・入口棟を過ぎると次は高層棟。私が訪ねたのはちょうど内装工事の時期(2018年2月28日)で、一度仕上げた内装をすべて外し、裏側の構造と設備を露わにするという日本の竣工検査にはないやり方が台湾の決まりだから、内装の完成形はよく分からず、ここでは触れない。

高層棟のポイントは内部より外観にある。上に行くにしたがって細くなる姿は、そう珍しく思わなかったが、細くなる姿が両手を合わせて祈るように2枚下ろしになっている点は初見であったし、それ以上に私の目を奪ったの

all the already installed interior furnishings and reveal the underlying structure and equipment, so I am not sure what the building looked like inside on completion, and I will not go into that here.

For the Office tower, the exterior is more important than the interior. Its basic form, tapering toward the top, is not so unusual, but I had never seen a structure quite like this one, where two slabs slant toward one other like a pair of praying hands. Even more, I was impressed by the thickness and strength of the mullions supporting the windows. In recent years many buildings, including Taipei 101 next door, are completely walled with glass, but here the mullions and the horizontal elements that connect them are emphasized more strongly than the glass. And the building looks even more powerful with the diagonals extending all the way down to the lower floors, certainly an unusual design. The highlight of the next zone, the commercial podium, is its façade, the surfaces of its prisms clad in lattices of small circular forms that give it a fuzzy look. These are said to reference plum blossoms, a flower symbolizing Taiwan.

After touring the site just prior to completion, I looked at it again from a distance. Seeing the three buildings at once answered questions that arose when seeing each one for the first time. The cultural + entrance podium is notably uneven like a turtle shell, the Office tower features accentuated mullions, the commercial podium is fuzzy. The question is, what is the unifying principle governing these seemingly disparate shapes and finishes? The materials used for these finishes are titanium for the cultural + entrance podium, aluminum for the Office tower, and stainless steel for the commercial podium. And that explains it: by using aluminum and stainless steel, in addition to titanium, known as the highest quality contemporary construction finish material, the architects must have wanted to give the skyscraper and the entire site an impressive metallic feel unachievable with a fully glass façade. While Taipei 101 succeeds as an icon thanks to its form, Taipei Nanshan Plaza succeeds in asserting an architectural presence that puts it on equal footing with the landmark next door, with a building plan and finish that captures the core intentions of the city's urban planning.

Mount Penglai in Taipei

In closing, I would like to touch on a surprising image that came to mind when looking at the three buildings as a group, namely the legendary Mount Penglai. The imagined appearance of this island of the immortals in Chinese mythology was based, they say, on both a sea turtle and an island. Of course we associate a turtle with the shape of its shell. This island consisted of the sharp peak of Mount Penglai, with the small hump equivalent to the turtle's head being the land of Fangzhang and the flat part corresponding to its tail the land of Yingzhou. Penglai, three forms in one, was envisioned as floating on the shell of a great turtle far offshore in the East China Sea.

On Mount Penglai pine trees grow, cranes fly, and immortal hermits dwell. Written in kanji, the word for these immortal hermits literally reads "mountain man," and it was believed that on Mount Penglai, they gained health and eternal youth by picking mountain herbs and making and drinking elixirs. The people of ancient China genuinely believed in the existence of Penglai and its immortal hermits, and it is said that Qin Shi Huang of the Qin dynasty (in the 3rd century BC) dispatched the scholar Cu Fu to the East China Sea to obtain elixirs. Various actual places including the Japanese islands and Taiwan were at one time believed to be Penglai. With this in mind, when I see the three buildings – the rugged turtle-like form of the Cultural + entrance podium is like Fangzhang, the tall tapered Office tower like the peak of Mount Penglai, and the commercial podium like the horizontal expanse of Yingzhou.

Of course the designers have not told me of any such requests from the client, but that was how it looked to me. If Taipei 101 represents a Buddhist's pagoda ornamented with coins, Taipei Nanshan Plaza might be an image of Penglai. It is surely appropriate for the client, a life insurance company, to express prayers for health and longevity.

環顧了即將完工的工地一周之後，我再走到基地外面，同時眺望三棟建築物後，終於解決了我個別觀看單棟時的疑問。藝文入口棟的外觀如同龜殼般的凹凸獨特，而辦公棟是強調窗框，商場棟則精雕雅緻。如上述看起來好像各有不同的形狀，因此，我很好奇是它以什麼原理來管控表面裝修？據說藝文入口棟的材質是鈦金屬板，辦公棟是鋁合金，商場棟則是不銹鋼。原來如此，我終於明白了！從現代大家最為熟知最頂級建材鈦金屬開始，接著使用鋁合金及不銹鋼，加強處理可令人印象深刻的表面材質的方式，是為了讓超高層大樓展現玻璃帷幕所缺少的金屬感與存在感。相對於「台北101」成功奠定了地標地位，「臺北南山廣場」則是以都市計畫的思維，透過建築規劃與裝修材質的力道，可以說是不受地標建築束縛，成功地展現了建築物本身的存在價值。

聳立於台北街道的蓬萊山

最後我想和各位分享，當我觀察三棟建築物的群體造型，腦中浮現了一幕出乎意料的景象，就是「蓬萊」。「蓬萊」為眾人熟知，意指古代中國的桃花源，以海龜及島嶼的模樣被圖像化流傳。說到海龜，就想到甲殼，而島嶼則意謂山頂處，稱之為蓬萊山。海龜頭部微小的隆起部為方丈，尾部水平的部分稱之為瀛洲。由這三者所形成的蓬萊，據說如同乘在巨大海龜的背上，漂浮於中國東海海上的遙遠某處。蓬萊山是松木高聳，仙鶴飛舞，仙人們居住的地方。仙人與蓬萊山，不僅意指「山居之人」，其採取的山上草藥調配成仙藥，飲用後可保證健康長生不老。古代中國人們深切相信蓬萊與長生不老仙人的存在。據說，秦始皇為求長生不老藥方，派徐福(西元前3世紀左右的秦朝學者)前往東海海上找尋。蓬萊又有一說，可能是日本列島與台灣島。如此思考後再回來眺望三棟建築，如海龜頭部般凹凹凸凸的藝文入口棟可視為方丈，往上筆直延伸的辦公棟就如同蓬萊山，商場棟看起來就似水平開展的瀛洲。

雖然沒有聽聞設計者或是業主有此思維，但映入我眼中的確實是如此的景象。若說「台北101」是寶塔與錢幣的形象，那麼「臺北南山廣場」，可以解讀是蓬萊的意象吧。非常符合祈求客戶健康與長壽的保險公司的企業精神！

は、窓を支える方立の太さと力強さだった。近年、多くのビルは隣のイコンのように全面がガラスだが、ここではガラスより方立と方立同士を繋ぐ水平材を強調している。おまけに、下層階を貫いて斜材を通しているから、ますます強い。珍しいつくりに違いない。その先の商業棟も見所は外観にあり、小さな円環状の外皮が四角い形を包み、毛深い。台湾を象徴する梅の花にちなみデザインしたという。

竣工直前の現場を一巡した後、再び外から眺めた。3棟を一度に眺めると、それぞれを見ている時に感じた疑問が初めて解ける。文化・入口棟の外観は亀甲的凹凸を特徴とし、高層棟は方立を強調し、商業棟は毛深い。このように一見バラバラな形と仕上げを統御する原理は何なのか、という疑問。仕上げ材を聞くと、文化・入口棟はチタン、高層棟はアルミ、商業棟はステンレス。そうか、そういうことだったのか。現代の最高の建築用仕上げ材として知られるチタンをはじめ、アルミとステンレスを駆使し、かつ印象深く表面を扱うことで、全面ガラスにはないメタルによる存在感を超高層に与えたかったのだろう。「台北101」がその姿によりイコンとなることに成功したのに対し、「臺北南山廣場」は、都市計画の意図をとらえた建築計画と仕上げの力により、このイコンに引けを取らない建築的存在感を示すことに成功していると評してよいであろう。

台北の街にそびえる蓬萊山

最後に、3棟の合体形を見ているうちに、私の脳裏に浮かんできたひとつの意外なイメージのことを述べておきたい。「蓬萊」である。古代中国の理想郷のイメージとして知られ、ウミガメと島の姿をもとに図像化されたという。亀でいえば甲殻、島でいえば山頂に当たる尖った山を蓬萊山といい、亀の頭にあたる小さな盛り上がりを方丈、尻尾にあたる水平部分を瀛州(えいしゅう)と呼ぶ。3つがひとつとなっている蓬萊は、中国の東海海上はるか、巨亀の背に乗って漂い浮かぶという。蓬萊山には松の木が生え、鶴が舞い、仙人が住む。仙人とは蓬萊山の「山の人」にほかならず、山の薬草を摘んで仙薬を調合し、その仙薬を飲むと健康になり不老長寿が保証される。古代中国の人びとは蓬萊と不老長寿の仙人の存在を本気で信じ、秦の始皇帝は仙薬を得るべく東海海上に徐福(紀元前3世紀頃、秦朝期の学者)を派遣したという。蓬萊とは日本列島とも台湾島だったとも伝えられる。そう思って3つの建物を眺めると、亀の頭のようにゴツゴツした文化・入口棟は方立に、上にスックと伸びる高層棟は蓬萊山に、商業棟は水平に伸びる瀛州に見えてくる。

設計者からは、むろん発注者がそのような意図を持っていたとは聞いていないが、私の目にはそのように見えてしまった。「台北101」を宝塔と銭のイメージとするなら、「臺北南山廣場」には蓬萊のイメージを読み取ることができよう。健康と長寿を願う生命保険会社にふさわしい姿に違いない。

Bird's eye view from the east. Offering an overview of the entire Xinyi Special District.

LOCATION: 100 Songren Road, Xinyi District, Taipei, Taiwan
PROGRAM: Office, Commercial, Cultural, Regional contribution facilities (Bus Terminal, etc.)
OWNER: Nan Shan Life Insurance
General Director:
　Samuel Yin　Y. T. Tu
Design Supervisor: Tsang-Jiunn, Jean
Landscape advisor: Tsunekata Naito
Development: Jonathan Tso, Chih-Cheng Chen, Kuo-Sheng Yeh, Hsiang-Jane Kao*
Supervision: Kuo-Chen Fu, Chin-Yin Hsu, Tien-Chen Hu, Ling-Chen Chen

DESIGN AND SUPERVISION
MITSUBISHI JISHO SEKKEI:
Design Director: Tetsuya Okusa
Chief Architect: Yasuhiro Sube
Competition: Yosuke Takahashi, Takaaki Fuji, Daisuke Maeda*
Concept Design: Yasuhiro Sube, Takaaki fuji, Tadayoshi Aori, Tsuyoshi Yoshino, Masayuki Yamazaki
Schematic Design/ Design Development: Yasuhiro Sube, Takaaki Fuji, Noboru Kawagishi, Shunichi Osaki
Urban Design Review: Yasuhiro Sube, Noboru Kawagishi
Design Supervision: Yasuhiro Sube
PM: Beckie Tiunn
Structural Engineering:
　Hiroshi Kawamura, Lin Lin
Mechanical Engineering: Yukio Moro
Electrical Engineering: Hiromitsu Mizutori

CS: Ken Kadokawa　Lin Lin
Project Architect: Ikki Nagasawa**
PM Cooperation: Lloyd Lin
(Schematic Design Phase: JPTIP Hiroaki Ebina, Fu-hsuan Kuo)
Drawing cooperation: Kentaro Uemura
CG Image: Feng Mingxuan, Shinichiro Hisashita, Shinji Oba
Model: Koichi Seki, Yoko Hirakawa, Yoko Wakabayashi, Manami Goto, Aiko Mita, Ai Suzuki
Lighting Design/Landscape design cooperation: sola associates:
　Lighting Design: Kazuhiro Kawamura, Atsushi Mitsui
　Landscape design cooperation: Hisakazu Fujita, Koichi Shioi
Interior and signage design cooperation:
　MEC Design International: Toshiya Yamasaki, Takaaki Mita, Hiroshi Fukuda, Akiyoshi Endo*

TAIWAN DESIGN
Architectural Design: Archasia Design Group:
Chief & Licensed Architect:
　Stan Hsing-Hua Lo, Eric Sao-You Hsu
Overall Supervision: Fan-Chou Meng
Competition & Execution Supervision:
　Leif Chen
Development Permit & SD: Leif Chen, Chung-I Shih, Nien-Jung Tu, Jianren Pan
Building Permit & DD: Zhen-Xing Liu, Andy Liu, Hsiu-Jung Chai, Hui-Yu Yu, I-Lin Chen
BIM & 3D Visualised Modeling: Leif Chen,

I-Kai Lin
Site Construction Supervision:
　Xiao-Chun Hua, Andy Liu
MEP Design Supervision: Tzu-Tung Lin, Tung-Sung Chao
Landscape Design Execution: Joyce Lin, Chun-Hui Su, Yi-Zhen Ding*, Hsing-Wen Wang, Yu-Ching Huang
Interior Design Execution: Jay Lin, Pei-Chun Ho, Grace Liu
Lighting Design Consultant:
　CMA Lighting Design: Ta-Wei Lin, Penny Lin, Catt Cheng
Traffic Impact Consultant:
　THI Consultants: Chun-Fu Lin, Lin-Ying Yang
Shop Drawing & BIM Analysis Consultant:
　J.E.T. DESIGN GROUP: Sheng-Yuan Fu, Yi-Ting Tang
Structure: Evergreen Consulting Engineering:
　Structure Design: Hsi-Ying Kan, Tsun-Huai Yao, Yuan-Hsing Li, Chien-Hong Mao
　Structure Construction Supervision: Chun-Hung Chung, Chiu-Chung Wu, Chun-Hsiung Chang, Wen-Lung Chang
Tuned Mass Damper System (TMD):
　RWDI Consulting Engineers and Scientists:
　TMD Design: Trevor Haskett, Brain Dunn, Chien-Shen (Tom) Lee, Navid Milani
Site Execution: GREAT Professional Construction Group:
　Jerry Huang, Yung-Jiang Yeh,

Ching-Chi Hsieh
Curtain Wall: H & K Associates:
　Joseph Huang, Amy Chiang, Sam Chou
MEP: General System Design:
　Sinotech Engineering Consultants:
　Electrical: Fuhbic International
　ICT & Smart Building System: Siemens Taiwan
　HVAC: Chien Yueh Technology Engineering
　Fire Safety System: Yuan Dah Fire Fighting Engineering
　Water Services: Johnson Engineering
(*former employee, **former partnering company)

CONSTRUCTION
Main Contractor: Futsu Construction:
　Duty Managers: Hao-Ching Wu, Hsien-Yao Liao, Chin-Ti Yang, Shih-Wei Wang, Chong-Rong Su, Hung-Chi Yu, Chun-Nan Chien
Electrical: Fuhbic International
ICT & Smart Building System: Siemens Taiwan
HVAC: Chien Yueh Technology Engineering
Fire Safety System/ Water Services: Johnson Engineering

PROJECT FIGURES
Site area:　　　　17,708 m²
Building area:　　10,271 m²
Total floor area: 193,843 m²
Building coverage ratio: A15 + A18: 65.87%
　A20: 36.39% (Allowable ratio: unspecified)
Floor Area Ratio: 685.95% (Allowable ratio: A15: 450% A18: 560% A20: 450%)
Number of floors: 5 Basement floors, 48

View from Northeast.

above ground floors, 2 penthouse floors

KEY DIMENSIONS
Maximum height: 272,000mm
Eaves height: 254,060mm
Floor height office: 4,800mm
Ceiling height office: 3,100mm
Main span office: 4,800 mm× 5,500mm

SITE CONDITION
Land Use: Specific working zone, General commercial district, Entertainment District
Road width: East 30m, West 20m, South 10m
Parking capacity: 487cars

STRUCTURE
Main structure: Aboveground:Steel frame, Underground: Reinforced steel frame concrete +Reinforced concrete structure (office tower 44th floor: 2 TMDs)
Pile and foundation: friction pile
Structure Accreditation Building

EQUIPMENT AND DACILITIES
ENVIRONMENTAL TECHNOLOGIES:
Taiwan Green Building Mark DIAMOND grade, LEED authentication GOLD grade

AIR-CONDITIONING FACILITIES:
Air conditioning system: cultural+entrance podium:AHU, office tower: PAH+FCU(heating and cooling), commercial podium:AHU
Heat source equipment: office tower and cultural +entrance podium: 950RT centrifugal chiller×3 units, 400RT spiral refrigerator ×2 units,commercial podium: 750RT centrifugal refrigerator×3 units, 400RT spiral refrigerator×1 unit

PLUMBING:
Water supply method: gravity method
Hot water supply method: instant electric hot water supply machine
Drainage method: Direct drainage

ELECTRICAL INSTALLATION:
Electric power inlet: high voltage power receiving (special high 22.8 kW)
Capacity: 31,500 kVA
Contract power: 11, 950 kVA
Standby power supply: Diesel generator: 2,500 kVA×7 units for office tower and cultural + entrance podium

DISASTER PREVENTION EQUIPMENT:
Fire extinguishing system: Sprinkler system, Foam fire extinguishing system
Smoke control system: Mechanical smoke control system

ELEVATORS AND ESCALATORS:
Elevator (offifce tower: Forecast System Double Deck Elevator×12×2 units, cultural + entrance podium:2 units, commercial podium: 5 units (Guest), 4 units(Guest luggage sharing), 2 units(Luggage), Escalator (Mitsubishi Electric)

SCHEDULE
Design period: Jul 2012 - Aug 2015
Construction period: Nov 2013 - Jan 2018

EXTERIOR FINISH
OFFICE TOWER
Roof: Urethane waterproof (Hydroseal Enterprise)
Exterior wall: AL louver / AL panel (YKK AP), Titanium panel (Alpolic), Glass (Taiwan Glass)
Opening unit: Curtain wall (YKK AP)
Exterior: Granite, Rock material tile (Olive Bricks)

CULTURAL + ENTRANCE PODIUM
Roof, Exterior wall: Titanium panel, Titanium composite panel (Nippon Steel & Sumitomo Metal), Aluminum composite panel (Mitsubishi Plastics), Stainless steel sheet waterproof
Opening unit: Aluminum Curtain Wall (Hard Engineering), Thermal Environment Glass (Saint-Gobain)
Exterior: Granite, Rock material tile (Olive Bricks)

COMMERCIAL PODIUM
Roof: Urethane waterproof (Hydroseal Enterprise)
Roof terrace: Artificial wood deck
External wall: Aluminum composite panel (Mitsubishi Plastics), Cast stainless steel + Hollow bent stainless (KINZI)
Opening unit: Aluminum Curtain Wall (Hard Engineering), Thermal Environment Glass (Saint-Gobain)
Exterior: Biotope, Granite, Organic tile (Olive Bricks)

PEDESTRIAN DECK
Roof: Urethane waterproof (Hydroseal Enterprise)
External wall: Aluminum composite panel (Mitsubishi Plastics)
Eave soffit: Artificial wood, Rock material tile (Olive Bricks)

INTERIOR FINISH
CULTURAL + ENTRANCE PODIUM
ENTRANCE HALL
Floor: Granite
Interiror wall: Travertine, Aluminum louver
Ceiling: Wood louver, PB+EP

NANSHAN HALL
Floor: carpet (MILLIKEN)
Interior wall: Wood louver, Shading rollscreen (SHY)
Ceiling: Wood louver

OFFICE TOWER
ENTRANCE HALL
Floor: Granite
Interior wall: SUS cut panel, Onyx light wall, Wall greening, Travertine, Decorative glass wall, Shutter (Sanwa Shutter)
Ceiling: PB+EP
Other
Screen art: Cast stainless steel (KINZI), Counter: Glass + Marble

TYPICAL FLOOR OFFICE
Floor: OA Floor h=150 mm (Inpel)
Interior wall: Shading rollscreen (SHY), Cloth
Ceiling: System Ceiling (Armstrong), System Lighting (Panasonic)

SHARED AREA, ELEVATOR HALL
Floor: Granite, Carpet (MILLIKEN)
Interior wall: Decorative glass wall, Sheet (TOPPAN)
Ceiling: PB+EP

TYPICAL FLOOR RESTROOM, SHOWER ROOM, GARBAGE ROOM
Floor: Ceramic tile
Interior wall: Ceramic tile, Mirror, System Toilet Booth (AICA)
Ceiling: PB+EP
Other: Sanitary equipment (TOTO), Hand dryer (DYSON)

INFORMATION
Commercial podium: Breeze Center
URL: https://www.breezecenter.com

位置　台灣台北市信義區松仁路100號
主要用途　辦公　商業　藝文設施　公共回饋設施(大型巴士停車場等)
業主　南山人壽保險
　總顧問／尹衍樑　杜英宗
　設計顧問／簡滄圳
　景觀顧問／內藤恒方
　開發／左昭德　陳志成　葉國勝
　　　　　高翔健*
　監造／傅滄珍　許金印　胡天禎
　　　　陳玲瑱
設計・監造
建築　三菱地所設計
　總監／大草徹也
　專案統籌・首席設計師／須部恭浩
　競圖階段／高橋洋介　藤貴彰
　　　　　　前田大輔*
　概念設計階段／須部恭浩　藤貴彰
　　　　　阿折忠受　吉野毅　山崎昌之
　基本・細部設計階段／須部恭浩
　　　　　藤貴彰　川岸昇　大崎駿一
　都市設計審議／須部恭浩　川岸昇
　監造顧問／須部恭浩
　專案經理／張瑞娟
　結構／川村浩　林林
　設備／茂呂幸雄
　電氣／水取寬滿
　業務／角川研　林林
　設計協助／永澤一輝**
　專案協助／林宣宇
　(基本構想階段: JPTIP 海老名宏明
　　　　　　　郭馥瑄)

製圖協助／上村健太郎
透視圖・CG協助／馮銘軒　久下真一郎
　　　　　　大庭慎司
模型協助／関浩一　平川暢子
　　　　　若林洋子　後藤Manami
　　　　　三田愛子　鈴木愛
照明設計・景觀設計協助
sola associates
　照明設計／川村和広　三井敦史
　景觀設計協助／藤田久数
　　　　　　　塩井弘一
室內設計、指標設計協助
MEC Design International
　山崎利也　三田高章　福田宏
　遠藤曉喜*
台灣設計
建築　瀚亞國際設計・瀚亞建築師事務所
　簽證建築師／羅興華　徐少游
　總監／孟繁周
　競圖統籌・細設統籌／陳列峯
　都市設計審議／陳列峯　施忠毅*
　　　　　杜念融　潘建任
　細部設計／劉振興　劉志鴻
　柴秀榮　游蕙瑪　陳怡霖
　BIM・模型／陳列峯　林義凱
　監造／華曉春　劉志鴻
　設備／林梓東　趙東崧
　景觀／林依璇　蘇春輝　丁怡貞
　　　　王星文
　室內設計／林榮華　劉憶萱
　　　　　吳翰翔　黃郁晴　何佩純
　照明設計　月河燈光設計

林大為　林佩縈　鄭玫君
交通顧問　鼎漢國際工程顧問
　林俊甫　楊林穎
細設・BIM設計協助　捷銳創意空間
　傅昇垣　唐翊庭
結構　永峻工程顧問
　設計／甘錫瀅　姚村准　李源興
　　　　毛建閎
　監造／鍾俊宏　吳秋仲　張俊雄
　　　　張文龍
TMD　RWDI Consulting Engineers
and Scientists
　　　Trevor Haskett　Brain Dunn
　　　李建生　Navid Milani
遠碩國際工程顧問
　黃治政　葉永江　謝慶琦
CW　康普工程顧問
　黃有立　江玉如　周子森
設備　系統構成　中興工程顧問
　電氣　福麟系統整合
　弱電　西門子
　空調　建越工程
　消防　元大消防工程
　給排水　兆申機電工程
(*為離職人員, **協力顧問)
施工
建築　互助營造
　吳豪卿　廖憲曜　楊金地　王士維
　蘇重榮　余鴻吉　簡俊男
電氣　福麟系統整合
弱電　西門子
空調　建越工程

消防、給排水　兆申機電工程
規模
　基地面積　17,708m²
　建築面積　10,271m²
　樓地板面積　193,843m²
　建蔽率　A15+A18: 65.87%
　　　　　A20: 36.39%(法定: 無規定)
　容積率　685.95%(法定: A15: 450%
　　　　　A18: 560%　A20: 450%)
　樓層數　地下5層　地上48層　屋突2層
尺寸
　絕對高度　272,000mm
　建築高度　254,060mm
　結構樓高　辦公棟標準層: 4,800mm
　天花板淨高度　辦公棟標準層:
　　　　　　　　3,100mm
　主要柱距　4,800mm×5,500mm
基地條件
　使用分區　特定業務區　一般商業區
　　　　　　娛樂設施區
　道路寬度　東30m　西20m　南10m
　停車數量　487部
結構
　主體結構　地上: 鋼骨結構　地下: 鋼骨
　　　　　　鋼筋混凝土+鋼筋混凝土結構(辦
　　　　　　公棟44樓: 設置TMD阻尼二座)
　基樁、基礎　摩擦樁
　耐震標章認證
設備
環保節能技術
　台灣綠建築標章　鑽石級
　LEED 認證 金級

View from Southeast.

空調設備
空調方式 藝文入口棟: AHU 辦公棟: PAH＋FCU(冷暖氣) 商場棟: AHU
供熱機器 辦公棟及藝文入口棟: 950RT離心式冰水主機3部、400RT螺旋式冰水主機2部 商場棟:750RT離心式冰水主機3部、400RT螺旋式冰水主機1部

衛生設備
給水 重力方式
熱水 瞬間電能熱水器
排水 直接排放公共污水下水道

電氣設備
接收方式 高壓供電方式(特高22.8kW)
設備容量 31,500kVA
契約電力 11,950kVA
預備電源 柴油發電機: 2,500kVA辦公棟及藝文入口棟7部 商場棟5部

防災設備
消防 消防栓 撒水頭 放水型撒水設備 泡沫滅火等設備
排煙 機械排煙

昇降機 電梯(智慧型派車系統辦公棟客用雙層車廂電梯×12部 藝文入口棟客用×2部 商場棟客用×5部 全棟客貨兼用×4部 貨用×2部) 電扶梯(三菱電機)

工程
設計期間 2012年7月～2015年8月
施工期間 2013年11月～2018年1月

室外裝修

辦公棟
屋頂 拜鐵膜防水(易森)
外牆 鋁百葉/鋁板(YKK AP) 鈦板(ALPOLIC) 玻璃(台灣玻璃)
開口部 單元式帷幕牆(YKK AP)
景觀 花崗石 陶磚(織部製陶)

藝文入口棟
屋頂 外牆 鈦板 鈦複合板(新日鐵住金) 鋁複合板(三菱樹脂)不銹鋼防水
開口部 鋁帷幕牆(合特工程) 熱線反射玻璃(Saint Gobain)
景觀 花崗岩 陶磚(織部製陶)

商場棟
屋頂 拜鐵膜防水(易森) 屋頂露臺: 人工木平台
外牆 鋁複合板(三菱樹脂) 鑄造不銹鋼＋不銹鋼管彎曲加工(KINZI)
開口部 鋁帷幕牆(合特工程) 熱線反射玻璃(Saint Gobain)
景觀 生物棲地 花崗石 陶磚(織部製陶)

空橋
屋頂 拜鐵膜防水(易森)
外牆 鋁複合板(三菱樹脂) 屋簷人造木材 陶磚(織部製陶)

室內裝修
■**藝文入口棟**
入口大廳
地坪 花崗石
牆面 洞石 鋁格柵
天花 木格柵 石膏板補土＋EP漆

藝文中心(Nanshan Hall)
地坪 地毯(MILLIKEN)
牆面 木格柵 斜面遮光捲簾(SHY)
天花 木格柵
■**辦公棟**
入口大廳
地坪 花崗石
牆面 SUS實心平切板 透光石牆 植生牆 洞石 裝飾玻璃牆 捲門(安和)
天花 石膏板補土＋EP漆
其他 藝術金屬簾; 鑄造不銹鋼(KINZI)
櫃台 玻璃＋大理石
標準層辦公室
地坪 高架地板 h=150mm(英邦)
牆面 斜面遮光捲簾(SHY) 壁布
天花 系統天花(阿姆斯壯) 系統照明(PANASONIC)
標準層公共區域 梯廳
地坪 花崗石 地毯(MILLIKEN)
牆面 裝飾玻璃牆 貼膠片(TOPPAN)
天花 石膏板補土＋EP漆
標準層廁所 淋浴間 垃圾暫存室
地坪 磁磚
牆面 磁磚 明鏡 系統揭擺(AICA)
天花 石膏板補土＋EP漆
其他 衛生器具(TOTO) 烘手機(DYSON)

設施內容
商場棟租戶 微風南山
URL: https://www.breezecenter.com

所在地　台湾台北市信義區松仁路100號
主要用途　オフィス　商業施設　文化施設　地域
　　　　　貢献施設（大型バス駐車場等）
建主　南山人壽保險
　　總顧問／尹衍樑　杜英宗
　　設計顧問／簡滄川
　　ランドスケープ顧問／内藤恒方
　　開発担当／左昭德　陳志成　葉國勝
　　　　　　　高翔健*
　　監理担当／傅國珍　許金印　胡天禎
　　　　　　　陳玲瑱
設計・監理
　建築　三菱地所設計
　　全体統括／大草徹也
　　PJ統括・主任設計者／須部恭浩
　　コンペ担当／髙橋洋介　藤貴彰　前田大輔*
　　基本構想／須部恭浩　藤貴彰　阿折忠受
　　　　　　　吉野毅　山崎昌之
　　基本・実施設計／須部恭浩　藤貴彰
　　　　　　　川岸昇　大崎駿一
　　都市審議／須部恭浩　川岸昇
　　現場監修／須部恭浩
　　PM／張瑞娟
　　構造担当／川村浩　林林
　　設備担当／茂呂幸雄
　　電気担当／水取寛満
　　CS／角川研　林林
　　設計協力／永澤一輝**
　　PM協力／林宣宇
　　（基本構想時：JPTIP海老名宏明　郭馥瑄）
　　作図協力／上村健太郎
　　パース・CG協力／馮銘軒　久下真一郎
　　　　　　　大庭慎司

模型協力／関浩一　平川暢子　若林洋子
　　　　　後藤まなみ　三田愛子　鈴木愛
ライティングデザイン・ランドスケープ協力
　ソラアソシエイツ
　ライティングデザイン担当／川村和広
　　　　　　　三井敦史
　ランドスケープ協力担当／藤田久数
　　　　　　　塩井弘一
内装設計・サイン協力　メック・デザイン・インター
　ナショナル
　担当／山崎利也　三田高章　福田宏
　　　　遠藤暁喜*

建築　瀚亞國際設計・瀚亞建築師事務所
　簽證建築師／羅興華　徐少游
　全体統括／孟繁周
　コンペ統括・実施統括／陳列峯
　都市審議／陳列峯　施忠毅*　杜念融
　　　　　　潘建任
　実施設計／劉振興　劉志鴻　柴秀榮
　　　　　　游蕙瑀　陳怡霖
　BIM・模型／陳列峯　林義凱
　監理担当／華曉春　劉志鴻
　設備担当／林梓東　趙東崧
　外構担当／林依璇　蘇春輝　丁怡貞
　　　　　　王星文
　内装担当／林榮華　劉憶萱　吳翰翔
　　　　　　黃郁晴　何佩純
ライティングデザイン　月河燈光設計
　担当／林大為　林佩縈　鄭玫君
交通　鼎漢國際工程顧問
　担当／林俊甫　楊林穎
詳細図・BIM設計協力　捷銳創意空間

担当／傅昇垣　唐翊庭
構造　永峻工程顧問
　設計担当／甘錫瀅　姚村准　李源興
　　　　　　毛建閎
　監理担当／鍾俊宏　吳秋仲　張俊雄
　　　　　　張文龍
TMD　RWDI Consulting Engineers and
　Scientists
　担当／Trevor Haskett　Brain Dunn
　　　　李建生　Navid Milani
遠碩國際工程顧問
　担当／黃治政　葉永江　謝慶琦
CW　康普工程顧問
　担当／黃有立　江玉如　周子森
設備　系統構成　中興工程顧問
　電気　福麟系統整合
　弱電　西門子
　空調　建越工程
　消防　兆大消防工程
　給排水　兆申機電工程
（*元所員，**元協力事務所）
施工
建築　互助營造
　担当／吳豪卿　廖憲曜　楊金地　王士維
　　　　蘇重榮　余鴻吉　簡俊男
電氣　福麟系統整合
弱電　西門子
空調　建越工程
消防　兆申機電工程
給排水　兆申機電工程
規模
敷地面積　17,708m²
建築面積　10,271m²

延床面積　193,843m²
建蔽率　A15+A18：65.87%
　　　　A20：36.39%（許容：規定なし）
容積率　685.95%（許容：A15：450%
　　　　A18：560%　A20：450%）
階数　地下5階　地上48階　塔屋2階
寸法
最高高　272,000mm
軒高　254,060mm
階高　高層棟執務室：4,800mm
天井高　高層棟執務室：3,100mm
主なスパン　4,800mm×5,500mm
敷地条件
地域地区　特定業務区　一般商業区　娯樂施設区
道路幅員　東30m　西20m　南10m
駐車台数　487台
構造
主体構造　地上：鉄骨造　地下：鉄筋鉄骨コンク
　　　　　リート＋鉄筋コンクリート造（高層棟44階：
　　　　　TMDダンパー2基）
杭・基礎　摩擦杭
台湾・耐震標章取得
設備
環境配慮技術
　台湾緑建築標章　DIAMOND級
　LEED 認証 GOLD級
空調設備
　空調方式　文化・入口棟：AHU
　高層棟：PAH+FCU（冷暖房）　商業棟：AHU熱
　源　高層棟および文化・入口棟：950RT遠
　心冷凍機3台、400RTスパイラル式冷
　凍機2台
　商業棟　750RT遠心冷凍機3台　400RTスパイラ

View from Southeast.

ル式冷凍機1台
衛生設備
給水　重力方式
熱水　瞬間電気給湯機
排水　直接放流
電気設備
受電方式　高圧供電方式（特高22.8kW）
設備容量　31,500kVA
契約電力　11,950kVA
予備電源　ディーゼル発電機：2,500kVA　高層棟および文化・入口棟7台　商業棟5台
防災設備
消火　消火栓　スプリンクラー　放水型　泡消火等設備
排煙　機械排煙
昇降機　エレベータ（高層棟乗用行先予報システムダブルデッキエレベータ×12×2台　文化・入口棟乗用×2台　商業棟乗用×5台　客荷物兼用×4台　荷物用×2台）　エスカレータ（三菱電機）

工程
設計期間　2012年7月〜2015年8月
施工期間　2013年11月〜2018年1月
外部仕上げ
高層棟
屋根　ウレタン防水（易森）
外壁　ALルーバー・ALパネル（YKK AP）　チタンパネル（アルポリック）　ガラス（台湾玻璃）
開口部　ユニットカーテンウォール（YKK AP）
外構　花崗岩　炻器質タイル（織部製陶）
文化・入口棟
屋根　外壁　チタンパネル　チタン複合パネル（新日鉄住金）　アルミ複合パネル（三菱

樹脂）　ステンレス防水
開口部　アルミカーテンウォール（合特工程）　熱環境ガラス（サンゴバン）
外構　花崗岩　炻器質タイル（織部製陶）
商業棟
屋根　ウレタン防水（易森）
　　　屋上テラス部：人工木ウッドデッキ
外壁　アルミ複合パネル（三菱樹脂）　ステンレスキャスト＋ステンレス中空曲げ加工（KINZI）
開口部　アルミカーテンウォール（合特工程）　熱環境ガラス（サンゴバン）
外構　ビオトープ　花崗岩　炻器質タイル（織部製陶）
ペデストリアンデッキ
屋根　ウレタン防水（易森）
外壁　アルミ複合パネル（三菱樹脂）　軒裏人工木　炻器質タイル（織部製陶）
内部仕上げ
■文化・入口棟
エントランスホール
床　花崗岩
壁　トラバーチン　アルミルーバー
天井　木ルーバー　PB寒冷紗パテしごき＋EP
文化ホール
床　カーペット（MILLIKEN）
壁　木ルーバー　遮光ロールスクリーン（SHY）
天井　木ルーバー
■高層棟
エントランスホール
床　花崗岩
壁　SUSカットパネル　オニキス光壁　壁面緑化　トラバーチン　装飾ガラス壁　シャッター

（三和シャッター）
天井　PB寒冷紗パテしごき＋EP
その他　ウィンドアート：ステンレスキャスト（KINZI）　カウンター：ガラス＋大理石
基準階事務室
床　OAフロア h=150mm（英邦）
壁　遮光ロールスクリーン（SHY）　クロス
天井　システム天井（アームストロング）　システム照明（パナソニック）
基準階共用部　エレベータホール
床　花崗岩　カーペット（MILLIKEN）
壁　装飾ガラス壁　シート貼り（TOPPAN）
天井　PB寒冷紗パテしごき＋EP
基準階トイレ　シャワー室　ゴミ庫
床　セラミックタイル
壁　セラミックタイル　ミラー　システムトイレブース（アイカ工業）
天井　PB寒冷紗パテしごき＋EP
その他　衛生機器（TOTO）　ジェットタオル（DYSON）

施設詳細
商業棟テナント　微風南山
URL：https://www.breezecenter.com

写真撮影・提供　図版提供｜
Credits / Photographs
KMG建築事務所｜KMG Architects & Engineers｜pp.012-013
鈴木久雄｜Hisao Suzuki｜表表紙（cover）／p.142／p.143／p.145／pp.146-147／p.148／p.149／pp.154-155／pp.156-157／p.158／p.159／pp.162-163 上（Top）／pp.170-171／p.173／p.174／p.180 上2点（2 images on the top）／p.182／p.184／p.185／p.186 左下（Bottom left）／p.194／pp.202-203
南山人寿｜Nan Shan Life Insurance｜p.025／pp.062-063／pp.064-065／pp.072-073 下6点（Bottom）／pp.096-097／pp.098-099／p.103／pp.110-111／p.114 下（Bottom）／p.115／p.117／p.119／p.123／p.124 下（Bottom）／p.125／p.126／pp.132-133／pp.134-135／裏表紙（Back Cover）
三菱地所設計｜Mitsubishi Jisho Sekkei｜p.009右（Right）／p.017／pp.018-019／pp.022-023／pp.026-027／pp.028-029／pp.034-035／pp.036-037／pp.038-039／p.042 左下1点（Bottom left）／p.045／p.048／p.056／p.066／p.068／p.071／pp.074-075／p.77／pp.078-079／pp.080-081／pp.084-085／pp.088-089／pp.090-091／p.93／pp.100-101／p.102／pp.108-109／p.113／p.118／pp.128-129／pp.138-139／pp.140-141／pp.150-151／p.163 左下（Bottom left）／p.172上、左下（Top, Bottom left）／p.176／p.181 上（Top）／p.188／pp.192-193／pp.200-201／pp.204-205／pp.208-209
Chi Po-lin (itaiwan8.com)｜pp.014-015

All photos expect as noted by Shinkenchiku-Sha.

Author | Mitsubishi Jisho Sekkei
Tetsuya Okusa　Yasuhiro Sube
Takaaki Fuji　Noboru Kawagishi
Shunichi Osaki　Beckie Tiunn
Hiroshi Kawamura　Yukio Moro
Hiromitsu Mizutori

**Editorial Contribution |
Mitsubishi Jisho Sekkei**
Kentaro Furuya
Yoshiko Araki　Yuko Nemoto
Kaori Hayashi
Kyosuke Nakamura

Editorial Cooperation
Ikki Nagasawa　Ryuta Fujii

文字撰稿 | 三菱地所設計
大草徹也　須部恭浩　藤貴彰　川岸昇
大崎駿一　張瑞娟　川村浩
茂呂幸雄　水取寛満

編輯 | 三菱地所設計
古屋健太郎
荒木佳子　根本裕子　林華織
中村教祐

編輯協辦
永澤一輝　藤井隆太

執筆・編集 | 三菱地所設計
大草徹也　須部恭浩　藤貴彰　川岸昇
大崎駿一　張瑞娟　川村浩
茂呂幸雄　水取寛満

編集 | 三菱地所設計
古屋健太郎
荒木佳子　根本裕子　林華織
中村教祐

編集協力
永澤一輝　藤井隆太